Indigenous Peoples in Canada

Darion Boyington

John Roberts

emond ▪ Toronto, Canada ▪ 2017

Emond Montgomery Publications Limited
60 Shaftesbury Avenue
Toronto ON M4T 1A3
http://www.emond.ca/highered

Printed in Canada.
Reprinted December 2018.

We acknowledge the financial support of the Government of Canada.   Canadä

Emond Montgomery Publications has no responsibility for the persistence or accuracy of URLs for external or third-party Internet websites referred to in this publication, and does not guarantee that any content on such websites is, or will remain, accurate or appropriate.

Publisher: Mike Thompson
Managing editor, development: Kelly Dickson
Developmental editor: Heather Gough
Senior editor, production: Jim Lyons
Production supervisor: Laura Bast
Copy editor: Leslie Saffrey
Proofreaders: Jim Lyons, Lila Campbell, and David Handelsman
Permissions editor: Lisa Brant
Indexer: Belle Wong
Typesetter and cover designer: Tara Wells
Cover image: M. Cornelius/Shutterstock

Library and Archives Canada Cataloguing in Publication

Boyington, Darion, author
    Indigenous peoples in Canada / Darion Boyington, John Roberts.

Includes index.
ISBN 978-1-77255-299-7 (softcover)

    1. Native peoples—Colonization—Canada.   2. Native peoples—Canada—Claims.   3. Native peoples—Canada—Social conditions.   4. Native peoples—Canada—Economic conditions.   I. Roberts, John A., 1944-, author   II. Title.

E78.C2B695 2017   971.004'97   C2017-902298-9

To my students, who both challenge my mind and keep me young. As you move into positions of leadership in this country, lead with wisdom to create a fair and just society.

—*Darion Boyington*

Brief Contents

Detailed Contents

1 Colonization and Treaties

2 Current Issues over Land

3 Indian and Inuit Residential Schools

4 Current Socio-Economic Issues

5 Indigenous People and the Criminal Justice System

Preface

Following the final report of the Truth and Reconciliation Commission of Canada (TRC) in 2015, it seemed like the time was right to offer a new text that presented an overview of Canada's Indigenous peoples for students across the country. This text offers a concise history of the relationship between Indigenous people in Canada and the new populations of settlers, and in doing so lays the foundation for understanding their past and present interactions and relations.

The text explores the treaty process in which Indigenous people lost vast areas of their traditional lands, and with this necessary background discusses land claims, which are commonly misunderstood by many members of the Canadian public. The socio-economic issues facing Indigenous people today are a legacy of colonization and forced assimilation. The text examines the history of the residential school system and the TRC's report on that era. These chapters also examine the positive strides that Indigenous communities are making toward self-government and the stabilization of their economies in partnership with the government of Canada. New initiatives from the court system and Correctional Service Canada, as well as new approaches to policing, are evaluated with regard to their ultimate goal—to reduce the overrepresentation of Indigenous people in the criminal justice system.

At relevant points throughout these chapters, many of the TRC's 94 "calls to action" are highlighted, helping to underline the connection between the historical, economic, and social issues being examined, and the future direction of Canada's Indigenous peoples in the post-TRC era.

For Instructors

For additional information and resources, please visit the accompanying website for this book at http://www.emond.ca/IPC. Teaching supplements are available to instructors who have chosen this book for their courses. These resources include PowerPoint slides, test banks, and an instructor's guide. Please visit the *For Instructors* tab on the book's website, or contact your Emond Publishing representative for more information.

Acknowledgments

I would like to extend my thanks to the many instructors who reviewed earlier editions of the books from which this text has evolved, for providing their very useful feedback and suggestions, and to John Roberts for his contributions to an earlier edition. I would also like to thank the team at Emond Publishing for their guidance and help, especially Heather Gough, whose ideas, suggestions, and research improved this edition in countless ways.

Darion Boyington

About the Author

Darion Boyington teaches in the Justice and Wellness Studies program at Mohawk College. Before joining the faculty at Mohawk, she completed a degree at Wilfrid Laurier University, and also served 14 years as a police officer, occupying various roles such as coaching new recruits and developing community services programs.

Her passion for the study of Indigenous issues in Canada comes from her front-line experience with Indigenous people in the criminal justice system. Her research centres on understanding the past and present conditions of Indigenous people in Canada. Her research goal is to create accurate, quality curricula to enable all students to fully comprehend the multi-faceted challenges that currently face Indigenous populations in Canada, and to be prepared to partner with Indigenous communities in their efforts to improve their position in Canada, making a more equal society for everyone.

1 Colonization and Treaties

Six Nations Iroquois (Haudenosaunee) chiefs reading wampum belts on September 14, 1871.

LEARNING OUTCOMES

After completing this chapter, you should be able to:

- Identify the differences between the Western European world view and the world view of Indigenous peoples.
- Consider how differences in world view will affect the continuing relationship between mainstream culture and Indigenous cultures.
- Identify the core issues in the long-standing debate over Indigenous claims to land and authority in the Americas.
- Discuss the relationship between the new European arrivals and the Indigenous people in Canada up to the time of the *Royal Proclamation of 1763*.
- Explore the treaty-making process and consider the benefits and disadvantages to all parties involved.
- Identify the assimilation policies and legislation set out by the Dominion of Canada and discuss the moral and ethical implications of those policies.

Introduction

This chapter contrasts pre-contact Europe and pre-contact North America with the goal of understanding what the two cultures were like before they collided. Once this is established, we go on to examine the colonization of Canada and its effects on the original inhabitants of the land.

We gain insight into a culture's world view by examining its creation story. This chapter looks at Indigenous creation stories and at Western European creation stories. We will reflect briefly on Western creation stories. Not all Canadians today are familiar with the Christian religion. But at the time of colonization and well into the 20th century, the majority of Canadians were people of Western European origin—that is to say, overwhelmingly Christian. Their European culture was the dominant culture in Canada during colonization and arguably remains so today. Despite the fact that Canada is widely considered to be a cultural mosaic, the fundamental principles of Indigenous cultures have always been quite different from the European principles that underlie the mainstream world view in Canada.

After examining the creation stories and differences in world view between Indigenous culture and mainstream culture, we will examine the relationship between Indigenous people and Europeans as it developed from the time of first contact through to the period in which Indigenous people went from being partners in trade and allies in war to being displaced and subjugated peoples.

World View

A world view is the set of assumptions and beliefs on which a people's comprehension of the world is based. The stories, symbols, analogies, and metaphors that compose a people's mythology express a world view in coded form. Such expression occurs in informal, formal, unconscious, and conscious ways through family and community, through arts and media, and through economic, spiritual, governmental, and education institutions. (Cajete, 2000, p. 62)

What distinguishes the world view of the dominant culture in Canada? Amid the many cultures that compose Canada, there is a dominant, mainstream culture. Members of a mainstream culture are sometimes hardly aware of its existence, but people from outside that culture tend to be acutely aware of it. According to Cajete, our culture gives us a particular world view that affects the way we live and our social and political actions. What are the stories, metaphors, symbols, and myths that express the mainstream Canadian world view?

Foundations of the Mainstream Canadian World View

The foundations of the mainstream Canadian world view before and during the centuries of colonization include stories of creation, 17th-century philosophy, structures of governance, and capitalist assumptions about land and property.

Religious Creation Story

Our society is still influenced by the Christian religion. The Christian belief is that humans are created in the image of God and that they, alone among the world's creatures, are endowed with a spirit. God has given humans "dominion over the fish of the sea, and over the fowl of the air, and over the cattle, and over all the Earth" (Genesis 1:25). This belief has profoundly shaped mainstream Western culture's view of humanity's relationship with the natural world. Christian principles, including the concept of the Protestant work ethic, were in part responsible for the emphasis on industry in Western European society and the development of capitalism, which continues to be the dominant economic ideology in North America. The Bible's assertion that humans were made to cultivate the earth is in part responsible for the emphasis on agriculture in Western European society, while the biblical view that the human purpose is to populate the earth was, historically, one of the factors in the high populations of Western European societies.

Our conceptions of justice are rooted in religion. Until very recently, our principles of sentencing for criminal offences were based on notions of retribution and punishment that are biblical in origin. Although the purpose of sentencing, as expressed in section 718 of the *Criminal Code*, is now more in line with modern thinking, various signs and symbols within mainstream culture (for example, in film, books, and stories) still promote a biblical, "eye for an eye" view of justice.

Finally, the Christian faith is a proselytizing religion, based on the belief that there is only one God and one true religion and that others must convert to it or be damned. At the same time, it contains many factions. This state of affairs produced much religious intolerance and dissension and conflict in Europe, one of the many reasons Europeans came to settle in new lands. Christianity's proselytizing tendency has affinities with ethnocentrism—the idea that others must live as we do because ours is the best way to live and all other ways are inferior. Not just Indigenous people but all people from cultural traditions outside the mainstream one will have come across this ethnocentric propensity in members of the cultural majority.

Scientific Creation Story

Mainstream culture has a second creation story, the scientific one based on Charles Darwin's theory of evolution. This story locates the creation of humanity in the "Cradle of Humankind" in South Africa. (According to some Christian scientists seeking to validate the biblical story, this is the true site of the Garden of Eden.) It is a story that has humans evolving from apelike ancestors to their current form, then gradually migrating outward to occupy the earth.

Darwin's theory of evolution has had a huge impact on mainstream culture's world view. That impact is reflected in colloquialisms such as "dog eat dog" and "only the strong survive." The creation story based on Darwin's theory has profoundly affected the way we see both ourselves and life on this planet. It supports our view that life is about competition for resources and survival. For mainstream Western culture, the scientific view of creation has displaced to some extent the religious view of creation.

Philosophy and Governance

Philosopher Thomas Hobbes wrote *Leviathan* in 1651, after the discovery of the Americas but prior to their full-scale colonization. Hobbes theorized that life in a state of nature, where there is no strong centralized government with absolute power, is "nasty, brutish, and short." His view of human nature was not a positive one. He presumed that men would kill one another in order to survive. He advocated investing absolute power in a sovereign in order to maintain both structure and peace in society. Hobbes's historical circumstances influenced his opinion. Europe in that period experienced political instability, war, and plagues that wiped out large portions of the population. There were huge class divisions between the wealthy and the poor, with wealth concentrated in the Church and monarchy. Europe was a long way from democracy. The Church and the sovereign were seen as a single concentrated source of power, while ordinary people had very little political control. It was a top-down structure of governance. This is the conception of government that many Europeans subscribed to when they embarked on the process of colonization.

Our political structure today is very different. While the Canadian political structure is in many ways based on the British political structure, some academics maintain that our current form of democratic government was to some extent modelled on the forms of government practised by Indigenous peoples at the time of their first contact with European explorers.

Locke's Theory of Landownership

When we discuss land rights, we tend to think in terms of rights to private ownership of property; that is our cultural understanding of people's relationship to land. This understanding is rooted in biblical texts and in political structures that date back to medieval times. Early in European history, the division of the "haves" and "have-nots" was determined by private landownership. By the time the Americas were "discovered," most of the land in Europe was already in the hands of private landowners. Those who worked the land for landowners would almost certainly never own land; they would be labourers their entire lives. When the Americas were discovered, philosopher John Locke wrote a theory of landownership that reinforced the established Western European notion of man's relationship to land. Locke's theory would rationalize the European seizure of land in the Americas. In brief, his theory went like this:

1. All land is owned by all of mankind.
2. Land can be transferred from general to private ownership by mixing one's labour with it.
3. Once converted to private ownership, land requires delineated boundaries (physically represented by fencing).
4. In order to have delineated boundaries, a society must have an established government and laws for enforcing private ownership.
5. Proviso: A man could take as much land as he required, provided that he left "enough, and as good" for others. (Bishop, 2003)

Locke's theory is an important one: it will come up again later in this book in connection with the clearing of Indigenous people from the land and our society's justifications for doing so. It is also relevant to our discussion later in this chapter; it provides a contrast to Indigenous concepts of land and methods of government.

The concepts we have discussed thus far should be very familiar to all members of mainstream Canadian culture. They are the building blocks of our society's world view. Many other concepts could be discussed, particularly the rise of capitalism, but space limitations preclude a fuller treatment. Now we must look at another world view, one that is very different from the mainstream one.

Indigenous World View

Before Europeans arrived on the shores of what would become Canada, there were self-governing nations of people living in organized groups throughout the land. Archaeologists estimate that the land sustained 500,000 to 2,000,000 people in all (Dickason, 1997, p. 43). These nations have rich histories that are tens of thousands of years old; conservative archaeological estimates put Indigenous occupancy at around 15,000 years. (According to Indigenous people, they have been here since time began.) In other words, European history on the continent represents less than one-tenth of the histories of these nations, who occupied every territory of the continent, using natural resources for sustenance.

Pre-contact population density estimates demonstrate Indigenous peoples' symbiotic relationship with the land. The highest population densities were in areas of plentiful resources that could support many people. Population densities in deserts and in temperate zones, where there is a short growing season, were smaller. Although the population of what would become Canada was low because of the climate, the population in Central and South America has been estimated as high as 37 million. The Aztec population alone was estimated at 11 million; their main city was said to be larger than Madrid, Spain. On the Caribbean island of the Dominican Republic, the site of the first European landing, the population density was very high.

FIGURE 1.1   Cultural and Language Groups Prior to Contact

Tlingit	1
Tsimshian	2
Haida	3
Wakashan	4
Salishan	5
Ktuxana	6
Algonquian	7
Siouan	8
Eskimo-Aleut	9
Iroquoian	10
Athapaskan	11

In the 16th century, an estimated 2,200 languages were spoken across the continents of Central and South America (Dickason, 1997, p. 5). In what would become Canada, 50 languages were spoken, which have been classified into 11 language families (see Figure 1.1). Not all people who speak the same language can understand one another. Many languages have a number of different dialects—variations of a common language. Since language is the conduit of culture, we know that the cultures are as diverse as their languages. Often we approach Indigenous people across Canada as if they are all part of one homogeneous group. This misconception often damages relationships between Indigenous people and mainstream Canadians.

Oral Tradition

Language conveys culture from one generation to the next. Indigenous culture accomplishes this through an oral tradition in which storytelling is the means of conveying values, social expectations, history, and knowledge. Storytellers hold a special place in Indigenous communities; storytelling is a tremendous responsibility that is taken very seriously. Stories are not passed down in a spontaneous manner; they are told and retold by the storyteller in teaching circles and formal ceremonies. Traditionally, few Indigenous cultures found a need to write; their storytellers have always been like living books. The stories they tell have certain features in common:

- They include various aspects of the storyteller's physical environment—the people, the local animals, and plants. Mythical creatures in the stories combine human characteristics with characteristics of local animals.
- They provide spiritual guidance and ethical instruction, exemplifying cultural values and expectations.
- They often include places that would be familiar and of spiritual significance to the listeners.
- They are rich in symbolism that sheds light on the origin of the people as well as on their world view.

European historians have tended to question the reliability of oral histories, believing that they are susceptible to being embellished, misinterpreted, or misunderstood. But they have found that the earliest recordings of Indigenous stories, which were compiled by Jesuit priests in the early 1600s, are identical to the stories being told by Indigenous elders and other storytellers today. This attests to the accuracy and completeness of oral transmission from one generation to the next and to the fact that these stories are timeless. Heirs to the text-centred European tradition would do well to remember that many of their culture's central narratives—the Bible, for example, and the seminal works of Homer—were in fact derived from oral renderings that subsisted for hundreds or thousands of years before anyone wrote them down. The oral and the written modes are not as distinct as is sometimes assumed. Stories about the Garden of Eden and Noah's ark, and other European creation stories, are, like Indigenous stories, filled with allegory and symbolism.

Creation Stories

One of the most important subjects in First Nations and Inuit stories is their origins. In all stories, the people either were created from the land in which they have traditionally lived or came to the land from some other spiritual place. Creation stories are important to a culture because they situate it in the world and shape its world view. Animals figure prominently in Indigenous stories of creation, working collaboratively with humans. Not only humans but animals and other natural elements are endowed with spirit by the Creator. The Creator gives humans stewardship of the natural world and compels them to live in harmony with it. This is remarkably different from Western ideas about the role of humans, which were based on the Christian concept of humankind having dominion over the natural world.

Concepts of Land and Spirituality

From these creation stories come foundations for a distinct world view. Intrinsic to this view is the connection to land. In these stories, land is more than merely a geographic territory or a potential source of wealth. It is *Land*—a sacred living entity, with its own rhythms and cycles. The life and spirituality of Indigenous peoples have always been connected to the land in a close, symbiotic relationship. They believe that because the people were born with the land as part of the common creation, they cannot be separated or differentiated from it.

All Indigenous peoples' spirituality is connected to the land. Their spiritual practices developed to reflect this connection, and these practices are as diverse as the nations themselves.

Mi'kmaq Creation Story—Two Creators and Their Conflicts

Before the earth was new, the sun was all that existed in the great universe. The sun divided the earth into several parts separated by many great lakes. In each part he caused one man and one woman to be born. They bore children and lived for many years. Wickedness pervaded this family, and slowly they killed one another. The sun wept and wept with grief. The tears became rain that fell from the skies until water covered the entire earth. The family had to set sail in bark canoes to save themselves from the flood. A violent wind overturned their boats. All perished in the sea but the old man and the old woman, who were best of all people, and it was they who populated the earth.

Source: Whitehead (1991).

Community Organization

Indigenous people organized themselves in different ways depending on their unique environments and spiritual beliefs. Generally, they organized themselves into communal groups that were egalitarian, self-sufficient, and connected to the land and its resources. Often they were connected to other specific nations in cooperative relationships for trade and the sharing of resources. These relationships were often set out in treaties that outlined each nation's responsibility to the others and, at times, delineated territorial boundaries for the purpose of resource management and harvest. Several nations would often be unified in a confederacy.

The Haudenosaunee, for example, were a collection of five nations: Mohawk, Seneca, Oneida, Onondaga, and Cayuga. Each nation had its own distinctive clan system. The Mohawk were bear, turtle, or wolf clan. The other nations had their respective clans. The Five Nations were united in a "League of Peace," otherwise known as the Iroquois Confederacy. The Confederacy was governed by a council of 50 chiefs representing the participant nations. Decisions were made by **consensus** among the chiefs and by the chief's consultation with the people whose interests he represented. Women had tremendous influence in the governmental system since they selected the chiefs and had the right also to remove a chief who proved to be unsatisfactory. Clarkson, Morrissette, and Régallet (1992, p. 16) have described the Indigenous decision-making process as follows:

> [W]hen decisions had to be made that affected the whole community, each clan would sit around a central fire with all other clans. Decisions the clan made together may include when to move, conservation of the resources of the territories, the striking of alliances and relationships with other nations and how to implement these decisions. Usually after

consensus government
a form of government that requires all parties to agree with a decision

much discussion and further consultation with their clan members, decisions would be made that would respect the interests of all clans and their members. Decisions were not arrived at in the same manner as western society today through majority vote. When decisions had to be made it would be through a consensus process. All people had to agree with the action or no action would be taken.

These forms of government indicate that cooperation and consensus are among the foundations of the Indigenous world view. Their spiritual teachings, by advising that decisions be made in the best interests not only of all living people but also of all people of the next seven generations, encourage a far-sighted concern for the community. Indigenous forms of governments are based on equality and on balancing individual interests against group interests, with group interests always taking precedence.

Because everything is connected in the Indigenous world view, spirituality influences land use, and both influence governance structures. There is no separation between these elements as there is in mainstream tradition. The conception of individual rights is not alien to the Indigenous system of social organization; it just is less important than group or collective rights. Negotiated rights to harvest territories are not individual rights; they are collective rights of the group. The harvest does not belong to the individual harvester but to the collective group and is distributed according to subsistence needs. The focus of Indigenous teachings is the individual's responsibilities to the group rather than the individual's rights within the group.

International Organization

Individual Indigenous nations did not exist in a vacuum. They were very aware of one another and entered into relationships to exchange knowledge and to trade material goods. In this way, they influenced one another's cultures. Sometimes nations traded for natural resources not available within their own territory. Agricultural societies such as the Iroquois traded their excess agricultural products. Trade took place over vast areas of the Americas.

Contact

First contact with Indigenous peoples in what would become Canada was made not by the British or the French, but by Vikings travelling from Greenland, drawn by the great supply of fish. They arrived in Newfoundland sometime between the 11th and 13th centuries and settled at L'Anse aux Meadows, which is today a UNESCO World Heritage Site. Little is known about the presence of the Vikings in North America; however, they did record their encounter with the Indigenous people of Newfoundland, whom they referred to as the "Skraelings." Although this group is known by several names, the most common is Beothuk. They were a small community of hunter-gatherers who depended upon the coastline for the fish and seals that they stored for consumption throughout the winter.

Explorer John Cabot arrived on the coast of Newfoundland in 1497, then carried news of the rich fishing waters back to Europe. Many Europeans were drawn by the opportunity to make their fortune exporting fish to Europe. In 1501, Portuguese explorer Gaspar Corte-Real captured 50 Beothuk and took them back to Europe as slaves. Probably as a result of this incident, the Beothuk subsequently avoided contact with whites.

By 1578, over 400 European fishing ships came to the region every summer. They began to occupy the coastline to dry fish, limiting the Beothuk's access to the ocean. Growing hostilities by the Europeans forced the Beothuk further inland, and, without access to the resources of the sea, they faced great hardship.

In 1713, the French were expelled, and the British increased their coastal settlements, further cutting off the Beothuk from the ocean and the resources that had sustained them for thousands of years. After taking control of the land and the resources, the British decided to attempt to protect the remaining Beothuk, whose population they recorded in 1768 as a mere 400. The British captured the last few Beothuk in 1810. The last known Beothuk, Shanawdithit, died of tuberculosis in 1829 (Dickason, 1997, pp. 73–74).

The first true voyage of discovery into what would become Canada was Jacques Cartier's exploration of the Gulf of St. Lawrence in 1534. Cartier met with the St. Lawrence Iroquois and engaged in trade with them. They described to him the route to the interior of the continent, where he hoped to find gold. With the help of his Iroquois guides, Cartier made it all the way to Hochelaga, present-day Montreal. He counted 14 villages on the north shore, of which Hochelaga was the largest, numbering 50 longhouses, with an estimated population of 1,500.

Europeans continued to arrive on Canada's eastern shores, drawn by a variety of hopes—of growing wealthy through the region's natural resources, of acquiring land, or of escaping poverty or religious persecution in the Old World. These Europeans continued to make contact with various Indigenous nations, each with its own form of governance and economic system.

Initially, contact involved a spirit of cooperation between the Indigenous groups and the colonists, and respect for one another's sovereignty. The reasons were threefold, and quite practical:

1. The Indigenous nations vastly outnumbered the colonists, who were poorly equipped for the harsh conditions of the land.
2. The economic interests of the newcomers depended on maintaining a good relationship with the Indigenous communities, who in turn benefited in terms of trade.
3. Indigenous people were desperately needed as military allies by the French and the English in their wars against each other, and, later, against the newly independent United States.

In the relationship between the Europeans and the Indigenous nations, the latter clearly had the upper hand at this point. This was made most clear in the Two-Row Wampum, or the *Guswentha*, the first agreement entered into between the Five Nations of the Iroquois and the British. To the Iroquois, the *Guswentha* was international law, recorded in wampum beads as was their custom. The two coloured rows of wampum represented an English trading ship and an Iroquois canoe. They travel parallel paths along the river of life. These paths never meet; the two nations are bound together in peace and friendship, with an agreement for reciprocal aid and defence. At the same time, neither nation is to interfere with the other or attempt to impose laws on it.

This agreement is well documented by the British, referred to as the **covenant chain**. The covenant chain was a clear recognition by both sides that their political systems would remain separate even as their systems of trade and alliance bound them. The British historical record, until it reaches the early 1800s, contains many references to this agreement.

covenant chain
first agreement entered into between the Five Nations of the Iroquois and the British; a clear recognition by both sides that their political systems would remain separate even as their systems of trade and alliance bound them

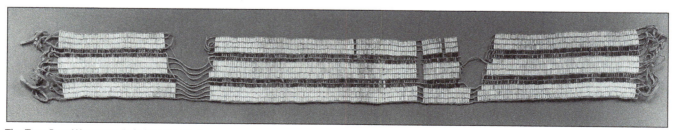

The Two-Row Wampum Belt (*Guswentha*).

This military alliance with the Iroquois served the British well and led to their defeat of the French in 1760. The French and British continually accused one another of bribing their allies with gifts and also of using Indigenous people, who during battles sustained great losses on the front lines, as "cannon fodder."

First Nations on both sides considered the battle to be between the French and the English and allied themselves with their traditional trade partners, viewing the outcome as a matter of trade dominance alone; they had no concept that their lands were at stake. They viewed the land as their sacred territory, which they had allowed Europeans to settle on under certain terms and conditions, such as trade alliances and gift distributions.

Upon the defeat of the French, many Indigenous leaders remarked to the English that it was not the Indigenous people that were conquered but the French. Ojibwe Chief Minweweh, whose warriors had fought on the side of the French, reminded the English: "Although you have conquered the French you have not conquered us. We are not your slaves. These lakes, woods and mountains were left us by our ancestors. They are our inheritance, and we will part with them to none" (Dickason, 1997, p. 155).

To address the Indigenous people's fears concerning the loss of their ancestral lands, the British included article 40 in the Capitulation of Montreal between the French and English. This section guaranteed First Nations protection of their lands from the encroachment of new settlers. It immediately proved difficult to enforce, however, as settlers began to pour in once peace had been established. Colonial governments displayed little will to enforce the legislation (Dickason, 1997, p. 153).

After the defeat of the French, First Nations found their position worsening. They had been holding the balance of power between two rivals, but now found themselves becoming irrelevant to both the British and the French. Gift distributions ended quickly, as did the supply of guns and ammunition. The Europeans no longer respected boundaries that First Nations set out as hunting grounds or sacred territories. Discontent among various nations led to a formidable uprising led by a remarkable man named Pontiac, an Odawa war chief, who was able to unite a number of nations in his quest to defeat the Europeans and drive them from the land. Within the span of two months in 1763, nine British forts fell to Pontiac with almost no casualties sustained by his men. The British feared being overrun and resorted to the first ever recorded case of biological warfare. They distributed smallpox-infected blankets to Indigenous settlements, wiping out entire communities, including women, children, and elders.

In this intense political climate, the British tried to justify their acquisition of land in the Americas. It was apparent to them that the land was in fact occupied by organized nations of people, albeit non-Christians. The British sought to reconcile their principles of justice with acquiring land for resource extraction and settlement. Securing the land for these purposes would be impossible without the help of the Indigenous nations. Britain was facing a growing rebellion in the 13 colonies and would require the allegiance of Indigenous nations again in war to avoid the loss of the New World altogether. Britain would never be able to secure the necessary allegiance if Europeans continued to trespass on the Indigenous peoples' territories, which was causing great animosity toward the British.

Royal Proclamation of 1763
the cornerstone of Indigenous land claims today; has been called the "*Magna Carta* of Indian Rights" and has been deemed by the courts to have the "force of a statute which has never been repealed"

The Royal Proclamation

In 1763, the British drew up an important piece of legislation to address the dilemma. The **Royal Proclamation of 1763** would become the cornerstone of Indigenous land claims today. This document has been called the "*Magna Carta* of Indian Rights" and has been deemed by the courts to have the "force of a statute which has never been repealed."

The first purpose of the Proclamation was to reserve a large piece of land for Indigenous occupation and use; under the Proclamation, the lands west of the Appalachian mountains were recognized as Indian lands. The second purpose was to appease Indigenous leaders in order to secure military allegiance and to stop the mounting Indigenous resistance movement. The third purpose was to create a treaty process by which the Crown alone could purchase Indigenous land for settlement.

Consider the wording of the Proclamation itself:

> And We do hereby strictly forbid, on Pain of our Displeasure, all our loving Subjects from making any Purchases or Settlements whatever, or taking Possession of any of the Lands above reserved [for Indians], without our especial leave and Licence for that Purpose first obtained.
>
> And We do further strictly enjoin and require all Persons whatever who have either wilfully or inadvertently seated themselves upon any Lands within the Countries above described, or upon any other Lands which, not having been ceded to or Purchased by Us, are still reserved to the said Indians as aforesaid, forthwith to remove themselves from such Settlements.
>
> And whereas great Frauds and Abuses have been committed in purchasing Lands of the Indians, to the great Prejudice of our Interests, and to the great Dissatisfaction of the said Indians: In order, therefore, to prevent such Irregularities for the future, and to the end that the Indians may be convinced of our Justice and determined Resolution to remove all reasonable Cause of Discontent, We do, with the Advice of our Privy Council strictly enjoin and require, that no private Person do presume to make any purchase from the said Indians of any Lands reserved to the said Indians, within those parts of our Colonies where We have thought proper to allow Settlement: but that, if at any Time any of the Said Indians should be inclined to dispose of the said Lands, the same shall be Purchased only for Us, in our Name, at some public Meeting or Assembly of the said Indians.

This powerful piece of legislation has never been repealed and therefore is still in effect and legally binding. The 13 colonies were very displeased with the limitations the Proclamation imposed on them; it became one of the many reasons for their rebellion against the British. The *Royal Proclamation* is legislation, drawn up by an imperial power, designed to protect the rights of Indigenous peoples to their land. As you continue to read, consider whether the British kept the terms of the Proclamation. Are we honouring these terms today?

The *Royal Proclamation* did accomplish what it set out to do: it drew a line between British territory and Indigenous land, and it convinced Indigenous people of Britain's "Justice and determined Resolution to remove all reasonable Cause of Discontent" where the Indigenous people were concerned. Its reassurances secured Indigenous support for the British in the upcoming American War of Independence and in Britain's later battles to repel the American invasion of what would become Canada.

The British government's third objective in establishing a treaty process to acquire land was to give the Crown a monopoly over land sales in Canada; it established itself as the only legal purchaser of Indigenous land. This was a source of enormous wealth for the British. In some of the first treaties in Ontario, the Crown purchased land for a mere 3 pence an acre from Indigenous people, who could not drive up the prices of their land by selling to any other party. The British then sold the land to private investors for settlement for 6 to 15 pence per acre, making a healthy profit.

The *Royal Proclamation* does not refer to Indigenous nations as sovereign nations, but neither does it refer to them as subjects of the Crown. It was not until after Confederation in 1867 that Canada began to aggressively and harshly subjugate Indigenous people.

The Fur Trade

During the early period of European–Indigenous contact, when settlement was still sparse, the fur trade was well under way. The French aligned with the Huron and other East Coast nations, and the English aligned with the Iroquois and their Indigenous allies. Both in trade and in war, the British and the French managed to exploit the divisions that had existed among Indigenous nations prior to contact.

The British set up the Hudson's Bay Company and the French, the Compagnie du Nord. The companies were in direct competition for the harvest and export of furs. Both attempted to extend their trade northward so as to gain control over trade routes. As early as 1632, the French were exporting up to 15,000 kilograms of furs a year. The French had 500 to 700 men on the canoe routes travelling to Huronia. Furs were the next best thing to gold (Dickason, 1997, p. 103).

The balance of power at this time was still very much in favour of the Indigenous nations. Consider, for example, that in 1633 the French colonies had 3,000 people, while the Huron nation alone numbered over 30,000. However, the Huron would shortly experience a rapid population decline as a result of European diseases brought by the missionaries and traders.

seigneurial farms
a system in which a man, usually a soldier, was granted land in the name of France

The French established a system of **seigneurial farms**, in which one man, usually a soldier, was granted land in the name of France. The soldier would bring over his family from France to labour on the farm to produce food for the fledgling colonies. The French did not enact any treaties to acquire this land for farming; they simply considered themselves as sole proprietors of the land by their mere presence. They declared the land to be *terra nullius*—empty land. The French did not recognize Indigenous nations as rightful possessors of land, on the grounds that the Indigenous people were not Christian. The French were, however, very careful to maintain good relationships with Indigenous nations and never made any open assertions to them about the ownership of the land on which they settled. The lack of treaties or legal arrangements to clear the land of Indigenous title became problematic later; upon the defeat of the French, the British also did not enact any legislation to clear the land of Indigenous title, assuming that the French had already done so.

As the fur trade expanded, forts were erected to house staff and government officials. The fur trade extended into northern Ontario in search of fresh supplies and to advance British interests. The fur trade was not conducted at a sustainable rate; beavers were all but extinct south of today's Canada–US border and soon neared extinction in southern Ontario in 1830 once the traders moved in.

The trading posts created new, non-Indigenous communities in Indigenous territory in the North, and had an impact on Indigenous people who came to sell furs. Posts were often established in strategic proximity to Indigenous campsites, and Indigenous groups who had traditionally been hunter-gatherers, travelling continuously with the seasons, began to create permanent dwellings around the trading posts.

Indigenous people began to barter for objects such as sewing needles, copper pots, knives, and hatchets. This improved their immediate quality of life; they traded for items they could not easily produce themselves. This trading system, however, could not create long-term economic prosperity in Indigenous communities. The real profits were being exported back to Europe in the form of furs, and the resources that had sustained Indigenous people for thousands of years were quickly being depleted beyond recovery.

Changes to Indigenous Communities

Contact with Europeans brought fundamental changes to Indigenous communities. For example, they began to develop notions of cumulative wealth. Before contact, Indigenous people had never viewed furs in terms of wealth. Animals were killed for food, shelter, clothing, and

CALL TO ACTION

The Truth and Reconciliation Commission (TRC) was established in 2008 with the goal of hearing the stories of First Nations people who had been affected by the residential school system, a part of Canada's systemic attempt to subjugate and assimilate Indigenous peoples. You will read more about this in Chapter 3. As part of its final report, issued in 2015, the TRC made 94 Calls to Action—steps to be taken to help redress the legacy of Canada's residential school system in particular and repair Canada's relationship with Indigenous peoples in general.

You will see some of these Calls to Action placed throughout the text near the historical incidents that they address. When you read them, consider how the repercussions of these historical incidents continue to affect the lives of Indigenous people today.

> 45. We call upon the Government of Canada, on behalf of all Canadians, to jointly develop with Aboriginal peoples a Royal Proclamation of Reconciliation to be issued by the Crown. The proclamation would build on the Royal Proclamation of 1763 and the Treaty of Niagara of 1764, and reaffirm the nation-to-nation relationship between Aboriginal peoples and the Crown. The proclamation would include, but not be limited to, the following commitments: Repudiate concepts used to justify European sovereignty over Indigenous lands and peoples such as the Doctrine of Discovery and *terra nullius*.

tools. Anything that the hunter did not need would be given to another family. The proceeds generated by the hunt were shared among community members. Hunting for more than the community needed simply did not make any sense; collecting and storing hides was ill-adapted to the Indigenous peoples' traditional lifestyle. Arrangements for trade of excesses could be made with neighbouring nations, but the scale of this trade was never such that it would outstrip the environment.

Economic imperatives, previously non-existent, began to influence the process by which Indigenous leaders were selected. The clan system, which had previously maintained the groups' cohesiveness by maintaining strict rules, values, and social mores, slowly lost its influence.

Indigenous groups became increasingly dependent on European traders and less reliant on their own natural environment and on the traditional web of trade established between Indigenous nations prior to contact. The introduction of alcohol through trade created new societal problems that have persisted to this day in some Indigenous communities. For many Indigenous nations, this dependence on European trade became entrenched; for others it remained insignificant. Europeans were eager to foster this dependence because it provided an advantage in trade. For Indigenous people, the fur trade did not provide economic stability; the prices of furs were dependent on the whims of fashion, and the fur harvest fluctuated according to environmental conditions and animal populations. The rate of harvest was unsustainable, and the fur trade was destined to collapse.

Many animals that were hunted for their fur neared extinction by the early 1800s. As a result, many trading posts closed, bringing extreme hardship to those Indigenous people who had come to rely on their commerce. Many faced starvation and diseases unknown before contact. The government provided food and other necessities but could never restore the economy of Indigenous people. Animal resources had been depleted beyond recovery in the first phase of harvest. Indigenous lands later underwent a second harvesting of natural resources in the form of logging and mining, which proved no less devastating to their society.

Along with trade goods, Europeans brought Christian religion—English Protestant and French Catholic—and missionaries to spread the faith. Indigenous people were not eager to accept missionaries or their faith. Traders brought practical benefits such as guns and copper pots, but new spiritual beliefs were something Indigenous people simply did not value. Eventually, however, most Indigenous groups began to accept missionaries into their communities, sometimes for self-serving reasons. In some instances, traders and missionaries assisted one another's causes; Indigenous trappers who had converted to Christianity were often given better prices for their furs and were permitted to purchase guns and ammunition while their non-Christian peers were not. The missionaries often became frustrated with these incentives, believing that Indigenous people were converting for convenience rather than from genuine desire for the Christian religion.

The Indigenous conversions may often have been half-hearted or purely mercenary, but the impact of European religion on Indigenous communities was unquestionably profound. Missionaries restricted or forbade Indigenous ceremonies, traditions, and cultural practices, pronouncing them "from the devil." With these elements of their culture gone—elements that had been the foundations of their values, unity, and governance for thousands of years—Indigenous communities began to unravel. Differences arose between those who accepted European religion and those who did not, and this disrupted communities and families. In extreme cases, such as in Oka, Quebec, the churches or religious orders were given authority to govern reserve land and resources. Resources were extracted and the churches reaped the financial profits while the Indigenous people were driven into poverty.

Following the American Revolution, a massive influx of settlers into Upper Canada began. Land was needed for settlement, and in keeping with the *Royal Proclamation of 1763* the British began the tedious process of acquiring Indigenous land through treaty. Although Indigenous people did not fully understand the treaty-making process, they had no choice but to engage in it; with Canada competing with its US neighbours for occupancy and therefore title over lands and access to resources, the British felt pressure to expand westward.

CLOSE-UP   Oka

In 1717, King Louis XV of France granted land 30 kilometres northwest of Montreal to the Seminary of Saint-Sulpice on the condition that it be used as a mission for the Mohawk people who had settled there. The grant was made to the seminary since it was deemed that the Mohawk could not manage the land themselves. The condition of the grant was such that if the Mohawk later abandoned the land, its ownership would revert to the Crown. The documents did not state whether the Sulpicians were the sole proprietors of the land or the trustees of the land for the Mohawk. As far as the Mohawk were concerned, the land had always been and continued to be their territory. The particular location was chosen so that the Mohawk territory, Kanesatake, was far enough from Montreal to limit negative influences from the French settler population, but close enough that the Mohawk could quickly be called into military action in defence of the French.

After the French lost their North American colonies, the Mohawk of Kanesatake unsuccessfully tried in 1781 to prove in court their proprietorship of the land. In 1841, the British issued a special ordinance confirming the seminary's title amid continuing disputes over the land and its resources. As the Mohawk began to turn from the Catholic faith to Methodism, the seminary encouraged them to leave Kanesatake so that French Canadians could settle there, establishing the town of Oka. To relieve tensions, in 1853 the Indian Department set aside land in Ontario and elsewhere in Quebec for the Mohawk of Kanesatake; however, most refused to leave. The Mohawk continued to assert

their rights to the land, cutting wood and building cabins. Some were jailed for cutting trees, since the seminary claimed rights to the timber. Violence ensued in many skirmishes, including one in which a church was burned down. In 1869, and again in 1878 and 1912, the government affirmed the seminary's ownership of the land.

In 1936, facing a financial crisis, the Church sold parts of this land for development, causing such strife that the Indian Department purchased the unsold portions of the land and managed it as a reserve, even though it was not granted reserve status. In 1961 the Mohawk requested that the land be granted reserve status so that it had protection from sale under the *Indian Act*; this was not granted. In 1975, as a new land claims process was outlined, the Mohawk put forward a comprehensive land claim, which was rejected. They filed a specific land claim two years later, which was rejected in 1986.

The claim, still unresolved, reached a boiling point in 1990 when the town of Oka announced that a nine-hole golf course on the contested land would be expanded and luxury condominiums built there also. In the resulting violent confrontation between Quebec police and the Indigenous residents of Kanesatake, an officer of the Sûrete du Québec was shot and killed. A 78-day standoff between the Canadian army and the Mohawk of Kanesatake cost millions and failed to resolve the land question.

Source: Dickason (1997, pp. 319–322).

Once occupancy was established, the "Indian question" remained. What would the colonies do with regard to the Indigenous peoples with whom they had entered into treaties? The newly formed government of Canada chose to embark upon a journey of forced assimilation by carefully enacting legislation designed to eliminate the Indigenous peoples as a special group within Canadian society.

Treaties Background

Most **treaties** in Canada were signed between 1800 and the early 1900s. They are documents drawn up by the Canadian government as purchase agreements for land recognized as having Indigenous title. In 1982 the treaties were protected in section 35 of the *Canadian Charter of Rights and Freedoms*, which reads as follows: "The existing aboriginal and treaty rights of the aboriginal peoples of Canada are hereby recognized and affirmed." This is a recent affirmation of the legitimacy of these treaty documents. Indigenous people continue to petition the government of Canada to fulfill its treaty promises and to have the original spirit of the treaties interpreted by the courts to uphold Indigenous rights to resources and land.

Treaties were not unknown to Indigenous people prior to the arrival of Europeans. Since time immemorial, Indigenous nations had made treaties among themselves to settle wars, establish ties of peace and friendship, create military alliances, delineate harvest territories, and facilitate trade. The records of these treaties were passed down orally and were honoured by the groups who entered into them.

When Europeans arrived, Indigenous people entered into treaties with them as well, such as the Two-Row Wampum treaty between the Iroquois and the British described above and the British–Mi'kmaq Treaty of 1725, which covered Nova Scotia as well as other territories. The British secured military neutrality and assistance from the Mi'kmaq in their war against the French in exchange for facilitating trade and guaranteeing protection of the Mi'kmaq people's traditional economy of hunting and fishing.

Indigenous people expected that the principles that had governed their earlier agreements—treaties of peace and friendship, military and trade alliances—would carry over into their negotiations with the Europeans over land. To them, mutual respect and understanding were essential components of negotiations. And they assumed, in keeping with the principles of their oral culture, that terms negotiated by way of discussion would be included in the final agreement.

This was not the case for Europeans; they had a different conception of written documents as opposed to spoken assurances, and different goals for the negotiations. Indigenous people believed that no one could own the land in the European sense of ownership. The land was a gift from the Creator, and they were stewards of the land, not owners of it. Indigenous people viewed the treaties as laying out the terms of a mutual sharing of resources, including their own compensation for consenting to share with Europeans.

Europeans understood the treaties, according to their own cultural context, as requiring First Nations to yield the land to the Europeans, thus giving the Europeans absolute ownership of the land. The intention was to erase First Nations title to the land so that it could be parcelled out for sale for new ownership. Although both parties had interpreters present, it was difficult to translate the European understanding of ownership into terms the First Nations negotiators would grasp. In retrospect, too, one must wonder how diligently the Crown tried to convey its intended meaning; a full understanding on the part of the First Nations people would most certainly have brought negotiations to an unsuccessful conclusion. Many times it was not until the Europeans began the process of removing First Nations people from their land that the latter fully understood what they had signed.

There are three categories of treaties in Canada: (1) pre-Confederation treaties, which were entered into before 1867; (2) numbered treaties, signed between 1871 and 1921, and intended

treaty
an agreement between two states that has been formally concluded and ratified

to unite the interior of Canada and formally recognize these territories as part of Canada, as well as to clear title to build a railway to facilitate the extraction of resources; and (3) land claims agreements, which were made after 1973, when the government established a formal land claims policy.

All treaties before 1973 were initiated by Europeans. Indigenous people never began any negotiations to sell their land. Following the defeat of the British in the American Revolution of 1776–1783, the British sought land to compensate both their Indigenous allies—primarily, the Six Nations (Mohawk, Onondaga, Cayuga, Seneca, Oneida, and Tuscarora), who had performed military services and sustained considerable losses for the British—and their other military allies. In 1784, Frederick Haldimand purchased 3 million acres (1.2 million hectares) from the Mississauga for £1,180 worth of goods to facilitate the settlement of the Loyalists. The Iroquois loyalists were granted a tract 6 miles (10 kilometres) wide on either side of the Grand River, a total of almost 1.2 million hectares in what is today southwestern Ontario. This is known as the Haldimand Grant, which provided a land base for the Six Nations reserve. In Chapter 2 we will look at this grant and discuss its implications for today.

Until 1798, the government had no problem obtaining Indian land, through treaty, for about 3 pence per acre in either cash or goods, then selling that land for a healthy profit to private investors and settlers for 6 to 15 pence per acre. By 1912, there were 483 treaties listed for Canada, comprising a considerable body of law (Dickason, 1997, p. 163).

Indigenous allies became the deciding factor in yet another war—the War of 1812—as the newly independent United States attempted to make its way north into British-held territory. The British were victorious and in the end established a border between the United States and Canada. In the following years of peace, the European population in Canada once again exploded. Between 1821 and 1851, the European population rose from 750,000 to 2.3 million (Dickason, 1997, p. 198). Once again the Crown was desperate for land to accommodate the population growth. With peace in sight, the British had less need of their Indigenous allies, who thus lost one of their key means of maintaining a balance of power. The government began to offer First Nations people annuities for their land rather than the considerably larger one-sum payments. This was a more economical way for the Crown to obtain land through treaty, since the annuities could be paid from the profitable sale of the land to settlers.

The treaty-making process was quite irregular. The Crown representative was included as a negotiator, but otherwise there seems to have been no standard policy, especially concerning the price of land. In 1790, for example, 2 million acres (809,000 hectares) were purchased by the Crown for £1,200 from the Ojibwe and Odawa in southern Ontario. Two years later, 3 million acres (1.2 million hectares) were purchased from the same group for the same amount (Dickason, 1997, p. 164). Many of these land transactions were not properly recorded or were imprecise in their terms regarding boundaries, giving rise to later disputes. For example, one treaty, aptly named the "gunshot treaty," describes a boundary as being "from the lakeshore to as far back as you can hear a gunshot." Many of the original treaties were lost. By the mid-1830s, a sequence of over 30 treaties had been concluded, effectively covering southern Ontario.

There were many problems with the treaty process. First, as discussed previously, there was the problem of making the First Nations people understand such concepts as exclusive possession of property. Second, there was the government's unscrupulous tendency to weight the written terms of the agreement more heavily than the oral ones that the First Nations negotiators considered binding. Today, efforts have been made to research the recorded minutes of council meetings before and after the signing of a treaty. This research has brought to light promises that were clearly made by the government but never written into treaty documents, which were then signed by individuals who could not read. Third, there was the problem of obtaining signatures from the leaders of First Nations affected by the treaty. Many First Nations were left out of the treaty-signing process simply because government officials did not know they were there. With a stroke of a pen, the government seized the land of these people without their permission or signatures. Adhesions (subsequent signings) had to be made later to the treaties to include some groups who had been overlooked.

Numbered Treaties

Following Confederation in 1867, treaty negotiations began with a large number of First Nations across Canada. These treaties are referred to as the "numbered treaties"; they were made in the interest of nation building and to acquire land for a national railway. These treaties cover very large land areas (see Figure 1.2). The terms of the 1850 Robinson–Huron treaty became a precedent for the other numbered treaties. These terms included the following:

- Sale of reserved lands and mineral rights was to be conducted by the government for the sole use and benefit of the First Nations.
- Negotiations were to be open and accessible to the public.

FIGURE 1.2   Treaties and Comprehensive Land Claims in Canada

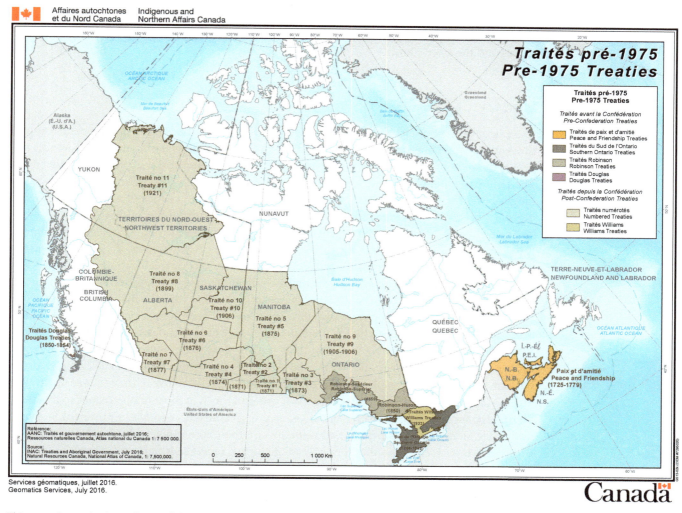

This map shows the boundaries of the land surrender treaties made between Indigenous peoples and the Crown between 1725 and 1975.

- Land was to be surrendered only to the Crown.
- Annexed to each treaty, a schedule of reserves was to be held in common by each group affected by the treaty.
- Annuities were to be paid in cash to signing members.
- First Nations retained "the full and free privilege to hunt over the Territory now ceded by them, and to fish in the waters thereof ... saving and excepting such portions of the said Territory as may from time to time be sold or leased to individuals or companies of individuals" (Aboriginal Affairs and Northern Development Canada, 1939).

The numbered treaties based the quantity of land reserved for First Nations people on their population in the treaty area at the time. These populations were smaller than pre-contact populations, since Indigenous peoples had sustained at least an 80 percent death toll due to European diseases. Among other items, agreements regarding schooling, annuities, and agricultural equipment for First Nations were included in most numbered treaties.

This brings us to a common misconception among Canadians. Some believe that federally funded education, housing, or taxation exemption are special and generous provisions from the federal government for First Nations. This is not the case; the federal government has frequently tried to escape these obligations but has been instructed by the courts that the treaties hold the force of law and must be honoured. These benefits were granted to First Nations people in negotiated treaties by which the Crown acquired the land that is now Canada. In the words of the treaties, these terms are to be upheld "as long as the grass is green, as long as the sun shines and the rivers flow."

Western Expansion

The pressure to populate the West with white settlers intensified following the conclusion of the American Revolution in 1783. It was apparent that the western lands and all the wealth and resources therein would belong to whoever could get there first and was prepared to defend it. The newly independent United States had severed its ties with Britain and therefore was no longer bound by the *Royal Proclamation*, and it embarked on a series of wars against the Indigenous inhabitants of the Americas in order to clear them from the land.

The British colonies created incentives for immigrants and other white settlers to move west, enticing agricultural settlers with 64 hectares of free "Crown land." Rapid work was required to obtain that land from the current occupants by way of treaty. The protection of this western land would be provided in part by the Indigenous peoples themselves. Recall that the United States concluded terms of independence in 1783. After this, the British were concerned about the Americans moving west and northward, as well as about the possibility of an American attack on the remaining British colonies, which would ultimately happen in 1812. The British had learned a valuable lesson in their wars against the French: the side with the most Indigenous allies would win. Between 1784 and 1788, the British spent £20,000 on gift distributions to Indigenous people, hoping to secure military allegiance as they moved westward. This was more than the British had paid to secure land through most of the treaties to that date. They were successful in securing the allegiance of Tecumseh, who was a powerful Shawnee leader. He sided with the British and united more than 30 nations to lead in the defence of British-held territories. Together they helped the British repel the Americans in the War of 1812. Tecumseh sided with the British not only for the gift distributions but also because he believed them to be the lesser of two evils, since the British continued to make assurances of protecting Indian lands, an assurance that the United States would not make.

VOICES

Tecumseh

My heart is a stone. Heavy with sadness for my people; cold with the knowledge that no treaty will keep the whites out of our land; hard with determination to resist as long as I live and breathe. Now we are weak and many of our people are afraid. But hear me; a single twig breaks but the bundle of twigs is strong. Someday I will embrace our brother tribes and draw them into a bundle and together we will win our country back from the whites.

Following the War of 1812, western expansion accelerated again. Northwestern Indigenous peoples such as the Sioux, Blackfoot, and Plains Cree, as well as the Métis, had built an economy based on the buffalo. Upon the arrival of traders, a market was quickly created for buffalo products. The hides became fashionable to wear, and the bones were exported to create bone china, popular in Europe. Bison bones were used in a wide variety of other applications as well, including as fertilizer; as part of the refining of sugar, liquor, and vinegar; and during the manufacture of dyes. At the peak of the bison slaughter, a ton of dried bones could sell for as much as $10. In less than a century, by 1889, the number of buffalo had been reduced from 70 million to 635. Needless to say, this caused extreme hardship among the Indigenous peoples of the plains at a time when treaty negotiations were fully under way.

Ultimately, Europeans made it all the way to the west coast of Canada. In 1785 the first trading ships arrived, drawn by the lucrative trade in sea otter pelts. Contact and trade were done by ship because an overland route was not found until 1804. Within the first 100 years of contact, West Coast peoples suffered an 80 percent population decrease due to European diseases, one of the most dramatic declines in an Indigenous population since first contact (Dickason, 1997, p. 180).

Sea otter pelt trading was in full swing by 1792, and by 1825 the sea otter population was devastated. One trader, John Kendrick, reported that he traded £100 worth of chisels and iron tools for 200 sea otter pelts. He then received £8,000 for the pelts in Europe (Dickason, 1997, p. 181).

In 1852, Vancouver Island had only 500 settlers; however, the discovery of gold brought 25,000 miners to Queen Charlotte Island in 1858. Salish First Nations and miners clashed regularly, sometimes violently. The destruction of Indigenous territories was rapid, and their land base eroded with the building of roads and mines.

Salmon resources were being exploited for export to European markets. Salmon was a main source of subsistence for many First Nations such as the Nisga'a, and the depletion of this resource caused them significant hardship. James Douglas, governor of Vancouver and the British Columbia mainland at this critical time, attempted to acquire land by way of treaty. He had signed 14 treaties with Salish bands on Vancouver Island by 1854, but this amounted to only 3 percent of the island's territory. The First Nations were not eager to enter into treaties, and James Douglas quickly ran out of money. Although the colony offered no further finances, Douglas was undeterred and continued to establish reservations for the First Nations people based on their favourite locations and on their numbers. He allotted 200 acres (81 hectares) per head of family, then simply assumed the rest of Vancouver Island and British Columbia to be territory of the Crown. He retired in 1864 and was succeeded by Frederick Seymore, who appointed a commissioner of Crown lands, Joseph Trutch. Trutch refused to recognize the legitimacy of the reserves established by Douglas, and was hostile to First Nations land claims. He wrote:

The Amerindians have no rights to the land as they were of no actual value to them, and I cannot see why they should either retain these lands to the prejudice of the general interests of the colony. Or be allowed to make a market of them to either the government or individuals. (Dickason, 1997, p. 234)

Trutch proceeded to reduce the size of the reserves surveyed by Douglas from 200 to 10 acres (81 to 4 hectares) per head of family, again without compensation.

British Columbia entered Confederation with Canada in 1871 and was allowed to retain control over "Crown land." But the federal government assumed responsibility for "Indians and lands reserved for Indians" as per the *British North America Act* of 1867. Arguments between provincial and federal governments began over how much land was to be granted for reserved First Nations land. British Columbia tried to reduce the lands even further, to 4 acres (1.6 hectares) per head of family, but the federal government insisted on 80 acres (32 hectares). British Columbia persisted in assigning reserves for First Nations without compensation, and by 1900 there were over 90 reserves established at an average of 185 acres (75 hectares) each (Dickason, 1997, pp. 234–235).

Note the emerging pattern here with regard to the seizure of land and resources. Most of the resources were exported to Europe; however, much of the wealth produced from the resources went toward building what is now our very affluent country. In fact, Canada still relies for its wealth on natural resources such as timber, oil, and gas; owners of land often grow wealthy from its natural resources. Unfortunately, Indigenous peoples generally do not share in this wealth. As we will see in Chapter 4, Indigenous people still suffer from higher than average levels of poverty and today live on only one-half of 1 percent of Canada's land mass.

EXERCISE 1

Consider the concept of "progress" from different cultural world views. How did the Western concept of progress affect Canada's Indigenous peoples?

Vanishing Race

The size of almost all reserves established through the treaty process was based on the population of the First Nation at the time of the treaty. But First Nations populations were low during this period, and the treaties made no provision for an increase in numbers. This seems evidence of a strong belief that Indigenous people were vanishing. And in fact they were dying at a rapid rate from disease, and many were lost in the numerous wars among the colonists. It was generally believed that within three generations of treaty-making there would be no Indigenous people left; they would either die of disease or be assimilated into mainstream Canada.

The Canadian government's intent regarding First Nations was never made so clear as it was by Deputy Superintendent of Indian Affairs Duncan Campbell Scott in 1920:

> I want to get rid of the Indian problem. I do not think as a matter of fact that this country ought to continually protect a class of people who are able to stand alone. That is my whole point. ... That has been the whole purpose of Indian Education and advancement since earliest times. One of the very earliest enactments was to provide for the enfranchisement of the Indian. So it is written in our law that the Indian was eventually to become enfranchised. ... Our object is to continue until there is not a single Indian in Canada that has not been absorbed into the body politic and there is no Indian question, and no Indian department, that is the whole object of this Bill. (Leslie & Maguire, 1978)

Scott's view was reflected in the actions of certain Canadians during this period. Indigenous graves, often fresh, were dug up so that the remains could be put on display at Wild West

Repatriating the G'psgolox Totem Pole

The G'psgolox totem pole was carved and raised in British Columbia in 1872 by the Raven Clan of the Haisla Nation after its chief, G'psgolox, had had a spiritual experience. An avalanche drove the nation to abandon its home, where the pole stood. Shortly thereafter, collectors from Sweden, who had been looking for a totem pole for their museum, found and removed it. The Haisla did not know where the pole had gone, and its whereabouts remained a mystery until it was located in the Museum of Ethnography in Stockholm, Sweden in 1991. The chief of the Haisla and a descendant of the pole's creator went to Sweden to request the pole's return. After long negotiations, the support of the BC government, and many delays, the return of the pole was celebrated in 2006 in Kitamaat, BC. The G'psgolox totem pole was the first to be repatriated to its people and began the return of many artifacts that have been housed for a century or more in European museums.

Source: Gersten (2007).

shows. Spiritual and cultural artifacts still in use by Indigenous people were taken and sold to collectors, who anticipated their value increasing as the Indigenous people themselves vanished. Today, Indigenous nations have undertaken serious efforts to repatriate these items and bring them back to their communities from museums around the world.

The idea of the Indigenous peoples' vanishing was appealing to the British for one very important reason: the treaties they had entered into with First Nations were binding in perpetuity. The British could see that the cost of maintaining these promises forever could be high, particularly because the depletion of resources was impoverishing First Nations people and creating a need among them for the relief assistance guaranteed by the treaties. Assimilation of those who survived disease and poverty became a paramount concern for the British in the years to come. The complete assimilation of First Nations meant no obligation to honour treaties and free access to reserve lands.

Assimilation Legislation

In the 1830s, as settlers and resource speculators increasingly encroached on reserve land, it became necessary to define who was an Indian and who therefore could reside on reserves. The following were considered Indians under the definition fashioned by the Crown:

- All individuals of Indian blood belonging to a tribe, band, or body of Indians and their descendants.
- Any person residing among such Indians whose parents were or are descended on either side from Indians, and the descendants of this person.
- All women lawfully married to an Indian and their children. First Nations women who married non–First Nations men would not be entitled to be Indian; nor would their children.

In 1830, the British began attempts to assimilate Indigenous people into mainstream culture, pushing them to become agriculturalists, to set up communities similar to white settlements, and to adopt the Christian religion and ways of life. Some Indigenous nations accepted this transition and requested assistance with it; they recognized that the industrialization of their lands would make the hunting way of life impossible. Furthermore, they believed that conversion to the "ideal" might help protect their lands. Model villages were set up and overseen by missionaries; many were quite successful. However, regardless of their success, as white communities expanded, the model villages lost land, and many were relocated. From the perspective of the British government, the genius of this plan was that the finances required to set up these communities and begin the "civilizing" process would come from the funds generated through the sale of reserve land or through the extraction of resources such as lumber from reserve lands. In effect, Indigenous people would pay their own way to "civilization" (Dickason, 1997, p. 199).

CALL TO ACTION

60. We call upon leaders of the church parties to the Settlement Agreement and all other faiths, in collaboration with Indigenous spiritual leaders, Survivors, schools of theology, seminaries, and other religious training centres, to develop and teach curriculum for all student clergy, and all clergy and staff who work in Aboriginal communities, on the need to respect Indigenous spirituality in its own right, the history and legacy of residential schools and the roles of the church parties in that system, the history and legacy of religious conflict in Aboriginal families and communities, and the responsibility that churches have to mitigate such conflicts and prevent spiritual violence.

The Crown passed legislation in 1857 called the *Gradual Civilization Act* to create a process of enfranchisement for First Nations people, so that they could cease being considered Indigenous. Enfranchisement began as a voluntary process. The legislation set out that if a First Nations male was self-supporting, debt-free, and deemed by the superintendent to be a suitable candidate for enfranchisement, he could forfeit his Indian status and receive 50 acres (20 hectares) of land cut from his people's reserve. Furthermore, he would thereafter have all the rights of a regular citizen, including the right to vote in provincial and federal elections. If it had been successful, this legislation would have eroded the reserve land base as well as First Nations sovereignty. Very few First Nations people accepted this offer (Dickason, 1997, p. 225).

In 1869, the *Enfranchisement Act* was introduced to limit blood quantum to at least one-quarter Indian in order to qualify to remain a status Indian. All others would be removed automatically from treaty entitlements. The purpose of this legislation, in the words of a bureaucrat in 1871, was "to lead the Indian people by degrees to mingle with the white race in the ordinary avocations of life" (Miller, 2004). The result would be fewer treaty Indians. Amazingly, this focus continued to be central to all legislation designed to administer Indian people until 1985.

During Confederation in 1867, at a time when efforts were focused on nation building, the British Parliament passed the **British North America Act**, also known now as the *Constitution Act, 1867*. Indigenous people were not consulted in the creation of the Act, and the Act did not recognize the right of Indigenous self-government. Section 91(24) of this Act gave Canada authority over "Indians, and Lands reserved for Indians." Many historians believe this was a turning point in history that marked the beginning of an era of serious oppression of Indigenous people in Canada. Through the BNA Act, the power of Indigenous governments was reduced to less than that of a municipality. Power would be held by the federal government with no regard to the diversity of First Nations peoples, their cultures, or their historical relationships with the Crown. They would all be treated as one homogeneous group and governed by a one-size-fits-all policy. They would no longer have the right to negotiate with the British

British North America Act
a statute enacted on March 29, 1867, by the British Parliament providing for the Confederation of Canada

Crown in regard to legislation affecting them or their lands; rather, they would have to negotiate with the federal government, which had a keen interest in acquiring the lands occupied by Indigenous people.

CALL TO ACTION

45. We call upon the Government of Canada … to … [r]econcile Aboriginal and Crown constitutional and legal orders to ensure that Aboriginal peoples are full partners in Confederation, including the recognition and integration of Indigenous laws and legal traditions in negotiation and implementation processes involving Treaties, land claims, and other constructive agreements.

The Indian Act

Within nine years of Confederation, the legislation regarding First Nations was consolidated into one act called the **Indian Act**. The *Indian Act* retained the earlier definition of an Indian but, continuing to broaden its scope of authority, now defined a band as well (Dickason, 1997, p. 259). The original *Indian Act* defined a band as follows:

> The term "band" means any tribe, band or body of Indians who own or are interested in a reserve or in Indian lands in common, of which the legal title is vested in the Crown, or who share alike in the distribution of any annuities or interest moneys for which the Government of Canada is responsible; the term "the band" means the band to which the context relates; and the term "band," when action is being taken by the band as such, means the band in council.

According to the current *Indian Act*, a band is

> a body of Indians
>   (a) for whose use and benefit in common, lands, the legal title to which is vested in Her Majesty, have been set apart before, on or after September 4, 1951,
>   (b) for whose use and benefit in common, moneys are held by Her Majesty, or
>   (c) declared by the Governor in Council to be a band for the purposes of this Act.

The lands mentioned in paragraph (a) refer to a reserve. Many First Nation groups are still awaiting designation as bands in accordance with this legislation; without such designation, the government does not afford them any benefits or protection. There are currently 617 recognized bands in Canada and 126 in Ontario.

The *Indian Act* did not include the Inuit because there was little contact between Canada and the Inuit at the time. The government was intent on reducing rather than increasing the number of status Indians. So when the Inuit question arose in the 1930s, Ottawa's position was that since the Inuit are not culturally Indians, they were not included in the *British North America Act*, section 91(24), which designated the federal government's responsibility for Indians. In the 1930s, the Inuit of northern Quebec were hard hit by a scarcity in the game that were their traditional source of sustenance, and they needed relief assistance. Neither level of government wanted any responsibility to provide this assistance, even though fur traders, miners, and whalers had spent decades extracting resources from Inuit land without compensating the land's inhabitants. The Quebec government took the federal government to court, arguing that the Inuit were Indians for all intents and purposes and should fall under the authority of the federal government. In 1939, the Supreme Court of Canada ruled that the Inuit, although culturally distinct, would be considered Indians, but would not be included in the *Indian Act*.

Despite the Inuit's being legally classified as Indians, the government neglected them until after the Second World War, when the need arose for military expansion into the North. Between

Indian Act
a statute created in 1876 to consolidate all policies aimed at the administration of Indian populations in Canada and giving the federal government exclusive jurisdiction over Indians and reserves

1941 and 1970, the federal government used a disk system to identify those Inuit for which it accepted responsibility. Each disk, which could be worn on a string around the neck, bore the Canadian coat of arms and the identity number of the wearer. This simplified record keeping, since the naming system used by the Inuit was unfamiliar to the government. The disk evolved into proof of status: those who had disks were eligible for government services; those without were not.

Other groups were also left out of the legislation aimed at Indians, including the Innu of Newfoundland and Labrador. When these territories entered Confederation in 1949, the rights of Indians to be defined and dealt with in accordance with Canadian legislation such as the *Indian Act* were originally included in the documents but were deleted prior to ratification, leaving the Innu with no protection for their territories and no guarantees of any assistance in times of need.

The Métis

As a result of the fur trade, many French and English traders married Inuit and First Nations women, creating a new and culturally distinct group of people in Canada. This group—the Métis—were also not included as Indians within the Act. The children of these unions grew up predominantly in their mothers' cultures—commonly Cree, Ojibwe, Saulteaux, or Inuit—but they were also introduced to French Catholicism and English Protestantism. As these communities grew in number, they became even more distinct as second and third generations intermarried. They occupied settled communities in Rupert's Land, owned under Crown patent by the Hudson's Bay Company; spoke French or English; and were predominantly employed by the Hudson's Bay Company or the North West Company as trappers, traders, buffalo hunters, exporters of pemmican, and interpreters. The Métis settlements in the Red River Colony (today's Winnipeg area) and Saskatchewan each developed a unique culture. When the government of Canada took over Rupert's Land in 1869, the ownership of the Red River Colony land was called into question.

The Métis as a distinct group did not enter into treaties but were occasionally included in treaty documents, listed as "half-breeds." They had settled all over Rupert's Land, and its sale to Canada left them with claims to settlements that had never been treated. The Métis united to set up a provisional government under Louis Riel, who negotiated the passage of the *Manitoba Act* in 1870, which brought the Red River Colony into Confederation as the province of Manitoba shortly thereafter. The Act provided Métis with 1.4 million acres (570,000 hectares) of reserve land. This was intended to give the Métis, who already lived there, a head start on land acquisition and to secure their settlements before a massive influx of European settlers arrived. After Manitoba joined Confederation, the transfer of land did not proceed as promised. However, the Supreme Court of Canada's recent decision in *Daniels v. Canada (Indian Affairs and Northern Development)* (2016) confirmed that Métis peoples are recognized as Indians under section 91(24) of the *Constitution Act, 1867*. This may open the door to the future settlement of historic Métis land claims.

When Ottawa sent out surveyors to assess and survey Rupert's Land to prepare for additional settlement, the Métis became very concerned over their position in their territories and the preservation of their unique culture. The Métis blocked the surveyors' access to the territory and rebelled against the settler government. Louis Riel, as leader of the rebellion, ordered the execution of one of its representatives and, as a result, was himself later hanged for treason.

The Métis did not fall under the strict definition of the *Indian Act* since they had no formally recognized bands, although they were defined as a distinct people. The *Indian Act* therefore did not provide the Métis land protection rights nor rights to education or relief. They are today recognized as one of Canada's founding Indigenous peoples, and their Aboriginal rights are protected under section 35 of the *Constitution Act, 1982*. To be recognized as Métis today, an individual must fulfill the following three conditions: self-identification as a Métis, ancestral connection to a historic Métis community, and acceptance by a Métis community (*R v. Powley*, 2003).

Imposed System of Government

The *Indian Act* quickly provided for the removal of First Nations traditional systems of governance and replaced them with a system called the band council. It is similar in nature to municipal governments in that it comprises one chief and several councillors elected through a process that is strictly regulated by the Act. This system was implemented for all First Nations in a one-size-fits-all fashion with no consideration given to the diverse forms of government and culture across First Nations. Furthermore, a person called the Indian agent (a white government official set in place to oversee the functions of the reserve) had authority under the Act to remove the chief or council members for any number of reasons.

Some nations resisted this intrusion on their established systems of government, the Six Nations being one of them. This band tried to resist the transition to an elected band council by agitating for change to the system and petitioning the Queen, insisting that they were allies, not subjects, of the British Crown, and had never given up their sovereignty. In 1924, Deputy Superintendent General of Indian Affairs Duncan Campbell Scott ordered the overthrow of the Six Nations' traditional council by force. Lt. Col. Morgan was charged with the responsibility of overseeing troops provided by the RCMP to overthrow the traditional council and oversee the institution of the first elected band council for the Six Nations.

Tax Exemption

The *Indian Act* included laws surrounding taxation. First Nations people living on reserves were not to be taxed either on any purchases they made while living on a reserve or on income generated from on-reserve activities. This provision was included in recognition of the special status accorded to "reserved territories" and was rooted in principles concerning nationhood and self-government. This tax exemption still exists today and is misunderstood by some non-Indigenous people, who perceive it as an unfair advantage. Many Indigenous people assert that this tax exemption signifies that Indigenous land is sovereign land and not a part of Canada, based on the fact that Indigenous people have never surrendered their sovereignty and right to self-government. Many non-Indigenous people overestimate the benefits of tax exemption. It is only for people living on the reserve and does not exempt income earned off-reserve. Since on-reserve employment is hard to find and on average generates income levels that are less

CLOSE-UP   The Métis National Council

Today, the Métis National Council is made up of five provincial organizations: Métis Nation British Columbia, Métis Nation of Alberta, Métis Nation—Saskatchewan, Manitoba Métis Federation, and the Métis Nation of Ontario. The provincial organizations have regional councils to represent Métis throughout each province. This council represents the voice of the Métis to the federal government and argues for the rights of the Métis under section 35 of the *Constitution Act, 1982*. The Métis have their own flag, which depicts the joining of two nations and the eternal existence of a people, represented by the infinity symbol on a blue background.

The councillors of the Métis Provisional Government in 1870. Louis Riel is seated in the centre.

than half the average Canadian income, most Indigenous people work off-reserve and are subject to income tax and all other taxes that other Canadians pay.

Sixty percent of First Nations people live off-reserve and therefore work off-reserve. Since tax-exemption status is attached to the territory of a reserve, not to the person, fully 60 percent of First Nations people pay all of the taxes that other Canadians pay, apart from provincial sales tax on purchases. Status Indians living off-reserve do not access provincial dollars to obtain services as non-First Nations members of the community do. They are the sole responsibility of the federal government and therefore must access federal funds allocated through Indian Affairs for services. For example, the province funds non-Indigenous education, while the federal government funds status Indians attending provincial schools in an agreed sum per student. It makes sense, then, that First Nations people are not forced to contribute to a provincial tax base that they are unable to access for services.

Changes Through Time

The first change to the *Indian Act* in 1880 was to withdraw "half-breeds" (Métis) from treaty agreements. This measure was calculated to quickly reduce the number of Indians that held status and therefore had treaty rights. At the same time, treaties were being made in the western plains area. The government could see that the buffalo population was in sharp decline and that the Métis, a distinguishable group who had already asserted their right to land, would require assistance in rebuilding their economy. In order to avoid any obligation of assistance, the government encouraged the Métis to accept **scrip**—a one-time payment and small land allocation—in lieu of the assistance they would have been entitled to as treaty Indians.

scrip
a one-time payment issued to Métis to discharge treaty rights

In the same year, the Indian Branch became its own department, with inside staff based in Ottawa, including a superintendent general, a chief clerk, an accountant, and clerical staff, as well as outside staff comprising 460 field workers responsible for the implementation of policies directed at Indians. These outside workers were called **Indian agents**, and were invested with tremendous authority over the reservation and the people with whom they worked.

Indian agent
a federal employee of Indian Affairs in charge of administration on reserves

A 1958 job study lists the authorities of the Indian agent as follows: dealing with the recording of property; registering births, deaths, and marriages; administering band funds; and holding elections. The Indian agent interviewed people who needed farming equipment, those who complained about land encroachments, and those applying for loans. He encouraged people to marry legally and to enlist in the armed forces. He adjusted property when members left or joined the band. He dealt with the estates of the deceased and supervised the building of infrastructure, including schools. He negotiated the surrender of band lands for highways or other purposes, and applied for relief funds to house those in need. He informed the court of matters concerning Indians who were on trial for criminal matters. He was the justice of the peace and the health inspector for the community and, later, for the schools. He presided over band council meetings and could vote to break a tie. Finally, he enforced the *Indian Act* and policies directed at Indians.

In some cases, Indian agents were capable people with integrity; in others, they were not. In all cases, they were non-Indigenous. This continued for decades. Slowly, bands have wrested authority for these matters back from the federal government.

In 1880, the "unmaking" of Indians continued, with mandatory enfranchisement of Indigenous people who held a university degree, joined the clergy or the armed forces, or voted in a federal election. The 1880 changes to the *Indian Act* dispensed with recognition of hereditary chiefs and recognized only elected band council chiefs. Indigenous peoples in the West were prohibited from selling their agricultural products because the government did not want them to purchase liquor or other "worthless" things.

In 1884, First Nations people complained that the government was not fulfilling the treaty agreements that would enable them to use the land; agricultural equipment promised in the treaties was not delivered. The government conceded that this was a legitimate complaint but excused the breach, explaining that the bands were not sufficiently advanced to benefit from the promised tools, livestock, and schools.

The potlatch and other Indigenous ceremonies were banned in 1884, with a two- to six-month jail term for those who contravened this prohibition. This prohibition was included in the Act but was not enforced until the 1920s under the leadership of Deputy Superintendent General of Indian Affairs Duncan Campbell Scott. Cultural practices and ceremonies went underground to avoid the watchful eye of the Indian agent. These practices had always played a critical part in the Indigenous oral culture, conveying to the next generation the people's history, their principles of governance, and their spirituality. Repressing these practices resulted in the beginning of loss of culture.

In 1889, the *Indian Act* was amended to allow the federal government to override a band that did not wish to lease land. By 1894, any Indian lands that were not worked (agriculturally) due to illness or injury could be leased to non-Indigenous Canadians under the authority of the superintendent. Idle or surplus Indian land was also seen as fair game.

In 1911, section 46 of the *Indian Act* allowed portions of land to be taken by municipalities or companies for roads or railways without consent of the band but with permission of the superintendent. Section 46(a) permitted the removal of Indians, against their wishes, from any reserve next to or partly within a town of 8,000 inhabitants. For example, a Mi'kmaq reserve in Sydney, Nova Scotia and the Songhees reserve in Victoria, British Columbia were moved outside these cities to free up urban land for development. In the West, between July 1, 1896 and March 31, 1909, First Nations received $74,343 for surrendered land. The Department of Indian Affairs subsequently received $2,156,020 for that land.

The promise of reserved lands through treaty was in some cases not fulfilled; in other cases, the power given to the Indian agent through the *Indian Act* resulted in large sections of reserved lands, coveted by settlers and resource speculators, being carved out of the First Nation's territory, sometimes without compensation. Railways expropriated reserved lands freely, often splitting communities down the centre. The railway towns that were springing up often grew to displace Indigenous people, and more land was seized, often without compensation, as the towns expanded.

In 1918, the enfranchisement of Indigenous people was made easier for those who wished to apply; however, the plan still did not meet with success. Subsequently, in 1921, legislation changed to provide the Indian agent with the authority to enfranchise any Indian who was deemed suitable regardless of his or her wishes. In other words, without giving consent, an Indian could lose his or her status with the stroke of a bureaucrat's pen.

You may be wondering why Indigenous people did not rebel against this oppressive legislation and continued seizure of their lands. In fact they did respond and organize resistance, but it seemed futile. In 1880, in response to political movement in the West to oppose land seizure, a pass system was implemented, requiring any Indian leaving the reserve to have a pass issued by the Indian agent. The goal of the system was to inhibit Indigenous people's mobility and discourage Indigenous alliances that might threaten Canadian authority. Many reserves were impoverished due to the depletion of resources, and any sign of political activism was quickly met with governmental threats of withdrawal of its relief funds.

In 1927, in a heavy-handed response to Six Nations' resistance to the authority of the Act and the West Coast Nisga'a's continued appeals to England, the *Indian Act* was again amended to proclaim that no person could raise money to fund any form of claims to land against the federal government without the express permission of the Indian agent.

VOICES

Deskaheh

Deskaheh was Cayuga, born in 1873 in western New York. He moved to the Six Nations reserve in Ontario, married, and had a family. In 1917, he became hereditary Chief of the Cayuga Nation. In 1921, Deskaheh travelled to London, England on a passport issued by the Iroquois Confederacy because the Canadian government would not allow him to travel. He went to Europe with an attorney hired by the band to speak on behalf of the Six Nations against the subjugation of his people by the Canadian government. He petitioned to join the League of Nations but was ultimately unsuccessful; he did, however, garner support from many European nations when he presented his "Petition and case of the Six Nations of the Grand River." With his lawyer, he returned to the United States to petition in Washington, DC. He was denied re-entry into Canada and spent his last days in Tuscarora, New York. Although he gained the support of nations such as Ireland, Switzerland, and the Netherlands, he was unable to achieve his goal of obtaining recognized international nation status for the Six Nations. In 1924, the hereditary council was forcibly removed from Six Nations and a band council imposed while Deskaheh was in exile in the United States. One of his most famous statements commented on Canadian policies of assimilation:

> Over in Ottawa, they call that policy "Indian Advancement." Over in Washington they call it "Assimilation." We who would be the helpless victims call it tyranny. If it must go on to the bitter end we would rather that you come with your guns and poison gases and get rid of us that way. Do it openly and above board.

It is believed that Deskaheh's actions resulted in Ottawa's oppression of Six Nations in the following years.

EXERCISE 2

The legislated disempowerment of Indigenous people through legislation such as the *Indian Act* led to the federal government assuming fiduciary responsibility for First Nations in Canada. **Fiduciary responsibility** is the legal or ethical responsibility to manage something, usually money or property, in trust for another person (or people) and act in their best interests. Do you think that the federal government has fulfilled this duty? Why or why not?

fiduciary responsibility
the legal or ethical responsibility to manage something, usually money or property, in trust for another person (or people) and act in their best interests

1951: Changes to the Act

The *Indian Act* was overhauled in 1951 in an attempt to create a more equitable piece of legislation. The ban on potlatches and other traditional dances and ceremonies was lifted. Over the previous 30 years, however, the passing of Indigenous culture and oral history to new generations, which was a central function of these practices, had been seriously disrupted. Added to this was the residential school system, to be addressed in Chapter 3, which all but eliminated Indigenous languages and culture through the education department's primary goal of assimilation.

The Act established the Indian Register as a centralized record of all individuals entitled to be registered as status Indians. The registrar was given authority to add or delete names from the general band lists. In response to complaints from Indians who were unilaterally removed from the band list or who could not be included on the band list because their births had never been registered, new rules required the posting of the band list. An appeal process was instituted for those who were removed from the list, with a limit of six months for appeal.

Despite the overhaul of the Act, there was still no agreement to set up a land claims commission as requested by Indigenous people. Furthermore, the 1951 revisions to section 88 of the Act allowed "all laws of general application in force in any Province to apply as well to Indians on and off reserves." This was undoubtedly a precursor to the federal government's intention to slowly devolve the responsibilities for Indians onto the provinces. The problem with this amendment was that certain provincial laws, such as hunting and fishing regulations, if applied to Indians, violated treaty rights. Today, Canadian courts are attempting to navigate their way through layers of treaty and provincial law to provide an equitable interpretation of that law and to define Indigenous rights in Canada.

It was not until the early 1960s that First Nations people were given the right to vote in federal elections. Soon after, they would use this right to become politically active in opposing the White Paper of 1969, proposed by Liberal Indian Affairs Minister Jean Chrétien. This paper called for the elimination of the *Indian Act*, reserved land for Indians, and the special legal category of status Indian. It further proposed to transfer all responsibilities for First Nations to the provinces and promised to look into land claims. Although it was claimed that the White Paper laid out a path to equality for First Nations people in Canada, they viewed it as the final stroke of assimilation. The National Indian Brotherhood stated: "We view this as a policy designed to divest us of our aboriginal, residual, and statutory rights. If we accept this policy, and in the process lose our rights and our lands, we become willing partners in culture genocide. This we cannot do" (Dickason, 1997, p. 364).

Once again, a policy had been created with little consultation with Indigenous people. In the words of Dave Courchene, president of the Manitoba Indian Brotherhood from 1967 to 1974: "Once again the future of the Indian people has been dealt with in a high-handed and arbitrary manner. We have not been consulted; we have been advised of decisions already taken. I feel like a man who has been told he must die and am now to be consulted on the methods of implementing that decision" (Dickason, 1997, p. 364). Cree leader Harold Cardinal wrote:

> We do not want the Indian Act retained because it is a good piece of legislation. It is not. It's discriminatory from start to finish. But it is a lever in our hands and an embarrassment to the government, as it should be. No just society with even pretensions to being just can long tolerate such a piece of legislation, but we would rather continue to live in bondage under the inequitable Indian Act than surrender our sacred rights. Any time the government wants to honor its obligation to us we are more than ready to help devise new legislation. (Cardinal, 1969, p. 140)

Many treaties had originally been made with the British, and legislation passed the responsibility to honour those treaties to the federal government upon the transfer of power during Confederation. The federal government could not simply exonerate itself of those obligations by passing them on to provincial governments. In 1971, the federal government abandoned the White Paper, but the idea of devolving responsibilities for First Nations onto the provinces had not disappeared. It resurfaced in 1986, when the Nielson report recommended that the cost of delivering services to First Nations be shared by the provinces. This was motivated by the rising costs of program delivery, since First Nations populations increased dramatically around this time, and their communities were suffering from the effects of the residential school system, which increased the need for social services. This recommendation was abandoned after much protest from First Nations people.

The fight against the White Paper resulted in a positive change to policy and practice under the *Indian Act*; for the first time, the federal government agreed to fund research into land claims and to set up processes by which those claims could be negotiated. We will discuss land claims in Chapter 2.

CHAPTER SUMMARY

Although the mainstream political structure in Canada today borrows from Indigenous government structure, the two systems are based on very different world views, particularly in regard to land and relationships between peoples and nations. Though Indigenous people held significant political power in their relationship with Europeans until the signing of the *Royal Proclamation*, they were quickly divested of that power following the collapse of their traditional economies during rapid expansion and multiple waves of harvest of natural resources by new arrivals.

The dispossession and disempowerment of Indigenous people in Canada has been a long process that has spanned generations. This dispossession was purposefully conducted by many levels of government to facilitate expansion and economic growth for Canada; however, Indigenous people in Canada rarely benefited from the economic growth. Aggressive policies of assimilation were created to ensure that status Indians with treaty entitlements would slowly disappear. But Indigenous people, against all odds, managed to cling to their heritage and status; today we grapple with the important task of defining Indigenous rights in Canada in accordance with the treaties. Indigenous people in Canada struggle to reclaim authority over their own affairs, to reclaim lost culture, to rebuild healthy communities, and to create economic growth and prosperity for themselves within Canada.

REFERENCES

Aboriginal Affairs and Northern Development Canada. (1939). Copy of the Robinson Treaty made in the year 1850 with the Ojibewa Indians of Lake Huron conveying certain lands to the Crown. https://www.aadnc-aandc.gc.ca/eng/1100100028984/1100100028994.

Bishop, J.D. (2003). The Lockean basis of Iroquoian land ownership. In R.B. Anderson & R.M. Bone (Eds.), *Natural resources and Aboriginal people in Canada: Readings, cases, and commentary*. Toronto: Captus Press.

British North America Act. (1867). 30 & 31 Vict., c. 3, reprinted in RSC 1985, app. II, no. 5.

Cajete, G. (2000). Philosophy of native science. In G. Cajete, *Native science: Natural laws of interdependence*. Santa Fe, NM: Clear Light.

Canadian Charter of Rights and Freedoms. (1982). Part I of the *Constitution Act, 1982*, being Schedule B to the *Canada Act 1982* (UK), 1982, c. 11.

Cardinal, H. (1969). *The unjust society: The tragedy of Canada's Indians*. Edmonton: Hurtig.

Clarkson, L., Morrissette, V., & Régallet, G. (1992). *Our responsibility to the seventh generation: Indigenous peoples and sustainable development*. Winnipeg: International Institute for Sustainable Development. http://www.iisd.org/pdf/seventh_gen.pdf.

Criminal Code. (1985). RSC 1985, c. C-46.

Daniels v. Canada (Indian Affairs and Northern Development). (2016). 2016 SCC 12.

Dickason, O.P. (1997). *Canada's First Nations: A history of founding peoples from earliest times* (2nd ed.). Toronto: Oxford University Press.

Gersten, P. (2007). Cultural heritage legal summary. *Journal of Field Archaeology*, *32*(1), 86.

Indian Act. (1985). RSC 1985, c. I-5.

Leslie, J., & Maguire, R. (Eds.). (1978). *The historical development of the Indian Act* (2nd ed.). Ottawa: Indian and Northern Affairs Canada.

Miller, J.R. (2004). *Lethal legacy: Current Native controversies in Canada*. Toronto: Macfarlane Walter & Ross.

Powley, R v. (2003). 2003 SCC 43, [2003] 2 SCR 207.

Royal Proclamation of 1763. (1763). RSC 1970, app. II, no. 1.

Whitehead, R.H. (Ed.). (1991). *The old man told us: Excerpts from Micmac history, 1500–1950*. Halifax: Nimbus Publishing.

REVIEW QUESTIONS

True or False?

_____ 1. Prior to European arrival in what today is Canada, there were 20,000 people living on this land mass.

_____ 2. In the oral tradition, spoken language is used to convey culture from one generation to the next.

_____ 3. The idea of collective rights was more prominent in European culture than in Indigenous culture.

_____ 4. According to Iroquois history, the Two-Row Wampum is an agreement between the British and the Iroquois to respect each other's sovereignty and to form a military alliance.

_____ 5. The *Royal Proclamation of 1763* is deemed to carry the force of law and has never been repealed.

_____ 6. Through the *Indian Act*, the government recognizes traditional forms of Indigenous government.

_____ 7. The *Constitution Act, 1982* recognizes existing treaty rights.

_____ 8. Treaties are a strictly European creation; Indigenous peoples never entered into treaties prior to European arrival.

_____ **9.** It was not until the 1940s that First Nations people were given the right to vote in federal elections.

_____ **10.** The White Paper of 1969 proposed the elimination of reserved lands for Indians.

Multiple Choice

1. Indigenous peoples' creation stories most often assert that
   a. they travelled across the Bering Sea
   b. they travelled across the Atlantic Ocean
   c. the people were born from the land or came to the land from a spiritual place
   d. they travelled from the South Pacific on ocean currents

2. Many academics assert that our current form of democracy was influenced by
   a. Locke's theory of landownership
   b. Indigenous forms of government at the time of European contact
   c. Thomas Hobbes's philosophy
   d. Charles Darwin

3. In Europe, the Christian religion was a "proselytizing religion." This means that
   a. Christians believed in one God manifested in many forms
   b. Christians believed that others must convert to Christianity or be eternally damned
   c. Christians were very tolerant of others' spiritual beliefs
   d. the Christian religion was not central to European culture at that time

4. Which of the following is not true of the outcomes of the fur trade as it affected Indigenous people?
   a. Indigenous people became increasingly dependent on European traders for goods.
   b. Many animal species neared extinction due to overhunting.
   c. Indigenous people incorporated the accumulation of wealth into their culture, which upset traditional balances.
   d. The fur trade created long-term and permanent economic stability for Indigenous nations.

5. The term _terra nullius_ means
   a. empty land
   b. unfertile land
   c. land whose ownership is contested
   d. lawfully purchased land

6. A treaty is
   a. a promise that is not legally binding
   b. an agreement between states in written form and governed by international law
   c. an agreement that is informal in nature
   d. an agreement between two states that has been formally concluded and ratified

7. The Robinson–Huron treaty of 1850 set a precedent for all future treaties made to acquire lands for settlement. Which of the following is not true of those precedent-setting inclusions to treaties?
   a. Sales of reserve lands and mineral rights were to be conducted by the government for the sole use and benefit of the Indians.
   b. Land was to be surrendered only to the Crown.
   c. Annuities were to be paid.
   d. Indigenous people were to forfeit hunting and fishing rights over the land that was ceded in the treaty.

8. The government accepted fiduciary responsibility for First Nations people when it passed the _Indian Act_. Fiduciary responsibility means
   a. the responsibility to cultivate the natural resources on land granted by the government
   b. the responsibility to educate
   c. the legal or ethical responsibility to manage something, usually money or property, in trust for another person (or people) and act in their best interests
   d. the responsibility to civilize

9. Indigenous people opposed Chrétien's White Paper, which proposed legislation that would in effect eliminate the _Indian Act_. Why?
   a. Because they believed that the _Indian Act_ was fair and equitable.
   b. Because they were resistant to change of any kind.
   c. Because the White Paper did not address the issue of land claims.
   d. Because the White Paper proposed to eliminate reserve land and treaty status for Indians.

10. Special rights accorded to Indigenous people in Canada today in the areas of education and taxation are
   a. an attempt at reconciling the inequalities of the past
   b. acts of generosity by the Canadian government
   c. attempts to resolve social problems prevalent on reserves
   d. obligations of the federal Crown that are rooted in treaty law

11. After the _Indian Act_ was established, who had control over the sale of Indian reserve lands?
   a. Indians
   b. the federal government through the Indian agent
   c. band-elected First Nations representatives
   d. traditional councils established by the band

2 Current Issues over Land

Tensions flare and police advance during an anti-fracking (hydraulic fracturing to extract shale gas) protest at Elsipogtog First Nation, New Brunswick, in October 2013.

Introduction

In January 2013 the *Globe and Mail* reported on a recent Ipsos Reid survey of Canadian attitudes toward Indigenous peoples and issues (Mahoney, 2013). This coincided with the Canada-wide "Idle No More" campaign in which Indigenous people protested their unequal living conditions in Canada. The protests included the blockade of some railway lines and highways, as well as many generally peaceful gatherings. There were harsh feelings expressed by non-Indigenous Canadians in response to the poll questions. Two-thirds of those polled felt that Indigenous Canadians get too much support from tax dollars and 81 percent believed reserves should not get any further funds until external auditors reviewed their financial records. Only 31 percent felt that shutting down roads and rail lines was a legitimate form of protest. However, 63 percent felt that immediate action was required from government to raise the standard of living for Indigenous Canadians, and the same number supported resolving land claims to provide Indigenous people with the land and resources necessary to become self-sufficient. Almost two-thirds of Canadians supporting land claims resolution is a remarkable move forward from 2003, when 50 percent of Canadians surveyed believed there was no validity to any Indigenous land claims in Canada (Curry, 2003).

Members of police services are drawn from all segments of the Canadian population, so we can infer that they are similar to the "average Canadians" polled by Ipsos Reid. And yet it is their responsibility to keep the peace when land claims issues arise in the form of roadblocks or peaceful (and sometimes not so peaceful) demonstrations and reclamations. Provincial and federal governments have sometimes used police as enforcement in resolving land and resource disputes with Indigenous people—for example, in the case of the Ipperwash incident (see Appendix 2.1 at the end of this chapter). The results of this have been disastrous for both officers and Indigenous people, ending in severely strained relationships between the two.

Police services today see the need to ensure that their officers have a broader understanding of the legal landscape surrounding land claims. If an officer believes that Indigenous protesters have no legal grounds for their actions or grievances, or does not understand the legal landscape that surrounds civil action, he or she will have trouble maintaining an objective and unbiased approach to peacekeeping. This chapter will outline the legal background of Indigenous land and resource claims in Canada. This will involve reviewing the constitutional rights granted to Indigenous people and the case law that has evolved to define those rights. It also requires understanding the current process for claims resolution in Canada and the challenges that it faces.

Background

The *British North America Act* of 1867 (also known now as the *Constitution Act, 1867*) established the legislative powers of Canadian government, dividing them between the federal government and the provinces. Under section 91(24) of the Act, jurisdiction and governance over territories reserved for Indigenous people were given to the federal government of Canada. Indigenous nations were not party to the creation of this Act, nor were they consulted about it. Nine years after the implementation of the BNA Act, policies regarding Indigenous people were consolidated in the *Indian Act*, an oppressive statute designed to strip away the governing rights of First Nations. The government also used the *Indian Act* to force relocations and land seizures upon Indigenous people. As the land base of Indigenous people dwindled, their level of poverty increased and their dependence on the government deepened. In a country whose economy was, and still is, based on the harvest and export of natural resources, Indigenous people, now divested of land, would become the poorest group in the country.

Many of the over 600 Indigenous territories in Canada today are economically dependent on the federal government for support, much to their dismay. Economic independence for these communities often hinges on gaining access to the harvest of natural resources on lands that are part of their traditional territory but outside their small reserves—that is, areas to which they have been granted access under the Constitution. Until recently, the government of Canada has used legislation to deny Indigenous people access to lucrative harvests, in favour of large corporations, and to trap Indigenous people in a cycle of economic dependency.

Historical Case Law

One of the first cases concerning the land claims of Indigenous people in Canada was *St. Catherine's Milling & Lumber Company v. The Queen* (1888). It set a precedent for the land claims of all Indigenous nations in Canada. Indigenous people were not represented and were not even involved in this litigation process.

The Ojibwe people in northern Ontario entered into Treaty No. 3 with the federal government of Canada in 1873. Shortly thereafter, Sir John A. Macdonald, acting in his capacity as prime minister of Canada and superintendent of Indian Affairs, issued a timbering licence to St. Catherine's Milling and Lumber Company (an interest with which he is alleged to have been closely connected) (Monture-Angus, 1999, p. 68). The company had cut 2 million feet of lumber when Ontario filed for an injunction to prevent both further cutting of the lumber and its removal. Ontario asserted that the province, not the federal government, was entitled to licensing fees and royalties for timber, since Treaty No. 3 areas fell within the boundaries of Ontario. The province cited section 109 of the BNA Act as its authority. Section 109 of the Act reads as follows:

> All Lands, Mines, Minerals, and Royalties belonging to the several Provinces of Canada, Nova Scotia, and New Brunswick at the Union, and all Sums then due or payable for such Lands, Mines, Minerals, or Royalties, shall belong to the several Provinces of Ontario, Quebec, Nova Scotia, and New Brunswick in which the same are situate or arise, subject to any Trusts existing in respect thereof, and to any Interest other than that of the Province in the same.

The federal government was the defendant in this case. Its argument was that the Indians had owned the land and had passed that ownership on to the federal government through Treaty No. 3; therefore, the federal government owned the land and the resources within it despite the fact that it lay within Ontario's provincial boundaries. The federal government cited section 91(24) of the BNA Act, which states that the responsibility for "Indians, and Lands reserved for the Indians" falls to the federal government. Ontario argued, successfully, that

Indian title to land did not constitute full ownership since Indians had no concept of property rights as recognized in British law. Ontario argued that the Crown had title to all lands of North America and that any rights to land asserted by Indians were granted by the generosity of the Crown. This, of course, is inconsistent with both the *Royal Proclamation of 1763* and the treaties themselves. Nevertheless, the result of the decision was that Indian title in the land was defined as less than full title. It was held that Indian interest in the land was mere "personal and usufructuary right"; in other words, Indigenous people's right to use the land was held at the pleasure of the Crown, which had the power to remove that right at any time.

Since this decision was made by the Judicial Committee of the Privy Council in England, the highest court in the land, it became binding on all future land issues involving Indian title to land. It is one of those precedents in the Canadian court structure that was a huge obstacle to anyone attempting to move forward in Aboriginal rights cases (Monture-Angus, 1999, p. 67), and it was followed for almost a century, until the *Calder* case in 1973. During the hundred years separating these two cases, the movement toward Indigenous land and resource rights was also hindered by amendments to the *Indian Act* in 1927, which prohibited First Nations from hiring lawyers or pursuing claims to land. These provisions were not repealed until 1951.

The *Calder* case began in 1971, when four Nisga'a communities in British Columbia's Nass Valley brought their case to the Supreme Court of Canada, asserting their claim to traditional territory that was outside the reserve created for them by the federal government. The communities based their claim on the fact that they had never entered into any treaties and had never relinquished their lands to either the federal government or the province of British Columbia. They and their ancestors had in fact occupied the land since time immemorial, and they had never agreed to relinquish any land or resources. The Supreme Court was split three to three on whether the claim to the land was valid (the seventh judge dismissed the case on a technicality). In his decision, Justice Judson stated:

> [T]he fact is that when the settlers came, the Indians were there, organized in societies and occupying the land as their forefathers had done for centuries. This is what Indian title means and it does not help one in the solution of this problem to call it a "personal or usufructuary right." What they are asserting in this action is that they had a right to continue to live on their lands as their forefathers had lived and that this right has never been lawfully extinguished. (*Calder et al. v. Attorney General of British Columbia*, 1973, p. 328)

Justice Hall discussed the process of extinguishment further. He stated that should the Crown claim to have extinguished Aboriginal title to land, it must do so in a clear and plain manner; it cannot rely on implied extinguishment. The most significant part of this judgment is that all six judges agreed that

- Indigenous title to land existed, as defined by British law, prior to and at the time of colonization; and
- the Crown must act in a clear and plain way to extinguish that title.

Although the *Calder* case did not provide a clear test of extinguishment—this did not come until the case of *Sparrow*, in 1990—it did force the federal government to work toward settling Indigenous claims in regions of the country where treaties had not extinguished Indigenous title. This was something Indigenous activists had long wanted; since the 1951 revision of the *Indian Act*, which had repealed the prohibition against First Nations' pursuit of land claims, they had been pressing the government, to no avail, to create a process for settling land claims.

Another case that significantly affected Indigenous land and resource claims in Canada was *Guerin v. The Queen* (1984). Prior to the verdict in *Guerin*, the Department of Indian Affairs had a *moral duty* to act in the best interest of First Nations in the administration of reserve lands and resources. But this duty, known as a *fiduciary duty*—in other words, the duty to act in the best interest of another—was not recognized in law. Accordingly, the department had limited accountability to the Indigenous people it administered; it was accountable only to the federal government, whose interests were opposed to those of the Indigenous people, particularly in financial matters.

In *Guerin*, the Musqueam Indian Reserve had agreed to lease 66 hectares of reserve land in the city of Vancouver to the Shaughnessy Golf Club in 1955. In keeping with the *Royal Proclamation of 1763*, which provides that Indian land is "alienable"—in other words, can be surrendered or leased—only to the Crown, the band was required to surrender the 66 hectares to the Crown before the lease could take place. In a meeting, the band and the Indian agent agreed upon the terms of the lease to be put in place with the golf club. However, these terms were misrepresented to the band. The land was surrendered and the Crown entered into a lease agreement with the golf club on terms that were unfavourable to the band and inconsistent with what it had agreed to. The band attempted to grieve this action, but to no avail. The band was unable even to procure a copy of the lease agreement, which it had never received at the time the land was transferred, until 1970. When the band obtained a copy of the lease, it attempted to sue the Crown for damages. The case made its way to the Supreme Court of Canada, which issued its decision in 1984. At the heart of the argument was the Crown's responsibility to act in the best interest of the band. The Crown argued that the responsibility amounted to a "political trust" enforceable by Parliament but not to a "true trust" enforceable by the courts. The Crown was unsuccessful in its argument, and the SCC ruled as follows (*Guerin v. The Queen*, 1984, p. 376) in its final verdict:

> An Indian Band is prohibited from directly transferring its interest to a third party. Any sale or lease of land can only be carried out after a surrender has taken place, with the Crown then acting on the Band's behalf. The Crown first took this responsibility upon itself in the Royal Proclamation of 1763. It is still recognized in the surrender provisions of the *Indian Act*. The surrender requirement, and the responsibility it entails, are the source of a distinct fiduciary obligation owed by the Crown to the Indians.

Justice Dickson also stated the following:

> After the Crown's agents had induced the Band to surrender its land on the understanding that the land would be leased on certain terms, it would be unconscionable to permit the Crown simply to ignore those terms. ... Equity will not countenance unconscionable behaviour in a fiduciary, whose duty is that of utmost loyalty to his principal. (*Guerin v. The Queen*, 1984, pp. 388–389)

There have been many cases like *Guerin*—that is, cases that bring into doubt the Crown's responsible administration of band resources and band land. *Guerin* set a precedent; the government would be held responsible for mismanagement. In the *Guerin* case, the band was awarded $10 million in restitution. The sum of the settlement was based on what the lease value of the land would have been to that point had the band never surrendered the land to the government to facilitate the unfavourable lease (Henderson, 1996). The settlement of the case came at the end of a long, slow process. There were a number of appeals; the final decision was rendered a full 14 years after the band first obtained a copy of the lease and the Crown's misdealings were seen in their full extent. This was 29 years after the original proposed lease.

Constitution

During the litigation of the *Guerin* case, the Canadian Constitution was **patriated**. Prior to the patriation of the Constitution, Indigenous activists had appealed to international powers and to governments in Canada and Europe for the inclusion of Aboriginal rights within the Constitution. Their work culminated in the inclusion of section 35 of the *Constitution Act, 1982*, which states the following:

patriation
the process by which Canada gained control over the Constitution; previously, amendments to the Canadian Constitution required an act of British Parliament

35(1) The existing aboriginal and treaty rights of the aboriginal peoples of Canada are hereby recognized and affirmed.

(2) In this Act, "aboriginal peoples of Canada" includes the Indian, Inuit and Métis peoples of Canada.

(3) For greater certainty, in subsection (1) "treaty rights" includes rights that now exist by way of land claims agreements or may be so acquired.

(4) Notwithstanding any other provision of this Act, the aboriginal and treaty rights referred to in subsection (1) are guaranteed equally to male and female persons.

Since the introduction of this provision in 1982, Canadian courts have been trying to clarify the extent of Aboriginal rights in this country. It is important to note the wording of the section; the *existing* rights of Aboriginal people are *recognized and affirmed*. This section does not provide any new rights for Indigenous people in Canada. Of course, Aboriginal rights existed in common law in Canada prior to the enactment of the Constitution. The source of those common law rights was the Indigenous people's original occupation of land and their social and political organization, which existed prior to Canada's assertion of sovereignty. Some of those rights were expressly terminated by the Crown through treaty, but many were not. Some Indigenous rights were established through the treaty process. Section 35 of the Constitution, rather than creating new rights, elevates the rights that existed already, through common law and treaty, to constitutional status. This restricts the right of the Crown to modify or extinguish Indigenous rights (Bell & Paterson, 2003, p. 108).

Section 35 provided protection for Aboriginal rights but did not simplify the process of defining what is and is not an Aboriginal right. So—what is protected under section 35 of the Constitution? Indigenous people have been taking their cases to court continually over the years to have the courts define these rights.

EXERCISE 1

Indigenous activist, author, and lawyer Ardith Walkem (2003, p. 198) has written the following about the purpose of Indigenous people's battle for rights in the Canadian courts:

When Indigenous Peoples speak of Aboriginal Title and Rights, it is a much broader conception than that which has evolved under Canadian Law. Indigenous Peoples are not seeking to have distinct practices protected, nor title recognized to small parcels of land. The reason that Indigenous Peoples engage in the court process stems from a simple desire and imperative: Our continued existence as peoples and maintenance of our ability to continue to exist and thrive on the territories on which the Creator placed us and according to the laws which bind us to the lands and waters and govern the relationships between all living things and the spiritual beings that also live within and through the lands and waters. These elements, at a minimum, embrace the fundamental aspects of Indigenous Peoples' aspirations:

1. Territory (both land and water) and recognition of our responsibility to manage, protect and benefit from that territory.
2. Recognition of the laws, traditions, languages and cultures of Indigenous peoples which flow, and are intricately tied to, our territories, and
3. Recognition of a right to self determination which ensures that we are able to survive into the future governed by, and accountable to, our own laws.

With reference to Walkem's description above, consider the importance and role of land within an Indigenous and a non-Indigenous framework, including its connection to identity and survival. How do you think this has shaped modern conflicts over land rights?

The right to self-determination is one of the fundamental aspirations of Indigenous people, and achieving it requires a certain degree of independence from the control of the Canadian government. This independence will require a degree of economic self-sufficiency, which means, in turn, that Indigenous people must rebuild their economies to thrive in today's world. Such rebuilding will require both land and control over resources of the land.

Many cases that have been brought before the Supreme Court involve rights to the harvest of natural resources—hunting and fishing rights, for example, as in *R v. Sparrow* (1990). Ronald Sparrow is a Salish and lives on the Musqueam Indian Reserve, which is located within Vancouver's city limits. He fishes commercially and for food. In May 1984, he was charged with using a drift net that was longer than British Columbia fishing regulations allowed. Sparrow did not dispute the facts at issue in the case but argued that he had an Aboriginal right to fish in the area, as his forefathers had for generations, and that this right was protected under section 35 of the Constitution. An *Aboriginal right* to fish in the area—so Sparrow's argument went—meant that he was not bound by the British Columbia fishing regulations applicable to non-Indigenous fishers. Sparrow did not decide lightly to embark upon this case; he was aware that the outcome would affect Aboriginal fishing rights across Canada. He was supported in his decision by the band. Its members were being charged more and more frequently under the fishing regulations, and relations between the band and the Department of Fisheries were growing hostile. Sparrow's decision to embark on the case was in the interest of his community, not simply himself (Monture-Angus, 1999, pp. 88–89).

Sparrow's case was heard by the Supreme Court of Canada in 1990. In reviewing the case, the court recognized that the main issue was whether Parliament had the right to regulate Indigenous fishing in light of section 35 of the Constitution. The first matter to be decided was whether the rights of the Salish to fish were "recognized and affirmed" in the Constitution at the time of its patriation in 1982. The Crown's position was that the right claimed by Sparrow was extinguished prior to 1982 amid the myriad provincial fishing regulations enacted over time in British Columbia. The Crown was unsuccessful in its argument due to the precedent set by the *Calder* case in 1973, wherein the court stated that the Crown must articulate in a plain and clear manner its intent to extinguish an Aboriginal right and cannot rely on implied extinguishment. Justices Dickson and La Forest stated the following in the *Sparrow* case: "The test of extinguishment to be adopted, in our opinion, is that the Sovereign's intention must be clear and plain if it is to extinguish an aboriginal right" (*R v. Sparrow*, 1990, p. 1099).

The Supreme Court found that the enactment of provincial regulations prior to 1982—the rationale for extinguishment cited by the Crown in the *Sparrow* case—is implied extinguishment only and did not meet the test for extinguishment. On this basis, the Supreme Court concluded that Sparrow's right to fish was constitutionally entrenched in 1982.

Since the Constitution is the supreme law of the land, statutes cannot be enacted to alter rights guaranteed in it. However, the Supreme Court in *Sparrow* recognized that the rights of Aboriginal people to the fisheries are not absolute. In *Sparrow*, the Supreme Court set out a two-part test for determining whether infringement on an Indigenous people's constitutional right to fish is justified. The first part of the test asks whether the Crown has "compelling and substantial objectives" for infringement—for example, the protection of the resources in order to ensure the continuation of the right. The second part of the test requires that any legislation aiming to limit Indigenous people's constitutional rights to fisheries must be consistent with the Crown's fiduciary obligation to Aboriginal people. Other compelling objectives may involve balancing the constitutional rights of Indigenous people to the fisheries with those of non-Indigenous people. In the latter circumstance, the test of fiduciary duty would come first.

The judgment rendered in *Sparrow* was seen as a victory for Indigenous people, whose aim in establishing a right to the resource was not to exclude non-Indigenous access but to increase their own economic self-sufficiency. Ultimately, of course, this victory was significantly limited by the power the decision gave the Crown to restrict Indigenous access through the two-part test. Still, the onus was now on the Crown to justify infringement, including minimal infringement. If the rights were to be infringed for justifiable reasons, this must be established through a process of negotiation. Bell and Paterson (2003, p. 107) offer a concise summary of the litigation process used to determine what Aboriginal rights are constitutionally protected:

1. identification of the nature and content of the right;
2. determining whether the right is an "existing right" recognized and affirmed by section 35 (or whether it has been lawfully extinguished prior to the enactment of section 35);
3. determination of whether federal or provincial legislation constitutes a prima facie infringement with the exercising of an existing Aboriginal right; and
4. analysis of the legitimacy of justification for government interference.

The *Sparrow* decision shows how a common law Aboriginal right to fish becomes protected under the Constitution. Later, in *R v. Badger* (1996), the Supreme Court clarified that rights set out in treaties must be protected in the same manner. This will have far-reaching consequences; many of the more than 500 treaties give Indigenous people the right to hunt and fish without interference by the Crown, and many treaties give them hunting and fishing rights over territories ceded in the treaties that are now Crown land or over territories in which interest has been vested in third parties due to grants by the Crown. The same two-part test set out in *Sparrow* must be applied to infringement of an Aboriginal right that is set out in a treaty.

A number of cases since *Sparrow* have elaborated on the two-part test. The *R v. Van der Peet* case, decided by the Supreme Court of Canada in 1996, offered a new twist on the *Sparrow* two-part test. Dorothy Van der Peet was charged with violating BC fishing regulations, which prohibited the sale and barter of fish. Van der Peet was a member of the Sto:lo First Nation. She sold 10 salmon for $50 to a non-Indigenous person. In this case, the Supreme Court set new criteria for characterizing and interpreting Aboriginal rights. It narrowed the definition of what could be considered an Aboriginal right to a right that existed pre-contact. It held that a right is not an Aboriginal right if it exists because of European influence. In this case, the Supreme Court held that the pre-contact activity of exchanging fish among nations or people did not correspond to an unlimited commercial right to fish for contemporary Indigenous people; it corresponded to a right to fish for livelihood. According to the principle in *Van der Peet*, contemporary Aboriginal rights must in some cases be grounded in pre-contact activities. This decision would set a precedent for the battle between mainstream Canada and Indigenous people over the latter's right to access the forestry industry, one of Canada's greatest exports and sources of wealth. The Supreme Court would later rely on the *Van der Peet* decision to disallow Indigenous people increased commercial access to the forestry industry, on the basis that logging is not an activity in which they engaged pre-contact.

Indigenous Title to Land

The *Delgamuukw v. British Columbia* case (1997) began its journey through the Canadian court system in the early 1980s. It developed in the following way. The Gitksan and Wet'suwet'en people sought to force the province of British Columbia to recognize Aboriginal title over the two bands' traditional territory, which they had never ceded to the province or federal government through treaty or by any other means. The area encompasses approximately 58,000 square kilometres in north-central British Columbia. The province asserted that Indigenous title to land in British Columbia had been extinguished in 1871, upon the incorporation of the province into the Dominion of Canada. The case was decided by the Supreme Court in 1997.

The case set precedents for Aboriginal rights, including Aboriginal title to land, and for Crown sovereignty, which the courts assert can coexist with Aboriginal rights.

The BC Crown argued the following:

1. Indigenous peoples were so low on the scale of social organization that their lands can be treated as vacant and unoccupied for the purpose of issuing Crown grants pursuant to laws enacted by settler governments without regard to the prior occupation of Indigenous peoples (Mandell, 2003, p. 166).
2. Colonial land legislation before Confederation extinguished Indigenous peoples' relations to the land; once the colony (soon to become a province) enacted legislation regulating Indigenous peoples' rights to the land and resources, their rights were extinguished by implied extinguishment and by the powers vested in the colony/province (Youngblood Henderson, 1999).
3. The creation of land grants by British Columbia to settlers extinguished Aboriginal tenure because Indigenous people were precluded from sustaining their relationship with the land; once settlers were granted land and began occupying it, Indigenous peoples' relationship to the land was broken. The existence of third-party interests displaces Aboriginal use, right, and title (Youngblood Henderson, 1999; Mandell, 2003).
4. The establishment of federal First Nations reserves in British Columbia extinguished Aboriginal tenure because Indigenous people "abandoned" their territory (Youngblood Henderson, 1999). An underlying assertion of this argument is that the benefits of colonization, such as "civilization" and "Christianity," were compensation enough for voluntarily vacating traditional lands (Mandell, 2003).
5. Section 88 of the *Indian Act* allowed provincial laws of general application to apply as well to Indians, extinguishing Indigenous title and rights (Youngblood Henderson, 1999).
6. Indigenous title and rights vanish with the passage of time (Mandell, 2003, p. 169).

These arguments, made by the Crown to assert the absence of Aboriginal title over the land, are the same ones put forward initially by many students who are studying land claims for the first time. It is important to understand that the Supreme Court heard—and rejected—all of these arguments in the *Delgamuukw* decision. Arguments 2 to 5 rest on the assumption that the colony or province of British Columbia has the power to extinguish Indigenous title to land. The court ruled that the province never had the constitutional authority to extinguish Indigenous title, and since that title had never been extinguished, it is protected under section 35 of the Constitution.

The court did not recognize the passage of time as extinguishing title or rights, nor did it recognize the argument that Indigenous people, because "uncivilized," were not a people capable of holding territory.

In its decision, the court identified three components of Indigenous title:

1. It encompasses the right to exclusive use and occupancy of the land.
2. It gives Indigenous people the right to choose what uses the land can be put to, with the limitation that the land cannot be altered so as to destroy its capacity to sustain future generations of Indigenous people.
3. The lands held pursuant to Indigenous title have an economic component.

The first component of the Supreme Court's ruling in *Delgamuukw* displaced the *St. Catherine's* ruling of 1888, which had stated that Indigenous interest in the land was merely "personal and usufructuary"—that is, held at the pleasure of the Crown. It elevates the Indigenous interest in the land to exclusive use and occupancy. The second component of the ruling states that Indigenous people must be consulted over decisions pertaining to the uses of the land held under

Aboriginal title. In other words, holding title to land gives Indigenous people mineral rights and rights to make decisions over resource harvesting and development. The third part of the court's ruling in *Delgamuukw*, by which the economic component of the land's value is recognized, suggests that the fiduciary responsibility of the Crown must be scrutinized in the dealings with Indigenous land, and that Indigenous people must benefit from the lands and resources. The Supreme Court also established a test for infringement on the rights inherent in Aboriginal title. It specified that the Crown must provide justifications for infringement and that compensation must be paid for the infringement based on the nature of the infringement, in recognition of the economic component of Aboriginal land title.

As in all cases involving Aboriginal rights, a move forward would not be complete without a limitation being placed on it. The *Delgamuukw* decision set out a two-part test for determining whether infringement on Indigenous title is justified. The first requirement is that the infringement be for a valid legislative directive. The Supreme Court definition of "valid legislative directives" was very broad; it included the following:

1. the development of agricultural, forestry, mining, and hydroelectric power;
2. the general economic development of the province;
3. the protection of the environment or endangered species;
4. the building of infrastructure; and
5. the settlement of foreign populations to support those aims (McDonald, 2003, p. 231).

The second part of the test for justifiable infringement asks whether the infringement is consistent with the fiduciary responsibility of the Crown to Indigenous people. It makes it mandatory for the government to consult with Indigenous people before reaching a decision about infringement and compensation. This consultation process has not always gone smoothly, and breakdowns can lead to serious and sometimes dangerous confrontations. For an example of such a breakdown, we will look briefly at the East Coast lobster fisheries dispute between the Crown and the Mi'kmaq.

Case Study: Mi'kmaq Fishing Rights

Originally, the Mi'kmaq were partners in the Wabanaki Confederacy, which comprised five nations: Mi'kmaq, Passamaquoddy, Penobscot, Maliseet, and Abenaki. The traditional territory of this group included Atlantic Canada, Maine, and parts of Quebec. Post-contact, the Mi'kmaq were aligned with the French but made treaties with the British after France was forced to cede its territories in Acadia to the British. Settlers and the original inhabitants of the territory signed a series of treaties, beginning in 1725, to establish peace. These treaties reserved the Mi'kmaq the right to fish and hunt in the territory as they had always done. The treaties did not contain any provisions about transferring the land's ownership. Renewed in 1749, 1752, 1760, 1761, and 1794, this series of treaties was characterized as a covenant chain, with each treaty connected and linked to the others. The highlights of those treaties were as follows:

> British laws would be a great hedge about the Mi'kmaq property and rights. Mi'kmaq could traffic and barter or exchange commodities in any manner with managers of truck-houses (trading posts). Mi'kmaq would receive gifts in the form of goods on the First day of each October and the nation to nation relationship between the British and the Mi'kmaq would be respected and the Mi'kmaq way of life would be preserved. (Knockwood, 2003, p. 47)

This is the same chain of treaties that currently affects New Brunswick in terms of protection of land use for traditional purposes and conflict with the development of a shale gas extraction industry.

Following this chain of treaties, the BNA Act was instated, followed by the *Indian Act*, which essentially denied the treaty rights of the Mi'kmaq. Following this, myriad federal and provincial laws were enacted to regulate and limit the Mi'kmaq rights to fish and hunt. Nevertheless, the Mi'kmaq continued to press for the recognition of the treaties and continued to hunt and fish outside the regulations that had been unilaterally imposed. In 1928, Mi'kmaq Gabriel Sylliboy was charged with hunting out of season. He was found guilty when the trial judge asserted that the treaty protection did not extend to Mi'kmaq outside the small band of the Shubenacadie, and since Sylliboy was not a member of that band, he had no protection under the treaty. Furthermore, the judge ruled that even if Sylliboy were a member of that small band, he would still be found guilty on the following grounds: when the treaty was signed in 1752, the Mi'kmaq were not an independent power legally capable of entering into a treaty. One must question the logic of this statement. Why would the British negotiate a treaty with a group whom they did not recognize as having the legal capacity to enter into a treaty?

The precedent was set; in a subsequent case, *Francis v. The Queen* in 1969, Justice Richard of the New Brunswick Magistrate's Court convicted Martin Francis of fishing without a licence (Knockwood, 2003, p. 52). Francis asserted that the treaties set out his right to fish. Although the judge was sympathetic to the issues, he found it his "painful duty" to convict because, he said, previous case law meant that the law did not recognize the treaty.

A number of cases ensued involving the Mi'kmaq, who, seemingly undaunted, continued to battle in the courts to assert their rights. The first case that followed the constitutional provisions enshrined in section 35 was *Simon v. The Queen*, in 1985. The *Sylliboy* decision, stating that the Mi'kmaq were not capable of entering into treaties, was overturned. James Simon, charged with hunting infractions, was not convicted. The basis given by the Supreme Court for his acquittal was that the treaty of 1752 was a valid treaty that the Mi'kmaq had legitimately entered into and that ought to protect them against infringements on their hunting rights. The Supreme Court also found that the right was not an "absolute right" and was subject to federal regulation. Nevertheless, this was a victory, since it was the first time the Mi'kmaq treaties had been recognized, affording them protection under section 35.

The last relevant decision of the Supreme Court came in 1999, in the case of *R v. Marshall*. Donald Marshall Jr., a Mi'kmaq fisherman, was charged with violating federal fishing regulations by selling eels without a licence, fishing without a licence, and fishing during the closed season with illegal nets. Marshall had caught 463 pounds of eels that he sold for $787.10 (*R v. Marshall*, 1999, para. 4; Donham, 2003, p. 366). Entered into evidence for the defence were minutes from the treaty negotiations from 1760–61. Those minutes included requests from the Mi'kmaq for truckhouses in which to sell their peltries (animal skins), and agreements by which the Mi'kmaq could barter and trade their catches and hunting spoils with the managers of the truckhouses for "necessaries." In 1999, the Supreme Court interpreted this as the Mi'kmaq having retained not only their right to harvest resources but also the right to sell and trade to their best advantage. The court interpreted "necessaries" to mean "a modest livelihood." The court, as in other cases previously discussed, did not give the Indigenous group the right to an unlimited commercial harvest; it provided that federal regulations might restrict the Aboriginal right if the resource needed to be protected. In keeping with the *Delgamuukw* decision, it was agreed that decisions about restricting or impinging on Aboriginal rights must involve negotiation with the Mi'kmaq, as well as close attention to the Crown's performance of its fiduciary duty.

Approximately 40 Mi'kmaq boats took to the water to celebrate the recognition of their rights and began to fish lobster. The same waters were home to some 2,893 lobster boats owned by non-Indigenous people. The backlash from non-Indigenous fishers, particularly commercial fishers, was fierce. They lobbied the government to re-open the *Marshall* case and insisted that the conservation of lobster fisheries was at stake. Violence broke out in some communities between Indigenous and non-Indigenous fishers. The Department of Fisheries quickly pressured

Mi'kmaq and other bands to sign agreements limiting their newly recognized rights to fish. Twenty-seven bands signed agreements with the department within a year. Bands at Indian Brook and Burnt Church refused to sign, and continued to fish and develop their own conservation plan. They were portrayed in the media as renegades, adamant and unreasonable in their determination to fish illegally. The media failed to point out that the quantity of Indigenous traps was in fact less than 0.2 percent of the non-Indigenous traps (Donham, 2003, p. 371). (Similarly, today we see media portrayals of violent acts to oppose shale gas development but no explanation of the peace and friendship treaties, their history, and the duties mandated by the Supreme Court that exist as a result, as well as no media investigation of the level of consultation that is or is not happening surrounding those obligations.)

As Indigenous traps were destroyed by angry non-Indigenous fishers, and violence broke out, the RCMP was called upon to keep the peace, and the Department of Fisheries was sent in to save the lobsters from Indigenous fishers who, according to the media, were about to drive the lobsters to extinction. The Department of Fisheries arrested Mi'kmaq fishers and participated in sinking several of their vessels (Obomsawin, 2002). The RCMP did what it could to keep the peace. By 2002, the Mi'kmaq had acquiesced and signed agreements to severely limit their take of the resource. Ten Mi'kmaq fishers had been arrested for fishing violations and for further criminal offences related to resisting Department of Fisheries officers' arrests. The conflict is not over; the Mi'kmaq continue to attempt to inch their way into the commercial fishing business, but the conflict has taken on the form of constructive negotiations. The Mi'kmaq Rights Initiative has assembled a unified team of Mi'kmaq negotiators who together with the Province of Nova Scotia and the federal government meet to examine and agree upon the manner in which the Mi'kmaq will exercise their constitutional rights to land, fisheries, and natural resource harvesting. The Mi'kmaq had 300 consultation processes under way at the time of writing, and many of Nova Scotia's prominent corporations involved in resource industries participate in the consultation process (Mi'kmaq Rights Initiative, n.d.).

What all of this means is that in 2004 one of the poorest Indigenous groups on the East Coast, a group with the greatest right—according to the Supreme Court of Canada—to harvest resources, was assigned a negligible amount of the harvest. The Supreme Court decision in *Marshall* was intended to increase Mi'kmaq access to the fishery and to provide economic hope for the community. As constructive negotiations continue, the consultation process will lead to a more equitable distribution of resources and the inclusion of co-management plans, as discussed in the next section.

Shale Gas Extraction (Fracking) and Indigenous Rights

The chapter opening photo taken in October 2013 in Rexton, New Brunswick, shows the RCMP enforcing a court-ordered injunction to remove Indigenous protesters from a blockade of seismic exploration trucks on Highway 134. The trucks were being used by SWN Resources, a Houston-based resource extraction company, for shale gas exploration in the area. Forty protesters were arrested following a clash with police in which six police vehicles were set ablaze. The conflict once again brings Indigenous land issues to the forefront, highlighting the Supreme Court–mandated "duty to consult" Indigenous people who have an underlying interest in the lands under development. Two weeks following the incident, the Assembly of First Nations' Chiefs in New Brunswick issued a statement that condemned acts of aggression by protesters but at the same time said, "First Nations are not anti-development but will never support development at the expense of the environment" (Assembly of First Nations' Chiefs in New Brunswick, 2013).

First Nations in the exploration area have concerns over the impact of shale gas extraction on local land and water and are not satisfied with the level of consultation on the matter.

The New Brunswick government subsequently placed a moratorium on shale gas drilling, and in March 2016 SWN Resources closed its New Brunswick office. Despite this, many businesses continue to pressure New Brunswick to permit shale gas extraction to create jobs and increase income for the province.

Working Together

Thus far we have examined the litigious and adversarial nature of defining Indigenous rights to land and resources. Because our system is based on Western European legal structures, it is adversarial in nature. However, there are other ways of defining rights and reaching mutually acceptable agreements about resource sharing and management. Because pursuing land claims through litigation is so slow and costly, it often happens that development continues on the contested lands until, by the time settlements are reached, the land's resources are already harvested or the land is permanently altered by, for example, mining or oil or gas exploration.

One of the new approaches to land claims is co-management. Co-management is a more inclusive and consensus-based approach to resource harvesting and development; it involves government and private industry sharing decision-making power with non-traditional actors—environmental groups, Indigenous groups, and local users of the resources—in the process of resource management. Co-management emphasizes resolving conflict through negotiation rather than litigation (Campbell, 1996). It has been implemented in areas where Indigenous rights to lands have not been extinguished and seems to have been most successful in more remote areas, where settlement and the harvesting of resources are just beginning.

As discussed earlier in this chapter, particularly in the *St. Catherine's Milling* case, the protection of Indigenous treaty rights, such as hunting and fishing, is seen as the responsibility of the federal government. However, the management of natural resources is seen as a provincial responsibility. Confusion can result when Indigenous people choose to exercise their treaty rights to natural resources on provincial Crown land. Whether they are permitted to do so depends on how developed that provincial land is.

Concepts of co-management fit well with the Supreme Court ruling in *Delgamuukw*, particularly the second component of the ruling, which set out the right of Indigenous people to determine the uses to which the land can be put. The process of co-management is a good answer to that component of the ruling, which makes sincere negotiations over land usage mandatory.

Current co-management schemes vary in the degree of control they allow Indigenous people in the management of resources. Provincial governments sometimes call their proposals "co-management" when what they are actually doing is informing Indigenous people about decisions already made with regard to the contested territories; they are not consulting with them on how to minimize the harmful effects to their communities. This kind of process is inconsistent with the true spirit of co-management. Even with real co-management, the degree of control allowed Indigenous people tends to vary; it can range from cooperation, to communication with advisory committees, to participation on management boards, all the way to partnership and community control. Ideally, the co-management process means a partnership of equals and completely joint decision-making. This requires commitment and a delicate balance of interests.

Co-Management: Torngat Mountains National Park

Torngat Mountains National Park is the 42nd and newest national park in Canada, created when the Nunavik Inuit Land Claims Agreement came into legal effect on July 10, 2008. This agreement was the first comprehensive land claims agreement in Atlantic Canada. The Park Impacts and Benefits Agreement formalized the ongoing relationship between Parks Canada and the Labrador Inuit and includes provisions that allow the Inuit to continue traditional activities such as land and resource uses in the park. A seven-member cooperative management board comprises two members from Parks Canada; two from Makivik Corporation, which represents Quebec Inuit; and two from the Nunatsiavut government, as well as an independent chair appointed by all three parties.

Land Claims

comprehensive land claims
claims to territory that are not covered by treaty or land cession agreements

Land claims are divided into two categories: comprehensive land claims and specific land claims. **Comprehensive land claims** affect land that has not been covered by treaty, meaning approximately 50 percent of Canada's land mass. Since no treaty involving that land was made, Indigenous people have an interest in any land that, as per *Delgamuukw*, has a distinct economic nature. Treaties are not a thing of the past; the processes through which these contemporary claims are settled constitute modern-day treaties. Their settlement can involve terms and conditions touching on a variety of matters, including money, land, forms of local government, rights to wildlife, the protection of Indigenous language and culture, and the joint management of lands and resources. These modern treaties set out conditions concerning resource allocations, structures for self-government, and many other matters related to economic interests in the land. Government negotiators often offer an increase in the existing Indigenous land base in return for the extinguishment of Indigenous title over an even larger portion of land. Such exchanges are highly controversial for Indigenous people, since the extinguishment of rights over territory is precisely what they are fighting against. As previously discussed, Indigenous people have a special sense of their connection to the land.

Some negotiations have led to portions of urban land being added to reserve holdings. The Manitoba Treaty Land Entitlement Framework Agreement, signed in 1997 by Canada, Manitoba, and Indigenous representatives, sets out that land should be added to Indigenous peoples' reserved land base to compensate for land improperly expropriated from them. The land is to come from Crown holdings. But the agreement allows for the purchase of private land, on a willing buyer–seller basis, by Indigenous groups who do not have sufficient Crown land to choose from in their immediate vicinity, with the federal government supplying $76 million for this purpose (Treaty Land Entitlement Committee of Manitoba Inc., n.d.). The Manitoba Treaty Land Entitlement includes 21 First Nations. Purchases of this sort have gone forward in a number of agreements in Western Canada. In some cases, Indigenous bands have used settlement money to purchase properties in urban centres to provide housing for urban Indigenous people, and they have started economic ventures in traditionally non-Indigenous areas where proximity to urban centres increases their chances of business success.

FIGURE 2.1   Manitoba Treaty Land Entitlement

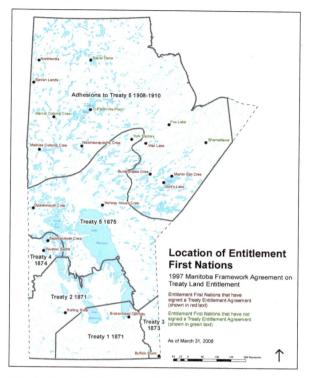

The First Nations involved in the Manitoba Treaty Land Entitlement, showing which nations have finalized their negotiations with the province and federal government in order to add to their reserve land base.

SOURCE: Implementation Monitoring Committee (2008).

Specific land claims are based on lawful obligation and involve claims related to the management of Indigenous lands and assets. With specific claims, the main issue is the loss of established band lands and their natural resources as a result of unilateral action by the Crown. The *Guerin* case discussed earlier in this chapter is an example of a specific land claim.

specific land claims claims that relate to specific misdealings of the Crown with relation to land or resources

---

EXERCISE 2

Research a specific land claim that interests you (for example, the Mississaugas of the New Credit claim regarding the Toronto Purchase) and reflect on the length of the process. Consider in what ways the land has changed while the claim was under way.

Each claim is distinct, reflecting the particular needs and history of each area. Take, for example, the claim put forward in 1988 by the Golden Lake Algonquin (Steckley & Cummins, 2001a). This claim is still under negotiation 30 years after the process began, and remains a long way from settlement. The Golden Lake Algonquin live 140 kilometres west of Algonquin Park, Ontario. They have never surrendered their rights to the land and have never signed a treaty. The government originally signed a treaty with an Ottawa band who spent a few years in the Algonquin area around 1680 but did not claim the area, at the time, as their traditional territory. The Algonquin, who claimed the area as traditional territory, were overlooked in the treaty process. This is not unusual and has happened to different Indigenous groups in Canada—the Lubicon Cree in Alberta, for example, and the Temagami Anishinaabe in northern Ontario.

The Golden Lake Algonquin have been asserting their claim to the land since 1772, when they petitioned the government to recognize their title. Sir William Johnson, superintendent of Indian Affairs for the northern district, assured the Algonquin that their title was protected under the *Royal Proclamation*—despite the fact that, at the time, they were being overwhelmed by white settlement. The government, after promising several times to keep settlers off the land, abruptly announced in 1836 that the Algonquin had already surrendered the land to the Crown under treaty and had been compensated accordingly. The 1845 Bagot commission, which investigated the uncompensated alienation of Indigenous people from their lands, looked at the Algonquin situation and recommended that the Algonquin be compensated for their land and that a tract of land be set aside for them. This recommendation was not followed.

In 1857, hemmed in by settlers on all sides, five Algonquin families petitioned the government for reserve land. Six years later, they were granted 631 hectares of land on which to live. Soon, other families joined the group and the population grew to the point that the established acreage could not sustain them. Algonquin Provincial Park was created in 1893 from Crown land that was for sale for settlement. Other groups of Algonquin were living in the area that would become the provincial park, and they petitioned the government to set aside lands for them, given that they had been displaced by the creation of the park. The government advised them to join the Golden Lake group on the area already set aside. (The government wished to avoid creating more reserves because it believed that the price of real estate would drop if there were too many Indigenous people in the area.) The Algonquin continued to petition the government, insisting that they had neither surrendered their land nor been compensated for its loss; furthermore, they had been told—and had believed—that their title to the land was protected under the *Royal Proclamation*. Their petitions were ignored.

In the mid-1980s, a Provincial Court judge agreed with the Algonquin that they had not ceded their traditional land and that therefore their title to the land was protected under the *Royal Proclamation*. The Supreme Court of Ontario overturned that decision; regardless, the Algonquin entered a claim that involved 8.8 million hectares, which included most of the park and much of the surrounding area, including small municipalities.

The Algonquin wished to reclaim unoccupied Crown land only, not private, commercial, or municipal lands. Four subjects were brought forward in this claim: land, natural resources, self-government, and compensation for the loss. The province began the negotiation process in response to the claim, but the public was outraged. The loss of the park and of Crown land meant that there was no room for non-Indigenous communities to expand.

By 1991, the two sides reached an interim agreement outlining hunting and fishing rights in the area. This agreement gave the Algonquin rights within the park, much to the dismay of non-Indigenous hunters. In 2013–14, members of the Ontario negotiations team scheduled over 150 meetings with landowners, cottage associations, and those who hold direct interests in Crown lands, including municipalities within the claim area. In June 2015, a proposed agreement-in-principle was finally reached and voting by the Algonquin was complete in March 2016, with the majority voting to accept the agreement-in-principle. An agreement-in-principle is something sought after in all negotiations. It is an interim point in the process; it is not legally binding, but it determines the scope of the negotiation and its goals. An agreement-in-principle requires ratification by all negotiating parties. The agreement-in-principle between the province, the federal government, and the Algonquins includes the following:

- the transfer of 117,500 acres of Crown lands to Algonquin ownership;
- defined Algonquin rights to resources, including hunting and fishing rights;
- $300 million as settlement capital from the federal and provincial governments;
- no creation of new reserves;

FIGURE 2.2   Algonquins of Ontario Settlement Area Boundary

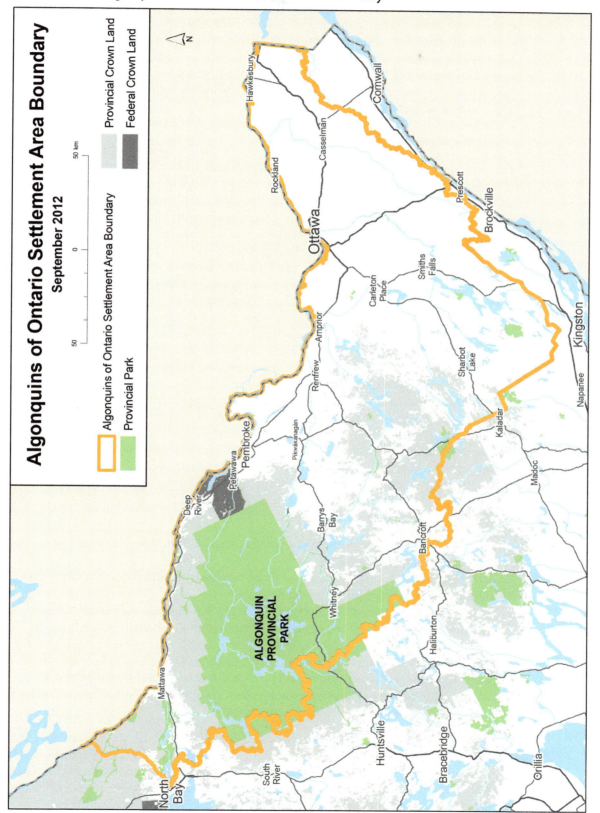

The original claim area of 36,000 square kilometres, or approximately 8.9 million acres; the claim settlement area is merely 117,500 acres, only a small fraction of the original claim area.

SOURCE: Aboriginal Affairs and Northern Development Canada (2012).

- the preservation of Algonquin Provincial Park for the enjoyment of all;
- no expropriation of land from private owners;
- the restoration of historically significant sites to the Algonquins;
- the development of moose harvesting plans by the Algonquin in consultation with the Ontario government;
- the development of fisheries management for the Algonquin settlement area by the Ontario government in consultation with the Algonquin, with the first priority being protection of the fisheries; and
- the continued provincial management of Algonquin Provincial Park in consultation with the Algonquin.

The next step is to begin drafting the detailed legal wording of a final agreement. In the case of the Algonquin land claim, the final agreement will be a modern treaty, which means it will be ratified by special legislation protected under the Canadian Constitution.

The considerable time it takes to negotiate a claim is obviously a major problem. Proposals have been put forward to speed the process along, but it remains painfully slow. Many claims have taken or will take much longer than the Algonquin's. Most claims are negotiated without protests or violence; however, when the negotiations break down, Indigenous people sometimes take action in the form of protests and/or setting up blockades. This most often happens when resource harvesting or development is occurring rapidly on contested land. Indigenous groups cannot afford to wait 20, 30, or 50 years while their claim makes its way through stages of research and negotiation. If they wait too long, there will be nothing left to negotiate for. These protests and/or blockades have the potential for violence: investors and construction or forestry crews become angry with the work stoppages, and Indigenous people become frustrated that their petitions are being ignored.

For specific claims, which are far easier to resolve than comprehensive claims, the resolution process has taken 13 years on average. In October 2008, the government passed the *Specific Claims Tribunal Act* (SCTA), which set a limit on how long a claim could remain outstanding. It was intended to reduce the backlog of 800 claims waiting for negotiation. The Act was given the slogan "Justice at Last" and was approved by the Assembly of First Nations. It was meant to increase impartiality and fairness, provide greater transparency, result in faster processing of claims, and provide better access to mediation.

The specific claims process has four steps:

1. Submission: A First Nation submits a well-researched claim to the minister responsible for Indigenous affairs.
2. Early review: The minister reviews the claim within six months to see if it meets the minimum standard articulated in the policy.
3. Research and assessment: The minister has three years to assess the validity of the claim and either accept it for negotiation or reject it on grounds that Canada has no obligation to negotiate. If a claim is rejected, the First Nation can file its claim with the Specific Claims Tribunal for a decision on the validity of the claim and compensation.
4. Negotiation and settlement: If a claim is accepted and negotiations cannot be concluded within three years, the First Nation can withdraw from negotiations and go to the tribunal for a binding decision on compensation.

As we approach the sunset of this program, scheduled for 2016–17, we reflect on the fact that the Act has not produced the results hoped for by Indigenous leaders. Aboriginal Affairs and Northern Development Canada (AANDC) reported in 2011 that the SCTA had resulted in the resolution of 445 specific claims since 2007. However, when the three-year deadline for negotiation (October 16, 2011) passed, the claims that had not been successfully negotiated started making their way to the new Specific Claims Tribunal. The tribunal opened in June

2011, after a delay in appointing judges and developing rules and procedural guidelines. A report published by the Union of British Columbia Indian Chiefs (2011) asserted that since the opening of the tribunal, Indigenous groups were being forced into take-it-or-leave-it offers from the government, on claims that have spent years under negotiation. They perceived that Canada had stopped negotiating in good faith and was intent on transferring the many outstanding specific claims to the newly created tribunal, which quickly became overwhelmed.

As Canada moves toward severely reducing the funding for the Justice at Last action plan in 2016–17, AANDC has published its success with the program, listing its achievements as

1. having fewer claims entering the system;
2. eliminating the backlog of claims;
3. negotiating specific claims that have been accepted by the minister;
4. establishing access to mediation for First Nations; and
5. fulfilling its requirements and meeting First Nations' expectations through the Specific Claims Tribunal providing final, just, and timely resolution of claims. (Aboriginal Affairs and Northern Development Canada, 2015)

However, in 2015 the Assembly of First Nations reviewed the process and refuted the AANDC statements of its achievements in a research document entitled *In Bad Faith: Justice at Last and Canada's Failure to Resolve Specific Land Claims*. While AANDC said that fewer claims are entering the system, the report's authors assert that AANDC omitted from its calculations the 230 claims that were in the research and development stage by the Claims Research Unit in 2014, which had yet to be submitted. AANDC also did not include 40 new claims that were rejected by the Claims Research Unit due to lack of funding; these claims also are yet to be submitted. Because the research and development process is so cumbersome and has had its funding drastically cut, there are an estimated 200 to 300 claims that will likely be submitted in the next five years, once the necessary funding is secured.

AANDC states that the backlog of 800 claims has been eliminated, but the way it has been eliminated requires closer inspection. First Nations claim that the "backlog" has been transferred to the Specific Claims Tribunal by the failure to negotiate in good faith to meet the three-year deadline, or by the rejection of claims through the early review, requiring additional research for resubmission.

Concerning AANDC's assertion that specific claims are being negotiated, First Nations point out that the early review includes a valuation of the claim. Claims are assessed as small value

FIGURE 2.3 Breakdown of Closed Claims per Fiscal Year

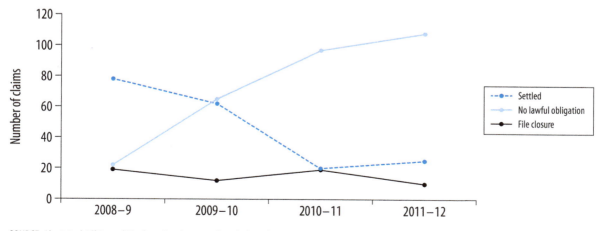

SOURCE: Aboriginal Affairs and Northern Development Canada (2013).

(less than $3 million), normal value ($3 million to $150 million), large value (over $150 million), or "unsure" value. This valuation allows proportional resources to be assigned to process the claim, including funding for negotiations and legal costs. Small-value claims are assigned limited funds and are often negotiated not in good faith but with a take-it-or-leave-it offer; however, these claims are listed as "negotiated" by the minister. The small-value claimants receive notification that their claim has been accepted for negotiation along with a one-time sum to cover legal costs and a 60- to 90-day window to accept the offer or have the file closed.

AANDC established a mediation unit as promised in the Justice at Last policy; however, this unit is housed within AANDC and the mediators are selected by AANDC, which brings into question their neutrality and independence in the mediation process.

The Specific Claims Tribunal, which is now handling the rejected claims and the claims that did not settle in the three-year time frame, has become overwhelmed. On November 14, 2014 the tribunal chair in his annual report warned that "crippling understaffing and considerable funding shortages will impair the ability of the Tribunal to function" (Assembly of First Nations, 2015, p. 27). He warns that the current and future caseload cannot be handled by the tribunal.

The Justice at Last negotiation and claims settlement process is to be completed by 2016–17. Time will tell what the final outcome will be as the measures of its achievements are presented in the future.

Ontario

Generally, there are three kinds of land claims in Ontario.

(1) **Claims relating to the fulfillment of terms of treaties.** These claims are usually the result of disagreements between the Crown and First Nations about the size and location of the reserves that were set aside in accordance with the treaties. These claims may also involve the wording of treaties and the understanding of the parties at the time of treaty signing. Claims can also arise as a result of events that occurred after the treaty signing, such as the flooding of reserve land for hydroelectric power and the expropriation of reserve land for public purposes such as highways, infrastructure, or military building without compensation. The Ipperwash land dispute falls into this category. (See Appendix 2.1 for details.)

(2) **Claims arising from the surrender for sale of reserve land.** These occur when an Indigenous community seeks compensation for, or the return of, land that had been surrendered to the Crown for sale for the benefit of the band. These surrenders did take place, and the funds generated from the sale of land were to be set aside for the sole benefit of the band. In many cases, however, the band did not receive these funds, or the land remained unsold and the band was not compensated.

(3) **Claims arising from Indigenous title.** There are few of these claims in Ontario, since most of the province is covered by treaty; however, other large areas of Canada are not covered by treaty. These claims are based on the allegation that lands traditionally used and occupied by Indigenous people were never surrendered to the Crown by Indigenous people. The Golden Lake Algonquin claim is an example of this type of claim in Ontario.

When it comes to negotiating land claims, the Ontario government has adopted the following policy:

> Ontario will not expropriate private property to reach a land claim settlement. However, when it would help to reach a settlement, Ontario may agree to buy land from an owner who wants to sell, in order to include it in a claim settlement.
>
> During negotiations, Ontario considers how Crown lands are being used. Potential impacts on current uses are reduced as much as possible. For example, the province will not cancel Crown land leases, easements, mining claims, timber allocations, and other licences and permits during their term. (Ontario Ministry of Aboriginal Affairs, 2011)

---

claims relating to the fulfillment of terms of treaties claims that are usually a result of disagreement between the Crown and First Nations about the size and location of reserves set aside by treaties

claims arising from the surrender for sale of reserve land claims occurring when First Nations seek compensation for, or the return of, land that had been surrendered to the Crown for sale for the benefit of the band

claims arising from Indigenous title claims based on the allegation that lands traditionally used and occupied by Indigenous people were never surrendered to the Crown by Indigenous people

In other words, Ontario residents need not fear a loss of land or loss of economic revenue as a result of a land claims negotiation or settlement. If a settlement indicates that acreage should be added to reserve holdings, the Crown would seek to negotiate the transfer of Crown land or would seek to purchase land from a willing seller.

Caledonia Land Claim

One well-known Ontario land claim involves the Six Nations of the Grand River, near Brantford, in what is now Caledonia. The history of this claim dates back to the Haldimand Grant of 1784, when Britain allowed the Six Nations to "take possession of and settle" approximately 385,000 hectares of land along the Grand River as a reward for their loyalty during the American Revolution. In 1792, the grant was reduced to 111,000 hectares by Lieutenant Governor John Graves Simcoe, and over the next two hundred years, much of the land was the subject of various transactions, with portions sold, leased to the Crown and then sold to third parties, surrendered (although this has been disputed), and set aside for a reserve.

In 1992, another element was added to the land's complex history when Henco Industries bought a company that owned about 40 hectares of land in the area. In 1995, Six Nations sued the Canadian and Ontario governments, asserting a land claim that included the land allegedly owned by Henco Industries. Ten years later, in July 2005, Henco registered plans for the Douglas Creek Estates subdivision with the province of Ontario and was granted title. In February 2006, when Henco began building homes on the land, a small group of Six Nations protesters moved onto the construction site and set up tents, a teepee, and a wooden building, and refused to leave. On March 10, Henco was granted a court order that required the protesters to leave the site by March 22, but they continued their occupation. During a pre-dawn raid by the OPP on April 20, which police stated was in response to "an escalation of activity," 16 people were arrested, and officers used pepper spray and Tasers against protesters. Protesters returned by 9 a.m. and blocked off the road using a dump truck and burning tires (CBC News, 2006a). OPP commissioner Julian Fantino underscored the role of law enforcement—it is to "preserve the peace, deal with offences and bring those who transgress the laws of the land to justice" (CBC News, 2006b).

The initial protests were followed by counterprotests from some residents of Caledonia, who were frustrated by the chaos and disruption of the protests; by the building and removal of barricades; and by general looting, vandalism, and violence. On May 19, the Ontario government announced an indefinite construction ban, and in mid-June the government bought out the disputed land for $12.3 million; the settlement was also to include compensation for the loss of future profits, to be determined later (CBC News, 2006a). Despite further judicial efforts to have the protesters removed, on August 27 the Ontario Court of Appeal ruled against ordering the protesters off the land.

In 2011, the government agreed to pay $20 million to compensate residents and business owners for the disruption caused by the protests. To resolve the claim, however, one must determine which part of the original land grant was surrendered by Six Nations legitimately, which part was kept, and which part was taken without Six Nations' consent (Darling, n.d.). Negotiations to settle the land claim are ongoing at the time of writing.

EXERCISE 3

Caledonia offers examples of the competing interests and obligations involved in any dispute over land—in this case, those of Henco Industries, the Six Nations protesters, the residents of Caledonia, the government, the court, and the police. In a dispute like this, what do you think the first priority should be? How would you balance the other interests against the priority you identified? Comment on the way this balance was struck in the case of Caledonia.

Political Activism

The cases discussed in this chapter, as well as the history of Indigenous people in Canada discussed in Chapter 1, have not progressed without organized political activity by Indigenous people. The earliest forms of activism were met with severe consequences from the federal government, which was able to control unrest through the *Indian Act*. However, since 1960 Indigenous people have been successful in bringing cases to court and pressuring the federal government to honour the treaties. Attempts have been made throughout Canada's history to organize political associations beyond the band level so that the common interests of Indigenous people in Canada could be advanced.

One of the first organizations to press land claims issues was the Allied Tribes of British Columbia, which formed in 1916 in an attempt to lobby the British Privy Council to adjudicate land claims. This organization folded in 1927 but was succeeded in 1931 by the Native Brotherhood of British Columbia, which emerged from Indigenous labour-related activities in the fishing industry.

In 1919 the League of Indians of Canada was formed in Ontario to address concerns over loss of reserve lands and the restriction of hunting and trapping rights, culturally destructive educational policies, poor economies on reserve, and poor health conditions. The league was ultimately unable to expand to include bands across Canada due to linguistic and cultural differences.

In the 1930s and 1940s the Indian Association of Alberta and the Union (later Federation) of Saskatchewan Indians were formed. In 1945 the North American Indian Brotherhood was another short-lived attempt to establish a national organization.

The National Indian Brotherhood emerged in 1967—finally, a national organization for Indigenous people in Canada. This was followed by a wave of activism sparked by the federal government's 1969 White Paper, which proposed to eliminate the *Indian Act* as well as transfer responsibilities for Indians to the provinces. The National Indian Brotherhood and affiliated activist groups successfully defeated the White Paper. The organization became the Assembly of First Nations in 1982, which today represents 634 member chiefs across Canada. The Native Council of Canada formed in 1970 to pursue changes in government policy with respect to Métis and non-status Indians. In 1993 this organization became the Congress of Aboriginal Peoples.

Indigenous protesters march through Ottawa to Parliament Hill in January 2013.

Between 1978 and 1982, all Indigenous political organizations worked together toward the inclusion of Indigenous rights in the Canadian Constitution. Today, much Indigenous political organization and activism centres on negotiating land claims and redefining treaties in the 21st-century political context, as well as pressing forward the issues of education, poverty, and equality. Indigenous activism and advocacy have helped achieve Canada's adoption of the United Nations' *Declaration on the Rights of Indigenous Peoples*, which the federal government at first opposed adopting. The advocacy of Indigenous political organizations was instrumental in obtaining the Indian Residential Schools Settlement Agreement as well as the Canadian government's apology for its part in the residential school system.

In December 2012, a younger Indigenous grassroots movement called "Idle No More" emerged. This movement effectively used social media to spread across Canada and into the United States, New Zealand, and Australia. It began as a "teach-in" in Saskatchewan about fears that federal omnibus Bill C-45 would weaken environmental protections and threaten Indigenous sovereignty. The timing of the event coincided with the announcement that Chief Theresa Spence of Attawapiskat First Nation was embarking on a hunger strike to bring attention to the poor living conditions on her reserve. The movement grew nationwide and included flash mobs of traditional dancing and drum circles as well as highway and railway blockades. It is important to understand that forward movement for Indigenous rights in Canada does not happen without political action, which sometimes takes the form of peaceful protest, blockades, and demonstrations. These actions inevitably require police involvement in one form or another. Today, police services plan ahead for the best interventions for all parties involved.

The Nishiyuu Walkers

In January 2013 seven Cree youth, wearing snowshoes and towing their supplies, began a 1,600-kilometre trek through the bush, in snow and freezing temperatures, from Whapmagoostui First Nation in Quebec to Ottawa. They became known as the Nishiyuu ("the people" in Cree) Walkers. They walked to Ottawa to bring attention to the poor living conditions in their community, to demonstrate unity among First Nations, and to show that the Cree are dedicated to keeping their language, culture, traditions, and laws of their ancestors. Along the way, around 270 others joined the trek. They reached Ottawa in March 2013, where they met with Aboriginal Affairs Minister Bernard Valcourt and invited him to visit their community.

Sources: CTV News (2013); Journey of Nishiyuu (n.d.).

CHAPTER SUMMARY

The Mi'kmaq fishing crisis and the dispute in Caledonia are two of the many conflicts between Indigenous protesters and police in Canada that have escalated into violence. Whenever these situations occur, police are called in to keep the peace, and it is vitally important that they remain neutral and understand the issues involved. Of course, police are not required to actually *resolve* the larger issues. When Caledonia residents called police to forcibly end the crisis by removing the demonstrators from the disputed land, then-OPP commissioner Julian Fantino underscored the role of law enforcement—to "preserve the peace, deal with offences and bring those who transgress the laws of the land to justice."

We all have biases that may emerge under stress. When it comes to Indigenous land and resources disputes, these biases are increasingly fed by the media. It is important to look behind the press coverage, and behind immediate events. It is crucial to look at the issue in its historical context to understand how emotionally charged these situations can be for all parties involved.

This chapter has shown that Indigenous land and resource claims have their foundations in law. The Supreme Court has clearly laid out the obligations of all parties in negotiating these claims. Problems arise, however, when governments allow the prospect of gaining income through development and commercial industry to take precedence over legal obligations.

REFERENCES

Aboriginal Affairs and Northern Development Canada. (2011). Fact sheet—Three-year time frames for negotiating specific claim settlements. http://www.aadnc-aandc.gc.ca.

Aboriginal Affairs and Northern Development Canada. (2012). Fact sheet: Algonquins of Ontario land claim negotiations. https://www.aadnc-aandc.gc.ca/eng/1355436558998/1355436749970.

Aboriginal Affairs and Northern Development Canada. (2013). *Summative evaluation of the Specific Claims Action Plan.* https://www.aadnc-aandc.gc.ca/DAM/DAM-INTER-HQ-AEV/STAGING/texte-text/ev_spcap_1385136300660_eng.pdf.

Aboriginal Affairs and Northern Development Canada. (2015). Specific claims. https://www.aadnc-aandc.gc.ca/eng/1100100030291/1100100030292.

Amnesty International. (2005, December 19). It is time to comply: Canada's record of unimplemented UN human rights recommendations. Ottawa.

Assembly of First Nations. (2015). *In bad faith: Justice at last and Canada's failure to resolve specific land claims.* http://www.ubcic.bc.ca/files/PDF/InBadFaith_JusticeatLast_CanadaFailureResolveSpecificClaims.pdf.

Assembly of First Nations' Chiefs in New Brunswick. (2013). First Nations, consultation, and fracking. http://www.chiefsnb.ca/index.php/news/item/first_nations_consultation_and_fracking.

Badger, R v. (1996). [1996] 1 SCR 771.

Bell, C., & Paterson, R. (2003). Aboriginal rights to repatriation of cultural property in Canada. In A. Walkem & H. Bruce (Eds.), *Box of treasures or empty box? Twenty years of section 35* (pp. 104–154). Penticton, BC: Theytus Books.

British North America Act. (1867). 30 & 31 Vict., c. 3, reprinted in RSC 1985, app. II, no. 5.

Calder et al. v. Attorney General of British Columbia. (1973). [1973] SCR 313.

Campbell, Tracy. (1996, March). Co-management of Aboriginal resources. *Information North, 22*(1). Arctic Institute of North America. http://arcticcircle.uconn.edu/NatResources/comanagement.html.

CBC News. (2006a). In-depth: Caledonia land claim, historical timeline. *CBC News.* http://www.cbc.ca.

CBC News. (2006b). OPP's job to "preserve the peace" in Caledonia: Top cop. *CBC News.* http://www.cbc.ca.

Churchill, W. (1992). *Last stand at Lubicon Lake: Struggle for the land.* Toronto: Between the Lines.

CTV News. (2013, March 25). "Nishiyuu Walkers" complete 1,600 km trek to Ottawa. *CTV News.* http://www.ctvnews.ca.

Curry, B. (2003, November 27). Half of Canadians disbelieve land claims. *The National Post.*

Darling, G. (n.d.). Land claims and the Six Nations in Caledonia Ontario. University of Alberta, Centre for Constitutional Studies. http://ualawccsprod.srv.ualberta.ca/index.php/constitutional-issues/aboriginal-rights/61-land-claims-and-the-six-nations-in-caledonia-ontario.

Delgamuukw v. British Columbia. (1997). [1997] 3 SCR 1010.

Donham, P.B. (2003). Fishery: Lobster wars. In R. Anderson & R. Bone (Eds.), *Natural resources and Aboriginal people in Canada: Readings, cases and commentary.* Concord, ON: Captus Press.

Francis v. The Queen. (1969). [1969] 1 NBR (2d) 886 (Prov. Ct.).

Friends of the Lubicon. (2006). United Nations holds Canada in continuing violation of Lubicon human rights. http://www.lubicon.ca/pa/humanr.htm.

Gibson, G., Higgs, E., & Hrudey, S. (1998). Sour gas, bitter relations. *Alternatives Journal: Environmental Thought, Policy and Action, 24*(2).

Goldi, J., & Goldi, J. (Producers). (2004). *Ipperwash: A Canadian tragedy*. [Motion picture].

Guerin v. The Queen. (1984). [1984] 2 SCR 335.

Henderson, B. (1996). Guerin v. The Queen [A brief introduction to Aboriginal law in Canada]. Welcome to my Virtual Law Office. http://www.bloorstreet.com/200block/rguerin.htm.

Implementation Monitoring Committee. (2008). Location of entitlement First Nations. http://www.tleimc.ca/index.php/entitlement-first-nations/map-of-entitlement-first-nations.

Indian Act. (1985). RSC 1985, c. I-5.

Journey of Nishiyuu. (n.d.). The quest of Wisjinichu-Nishiyuu, quest for unity. http://nishiyuujourney.ca/#!/?page_id=10.

Knockwood, C. (2003). The Mi'kmaq-Canadian treaty relationship: A 277-year journey of rediscovery. In A. Walkem & H. Bruce (Eds.), *Box of treasures or empty box? Twenty years of section 35* (pp. 43–60). Penticton, BC: Theytus Books.

Mahoney, J. (2013, January 16). Canadians' attitudes hardening on Aboriginal issues: New poll. *The Globe and Mail*. http://www.theglobeandmail.com.

Mandell, L. (2003). Offerings to an emerging future. In A. Walkem & H. Bruce (Eds.), *Box of treasures or empty box? Twenty years of section 35*. Penticton, BC: Theytus Books.

Marshall, R v. (1999). [1999] 3 SCR 533.

McDonald, M. (2003). Aboriginal forestry in Canada. In R. Anderson & R. Bone (Eds.), *Natural resources and Aboriginal people in Canada. Readings, cases and commentary*. Concord, ON: Captus Press.

Mi'kmaq Rights Initiative. (n.d.). Consultation. http://mikmaqrights.com/consultation/.

Monture-Angus, P. (1999). *Journeying forward: Dreaming First Nations independence*. Halifax: Fernwood Publishing.

Obomsawin, A. (2002). *Is the Crown at war with us?* [Motion picture.] National Film Board of Canada.

Ontario Ministry of Aboriginal Affairs. (2011). Ontario's approach to land claim negotiations.

Royal Proclamation of 1763. (1970). RSC 1970, app. II, no. 1.

Simon v. The Queen. (1985). [1985] 2 SCR 387.

Sparrow, R v. (1990). [1990] 1 SCR 1075.

Specific Claims Tribunal Act. (2008). SC 2008, c. 22.

St. Catherine's Milling & Lumber Company v. The Queen. (1888). 14 App. Cas. 46 (PC).

Steckley, J., & Cummins, B. (2001a). The Golden Lake Algonquin and Algonquin Park: Missed by treaty. In *Full circle: Canada's First Nations* (chap. 14). Toronto: Prentice Hall.

Steckley, J., & Cummins, B. (2001b). Social issues: The Dudley George story. In *Full circle: Canada's First Nations* (chap. 20). Toronto: Prentice Hall.

Sylliboy, R v. (1929). [1929] 1 DLR 307.

Treaty Land Entitlement Committee of Manitoba Inc. (n.d.). http://www.tlec.ca.

Union of British Columbia Indian Chiefs. (2011). Canada's undermining of the specific claims process—A summary and analysis. http://www.ubcic.bc.ca/News_Releases/UBCICNews07261101.html#axzz4JhOudtg6.

Van der Peet, R v. (1996). [1996] 2 SCR 507.

Walkem, A. (2003). Constructing the constitutional box: The Supreme Court's section 35(1) reasoning. In A. Walkem & H. Bruce (Eds.), *Box of treasures or empty box? Twenty years of section 35* (pp. 196–222). Penticton, BC: Theytus Books.

Youngblood Henderson, J. (1999). Impact of Delgamuukw guidelines in Atlantic Canada. Cape Breton University. http://www.cbu.ca/indigenous-affairs/unamaki-college/mikmaq-resource-centre/essays/impact-of-delgamuukw-guidelines-in-atlantic-canada/.

REVIEW QUESTIONS

True or False?

_____ 1. *St. Catherine's Milling & Lumber Company v. The Queen* concerned a dispute between the Ojibwe people and Ontario over logging leases.

_____ 2. Section 91(24) of the *British North America Act* gave jurisdiction over Indians and lands reserved for Indians to the provincial governments.

_____ 3. In the case of *Guerin v. The Queen*, the Supreme Court ruled that the Crown's responsibility was only a "political trust" rather than a true trust and that therefore the Crown was not accountable for the $10 million that had gone missing through the leasing of land to the golf club.

_____ 4. Section 35 of the *Constitution Act, 1982* created entirely new rights for Aboriginal people, which had never existed in law before.

_____ 5. In *Delgamuukw*, the Supreme Court ruled that the Crown can never infringe on an Aboriginal right in any circumstances.

_____ 6. Of the six arguments put forward by the Crown in the *Delgamuukw* case, the Crown was successful with the argument that a third-party interest in unceded Indigenous land displaces Aboriginal title.

_____ 7. In the *Marshall* case of 1999, the court gave an unlimited right to the Mi'kmaq to fish, which led to the lobster-fishing dispute in the Maritimes.

_____ 8. The *Calder* case, in which four Nisga'a communities asserted rights over traditional territory outside the reserve created by the federal government, is an example of a specific land claim.

_____ **9.** With reference to the *Sparrow* case, it has been found that the enactment of provincial fishing regulations is evidence of clear and plain extinguishment of an Aboriginal right.

_____ **10.** The management of natural resources is a provincial responsibility.

Multiple Choice

1. In the case of *R v. Sparrow*, a two-part test for limiting an Aboriginal right was created. The first part of that test says that the Crown must have a compelling and substantial objective if it is to limit an Aboriginal right. An example of this is

  a. protection of a resource

  b. protection of the economy

  c. obtaining votes

  d. there is no such thing as a compelling or substantial objective

2. The 1888 *St. Catherine's Milling* case set the precedent for the definition of Aboriginal title to land for ____ years.

  a. 10

  b. 30

  c. 50

  d. 100

3. In the *St. Catherine's Milling* case, the court came to the conclusion that Indigenous groups had a "personal and usufructuary right" to land, which means

  a. the right to use the land at the pleasure of the Crown, so that the Crown has the authority to remove the right at any time

  b. the right to use the land but never own it

  c. the right to sole possession of the land

  d. no rights to the land whatsoever

4. In the *Calder* case, the decision over whether or not Indian title to land can be extinguished without treaty resulted in the setting of a standard by which such extinguishment can occur. Which of the following defines that standard?

  a. by implication through other laws

  b. by a failure to occupy the land

  c. in a clear and plain way

  d. by assumption

5. In the *Sparrow* case, the Crown set out a two-part test for limiting an Aboriginal right. The first part was that the Crown must have a compelling and substantial objective, and the second part was that

  a. the limit must be fair

  b. the limit must be consistent with the Crown's fiduciary responsibility to Indigenous peoples

  c. the limit must protect the Canadian economy

  d. the limit must be temporary

6. The framework of the litigation process to determine an Aboriginal right has four steps. Which of the following is not one of those steps?

  a. identification of the nature and content of the right

  b. determining whether the right is an "existing right" recognized and affirmed in section 35 of the *Constitution Act, 1982* (or whether it was extinguished prior to the Constitution)

  c. determination of whether the provincial or federal legislation or regulation interferes with the right

  d. paying out for loss of the right

7. A comprehensive land claim is

  a. a claim to an entire province

  b. a claim to territory that is not covered by treaty or land cession agreements

  c. a claim to resources but not to land

  d. a claim to privately and individually owned land

8. Co-management of land and resources has been implemented in some areas where Aboriginal rights have not been extinguished. Co-management effectively is

  a. the inclusion of non-traditional groups such as environmentalist groups, Indigenous groups, and industry in decision-making over resources

  b. the division of management over resources strictly between federal and provincial governments

  c. the division of responsibility for the area among a vast number of government agencies

  d. the granting of exclusive authority to Indigenous groups to manage the area

9. A specific land claim is

  a. a claim that relates to a specific surveyed parcel of land

  b. a claim that relates to specific misdealings of the Crown with relation to land or resources

  c. a claim that results because Indigenous title was never extinguished by treaty

  d. a claim that cannot be legitimized

10. Which of the following is not one of the three types of land claims active in Ontario?

  a. claims relating to the fulfillment of terms of treaties

  b. claims arising from the surrender for sale of reserved lands

  c. claims arising from Indigenous title

  d. claims of abuse

APPENDIX 2.1
The Dudley George Story

During the American Revolution and the War of 1812, the Anishinaabe, originally from northern Ontario, were allies with the British. They settled in southern Ontario following the wars and became known as the Chippewa. The government of the Chippewa signed a treaty in 1825 that created four reserves: Sarnia, Walpole Island, Kettle Point, and Stoney Point. In 1928, the provincial government pressured the Stoney Point people to sell 152 hectares of prime waterfront land to private interests. Although they were against the idea of selling their land, the band had little control. Indian Affairs, through the oppressive *Indian Act*, sold the land without the band's permission. A large part of that land was reserved to create the Ipperwash Provincial Park in 1936. The Stoney Point people were unhappy about the sale and unhappier still when their burial site was disturbed in the creation of the park.

In 1942, the federal government asked the Stoney Point people to relinquish what remained of their land so that a military base could be built to support the war efforts. (Many of the Stoney Point men were, in fact, overseas serving as soldiers.) The federal government offered $23 per acre for 2,211 acres of land (895 hectares). The Stoney Point people voted on the offer and declined. Invoking the *War Measures Act*, the federal government expropriated the land regardless. The Stoney Point people were paid the said amount and were promised that the land would be returned to them at the end of the war, provided the military had no further need for it. The Stoney Point people were forced to leave and live with their neighbours at Kettle Point.

At the end of the war, the Stoney Point people requested to enter into negotiations for the return of their land. The armed forces continued, however, to make peacetime use of the land as a cadet training camp and therefore did not return the land. In 1981, 36 years after the end of the war, the federal government agreed to pay the Stoney Point band $2.4 million in compensation for the 40-year use of the land and agreed to return the land pending an environmental assessment. The cost of cleaning the area environmentally was expected to be high because of the way it was used by the military. The Department of National Defence then decided that it did not want to relinquish the land. The department promised to review the requirements for the training camp every three years; if the training camp was deemed unnecessary, the department would turn it over to the Stoney Point people.

A recommendation was put forward in 1992 by the Standing Committee on Aboriginal People that the federal government return the land. The committee insisted that the government's reasons for failing to relinquish the land were "without substance." The recommendation was not followed. In May 1993, the Stoney Point people, bringing tents and trailers, moved onto the military property. They maintained a tenuous relationship with the military they were living alongside. In September of that same year, they walked for three weeks to Ottawa to insist that action be taken to return the land. No action was forthcoming.

On September 4, 1995, Indigenous protesters moved into the adjacent provincial park after it had closed for the season. One of the contentious issues about the park was the burial ground, which the Stoney Point people had requested be protected and fenced off. This had never been done despite clear archaeological records of the existence and location of the burial ground. The Ontario government would deny that a burial ground was even located in the park; the government was subsequently proven wrong.

Newly elected Premier Mike Harris held an emergency meeting the day following the occupation. OPP Inspector Ron Fox was at that meeting. It was alleged that Premier Mike Harris insisted that the protesters be removed from the park. This allegation appears to have been substantiated: years later, at the 2006 inquiry into the incident, on a tape-recorded conversation from 1995 between Fox and OPP Inspector John Carson, made directly following the emergency meeting, Fox can be heard saying the following: "No question they don't give a shit about Indians";

and "They just want us to kick ass." During the course of the inquiry Mike Harris would deny saying, "Get the fucking Indians out of the park." Various people present at the meeting would testify that they heard Mike Harris say this; others would testify that he did not. Regardless, after four days of testimony at the inquiry, Harris stated that he would not make any changes in the way he had handled the Ipperwash incident.

Following the September 5, 1995 meeting, the OPP prepared themselves for the altercation they expected. They ordered night-vision goggles, gas masks, and helicopters, and brought in 250 officers from across the province. The OPP had received intelligence information that the protesters were unarmed.

On September 6, the order was given to the OPP to get the protesters out of the park. After dark, the OPP advanced on the 30 unarmed protesters in the park. Sergeant Kenneth Deane, a sniper for the Tactics and Rescue unit, then shot Indigenous protester Dudley George, who later died from his injuries. Deane would testify that he witnessed a muzzle flash and saw George with a rifle. The investigation would reveal that there was no rifle and that George was unarmed at the time of the shooting. The police did not call an ambulance for George; the protesters attempted to call for one but were arrested. George was driven to the hospital by family members; a car breakdown en route delayed medical treatment even further. George's family members were arrested at the hospital; it was too late to save George, who died from his wound.

Kenneth Deane was charged and found guilty of criminal negligence causing death. He was sentenced to two years less a day to be served in the community plus 180 community service hours. He appealed his conviction unsuccessfully. Deane did not testify at the 2006 inquiry because he died in a car accident before it took place.

The Indigenous protesters were arrested and faced 62 charges, most of which were dropped. Charges that stemmed from their entry into the park were dismissed because it was decided that they had colour of right to the park—that is, interest in the property—because the burial ground, previously alleged to be non-existent, was now acknowledged to be there.

Indigenous rights groups immediately demanded an inquiry into the incident. Ontario's Conservative government refused, and it was not until the election of a new government in 2003 that an announcement was made that an inquiry would begin.

Following the announcement of the inquiry, the CBC received OPP surveillance tapes that were aired on the news. The tapes show OPP officers at the scene just prior to the shooting making racist comments about the protesters. These tapes brought the OPP's actions and motives into question.

The inquiry's report, released May 31, 2007, ruled that the OPP, the government of former Ontario premier Mike Harris, and the federal government all bore responsibility for the events that led to Dudley George's death. Both federal and provincial governments had more than 50 years to resolve these issues and chose not to. This choice led to a violent confrontation between police and Indigenous protesters, which culminated in the death of Dudley George. This tragedy could certainly have been avoided. Police services in Canada would be wise to study and learn from these events to ensure that they are not repeated in the future, because confrontations involving Indigenous land and resources are likely to occur for decades to come.

In December 2007, the Ontario government announced that it would return the 56-hectare Ipperwash Provincial Park to the Chippewas of the Kettle and Stoney Creek First Nation, after a period of co-control between the Chippewas and the government. On May 28, 2009, the province officially signed over control of Ipperwash Park to the Chippewas. In April 2016, the military base Camp Ipperwash was also turned over to the Chippewas, along with the $95 million negotiated settlement.

Sources: Goldi & Goldi (2004); Steckley & Cummins (2001b).

APPENDIX 2.2

The Lubicon Cree

The Lubicon Cree were traditionally hunters and gatherers. From time immemorial, they had lived in a 10,000 square kilometre area surrounding Lubicon Lake in northern Alberta. In 1899, a delegation from the Canadian government travelled through northern Alberta to secure for Treaty No. 8 the signatures of bands occupying the area. However, treaty commissioners failed to contact a number of small bands scattered throughout the vast territory covered by the treaty. The Lubicon were one of those bands; members did not hear of the treaty until 1912. The band never signed a treaty, nor did they ever cede or relinquish rights to their traditional territory.

Under the provisions of Treaty No. 8, each band was to receive a "reserved" land, the acreage depending on the population of the band, and each member was to receive an annuity in payment for the alienation of the land. Bands that were not notified of the treaty could go to designated locations and be added to the pay list for annuities. When the Lubicon band members were notified of the treaty by other bands, they made their way to Whitefish Lake and received an annuity there. Government officials then added the Lubicon names to the band list at Whitefish Lake, although the Lubicon group had no connection to that band and were a separate and individual band, as they had always been.

In 1935, the Indian Department sent notice to the Lubicon band that they were living off their designated reserve, and must relocate to live at Whitefish Lake. The Lubicon protested that they had never lived there and were a separate and distinct band that resided at Lubicon Lake; they requested that they be declared a band by the Indian Department. The department investigated, concluded that the Lubicon were indeed a separate and distinct band, and approved the creation of a new reserve at Lubicon Lake. In 1940, that reserve was surveyed by the department according to the population of the band at the time, which was set by the Indian agent at 127 members. At 52 hectares per person, the reserve was surveyed for 6,500 hectares.

Prior to the completion of the deal in 1942, Indian Affairs official Malcolm McCrimmon was sent to northern Alberta to see that the pay lists for annuities for Indians were in order. Because Second World War expenses were mounting, the federal government was looking to reduce expenditures elsewhere, and the Indian Department seemed a logical place to cut costs. McCrimmon rewrote the rules for addition to treaty annuity lists and eliminated all members who joined after 1912. He insisted that birth records be provided to prove that only pure-blood Indians were on the lists—but this was in a remote area where children were born at home and it was common to have no birth record. McCrimmon eliminated 700 names from the annuity pay list, including 90 members of the Lubicon Cree band. He then argued against the establishment of a reserve for the Lubicon, saying that there were insufficient members of the band to warrant one. As a result, the Indian Department postponed the creation of a reserve indefinitely.

The Lubicon continued to live at Lubicon Lake, but a renewed interest in the area occurred in 1950 when Alberta Lands and Forest Division received inquiries from a large mining corporation regarding the Lubicon area. The company wanted the provincial government to open it for exploration. The province of Alberta requested that the Indian Department relocate the proposed reserve for the Lubicon to a "less isolated area." However, the federal government failed to respond to the province, which was anxious to lease the land. The province eventually sent a letter with an ultimatum, that the federal government respond within 30 days or the province would deem the proposed reserve not to exist. The federal government failed to respond. Alberta then requested that Indian Affairs strike the band from the record as an official band. The federal government could not comply with this request because it had declared the Lubicon a distinct band in 1939 even though it had failed to finalize a reserve for the band. Alberta insisted that the Lubicon band be reduced through enfranchisement where possible, and the remainder of the band be relocated to live with the Whitefish band. The two levels of government could not come to an agreement on how to resolve this issue.

In 1971, Alberta secured oil company financing to build an all-weather road into Lubicon territory for the purposes of exploration. The Lubicon lobbied the government to stop the encroachment of corporations, insisting on their right to their traditional territory. The Alberta government insisted that the Lubicon were squatters on provincial Crown lands with no land rights to negotiate. In 1975, as developers began exploration, the Lubicon filed a caveat under provincial law to place would-be developers on notice that title to the land was contested. The provincial government asked for a postponement of the caveat and rewrote legislation under Bill 29 to end grounds for Lubicon legal action.

In 1979 the all-weather road was completed and people poured into the area, severely disrupting the Lubicon way of life. In 1980, the Lubicon appealed to the federal government to provide them with financial assistance to seek an injunction to stop development until a resolution could be reached over the land title issues. The federal government denied the request. In 1981 Alberta declared the main settlement area of the Lubicon a hamlet, subdivided the area into 0.8 hectare lots, and proposed to lease or gift the lots to individual band members. The Lubicon were very concerned about how this "land tenure program" would affect their land claim and petitioned the federal government to look into the matter.

The minister of Indian Affairs discovered that the land in question could no longer be subject to a land claim because as a hamlet it was no longer classed as provincial Crown land.

In 1982, with the federal and provincial governments still unable to reach an agreement over the land allocation, the Lubicon filed a second legal action before the Alberta Court of Queen's Bench requesting the retention of Indigenous rights over their traditional area, which would void the leases provided by the province to oil companies. The band requested an immediate injunction to stop development until the land issues could be resolved. The concluding arguments in the case were heard on December 2, 1982, but the court postponed the delivery of its verdict until March 1983. At that time an injunction to stop development was received—too late. The companies had simply accelerated their exploration through the winter, and the area became irreversibly altered environmentally.

By 1983, 400 oil wells had been drilled within 15 kilometres of the Lubicon's main settlement. The typical trapper's income was reduced from $5,000 per year to $400, and the number of moose killed for food plummeted from 200 to 19. The Lubicon experienced a rash of suicides and rising alcoholism within the community. Welfare dependence in the community increased from 5 percent to 90 percent. The extreme poverty and a tuberculosis outbreak affecting one-third of the community demoralized the band even further.

Following the injunction, the companies returned to court to argue that the injunction was unnecessary since the drilling was already complete and the pumping process put in place would not cause any further environmental degradation. By 1987, it was estimated conservatively that oil and gas revenues from the area were in excess of $500 million per year.

In 1984, after the Supreme Court of Canada refused to hear their case, the Lubicon appealed to the United Nations Human Rights Commission. The United Nations conducted a study of the situation and concluded in 1987 that the Lubicon could not possibly achieve political redress in Canada. The United Nations appealed to Canada to do no further harm to Lubicon territory until a hearing could be held on human rights violations. However, in 1988, Alberta announced that it had granted timber rights in the Lubicon territory to a Japanese company, Daishowa, which planned to cut 11,000 trees daily to produce 1,000 tonnes of pulp per day.

In response to the news of the lease, the Lubicon toured Europe prior to the 1988 Olympics seeking support from other countries. Then, at the winter Olympics in Calgary, they boycotted the Indigenous art exhibition ("The Spirit Sings"), having discovered that its sponsors were the very oil companies that were undermining Indigenous land claims in Canada. Their boycott was supported by human rights organizations around the world. Also in 1988, the Lubicon, fed up with the system, withdrew all cases from Canadian courts, declared themselves a sovereign nation, and blockaded all roads leading into their territory. The RCMP arrested 27 people involved in the blockades, and the province refused to negotiate with the Lubicon until the blockades were removed.

Concerned that the situation could escalate into violence, Alberta returned to the negotiating table. Alberta negotiated the Grimshaw Accord, which called for the creation of a reserved land base for the Lubicon people that included subsurface rights to the land. The federal government disagreed, offering a reserved land base with no subsurface rights. The subsurface rights were critical for the Lubicon, since mining and drilling are the only ways they can now sustain their people—the degradation of the land made their traditional economy impossible. The subsurface rights are not forthcoming.

In 1989, the federal government exploited divisions within the band. Facing extreme poverty, with no resolution in sight, some members of the band wavered in their support of the band governance body. The federal government met with a dissident group and agreed to create a new band called the Woodland Cree, insisting that they have rights to the contested area. The federal government presented the rejected offer from the Lubicon band to the Woodland band, offering them an additional $1,000 each to sign the agreement that did not include subsurface rights. The federal government offered the same deal to the Loon Lake Cree, and subsequently pressured the Lubicon to sign the same agreement without subsurface rights. The chief of the Lubicon band, Bernard Omniyak, says the agreement is "deficient in the area of providing economic stability for the future. In essence, the Canadian government has offered to build houses for the Lubicon and support us forever on welfare like animals in the zoo who are cared for and fed at an appointed time" (Churchill, 1992).

In 1990, the United Nations charged Canada with human rights violations under article 27 of the *International Covenant on Civil and Political Rights*. Canada did not answer to the charges, which stand today.

In 1991, the Lubicon organized an international boycott of Daishowa. In response, Daishowa agreed to stay out of Lubicon territory until the land issue was resolved; however, in 1994, Daishowa sued the organizers of the boycott for $5 million in compensation for lost business. The suit was unsuccessful.

In 1994 the Lubicon protested oil and gas corporation Unocal's plans to build a sour gas processing plant within 4 kilometres of the proposed reserve. Alberta's energy board failed to convene a hearing on the matter until after the plant was built. The plant went into operation in 1995.

Following the opening of the sour gas plant, Alberta proposed that the size of the proposed reserve be reduced from the original 243 square kilometres specified in the Grimshaw Accord; their rationale was that the population of the Lubicon band had decreased due to the creation of the Woodland Cree band and the transference of members to that group (Gibson, Higgs, & Hrudey, 1998).

In 2002, an agreement was finally reached between the federal and provincial governments and the Lubicon Cree over the construction of a new reserve, although subsurface rights were still undetermined. On November 1, 2005, the United Nations Human Rights Committee reaffirmed its earlier conclusion that Canada is violating article 1 of the *International Covenant on Civil and Political Rights* insofar as it is denying the Lubicon basic subsistence by destroying their traditional economy and way of life. Furthermore, Canada is in violation of article 27 of the Covenant insofar as it is participating in the destruction of the Lubicon's culture, language rights, and way of life by refusing to negotiate a reasonable resolution to their land claim. The committee reiterated its 1987 recommendation (for which there is support in Canadian case law, established by the 1997 *Delgamuukw* decision) that Canada should consult with the band before granting licences for economic exploitation of the disputed land and ensure that in no case such exploitation jeopardizes the rights recognized under the Covenant. Canada has not responded to the committee's findings. However, Amnesty International provided the following statement:

> One of the most glaring failures to implement UN level human rights recommendations is the situation of the Lubicon Cree in Alberta. In 1990, the Human Rights Committee issued a detailed report documenting serious violations of the rights of the Lubicon, stemming from a decades-old failure to enter into an agreement with the Lubicon regarding their land rights. The Committee called on the government to ensure a prompt and just settlement of the dispute. Fifteen years later the dispute remains unresolved, the ability of the Lubicon to provide for themselves remains under threat, and there have been no negotiations between the government and the Lubicon for over two years. (Amnesty International, 2005; also see Friends of the Lubicon, 2006)

The issues regarding land rights have still not been resolved. The Lubicon band suffers economically and socially, and the resource that has brought economic wealth to the province of Alberta and Canada has led to economic collapse for the Lubicon. In 2009, the Alberta government approved the extension of an oil pipeline through the contested territory, and 2,400 kilometres of pipeline now snake through the Lubicon's traditional land. In May 2011, an oil spill leaked an estimated 28,000 barrels of oil onto the Lubicon's traditional territory, approximately 30 kilometres from the site of their community's main town, contaminating the surrounding areas.

While their land claim remains unresolved, the Lubicon are fighting not just for a resolution of their claim but for environmental protection for their community. In October 2014 Alberta Premier Jim Prentice met with the band to begin dialogue again on the 80-year outstanding claim. In December 2014 Aboriginal Affairs and Northern Development Canada signed a Negotiation Framework to move the claim forward after a long period of inaction on the claim. The framework sets out three priority issues identified by the band: the establishment of a reserve pursuant to the treaty; construction of the community on the future reserved land; and the resolution of claims to other treaty-related benefits. The next step will be to create an agreement-in-principle that can be signed and then negotiated into a binding legal decision in the form of a claim settlement that would then be protected under the Constitution. As we know from other claims examined in this chapter, settlement is years away, but progress continues.

3 Indian and Inuit Residential Schools

Cree child Thomas Moore, as he appeared in his traditional attire when admitted to the Regina Indian Industrial School in 1891, contrasted with his appearance afterward.

LEARNING OUTCOMES

After completing this chapter, you should be able to:

- Explain the Dominion of Canada's rationale for implementing residential schools.
- Understand the magnitude of the damage done to Indigenous societies by residential schools.
- Understand how the residential school experience led to the later seizure of children from Indigenous communities during the 1960s, 1970s, and 1980s.
- Understand why the Truth and Reconciliation Commission was created, what its goals were, and what it has recommended in its final report.
- Discuss the moral, legal, and ethical issues related to accountability and healing, as well as the current efforts being made by the government of Canada, in partnership with the Indigenous people, to promote healing.

Introduction

residential schools
church-run, government-funded boarding schools for Indigenous children, designed to prepare them for life in white society

From 1870 to 1940, Indigenous children were not allowed to attend any schools other than those designated specifically for their education. These schools were provided by the Canadian government in conjunction with the Roman Catholic, Anglican, United, and Presbyterian churches. The schools were chronically underfunded and poorly run, and the health of the children suffered. Due to poor nutrition and substandard living conditions, many children died of typhoid fever and tuberculosis. From the 1870s to the 1990s, when the last **residential school** was closed, a growing catalogue of crimes against humanity was compiled. The continued incidents of physical abuse, sexual abuse, emotional abuse, cultural extinguishment, and neglect resulted in psychological trauma for generations of Indigenous people in Canada. The forcible removal of First Nations children from their families to the schools was designed to "kill the Indian" but save the child and result in the assimilation of Indigenous children into white Canadian society.

Royal Commission on Aboriginal Peoples (RCAP)
a commission established by the federal government in 1991 to investigate the issues facing Indigenous people in Canada

Much of the information about residential schools and their impact on Indigenous communities was absent from the public consciousness until the final report of the **Royal Commission on Aboriginal Peoples (RCAP)** was released in November 1996. The commission's report gave society at large a clearer picture of the enormous damage done to Indigenous communities by the long-standing maltreatment and abuse of their children. The schools' presence in Canada and their effects on First Nations and Inuit children warrants careful study. Indigenous people working to heal their communities say that the education system's part in this damage cannot be overestimated.

The government of Canada made its first carefully worded apology in 1998, delivered by Indian Affairs Minister Jane Stewart. A second apology followed a decade later, in June 2008, delivered by Prime Minister Stephen Harper as he accepted responsibility on behalf of the Canadian government for the abuses that occurred in residential schools and concluded that the residential school system was wrong and had no place in Canada. Since the apologies, the government has partnered with Indigenous peoples to create both the Aboriginal Healing Foundation and the Truth and Reconciliation Commission (TRC) to improve the well-being of Indigenous communities and repair the relationship between Indigenous and non-Indigenous people in Canada. In 2015, after the release of the TRC's final report, Prime Minister Justin Trudeau committed to working with Indigenous communities to implement the TRC's recommendations (Prime Minister of Canada Justin Trudeau, 2015).

It is startling how many Canadians today are either unaware or only vaguely aware that Indigenous children, until relatively recently, were forced to attend residential schools. Many young non-Indigenous Canadians have not been taught—and many adults have chosen not to inquire—about the residential school legacy. This situation is very unfortunate. Just resolutions and reconciliation in the issues involving Indigenous people in Canada depend on all Canadians, Indigenous and non-Indigenous alike, having the same awareness of past and present.

This chapter examines and discusses the political environment that made this whole episode possible—and possible, moreover, in a country that is today renowned for its attention to civil rights. To help us understand the survivors' pain, we recount some of their stories. This chapter also examines some of the current efforts to help Indigenous people recover and to bring about reconciliation between them and the rest of Canada.

Education as a Tool for Subjugation, Socialization, and Assimilation

Indigenous and non-Indigenous people agreed from an early point in their relations that education was important. As a result, guarantees for education funding were set out in certain treaties. The Stone Fort Treaty (1871), for example, stated the following: "And further, Her Majesty agrees to maintain a school on each reserve hereby made, whenever the Indians of the reserve should desire it" (Morris, 1971, p. 315). Indigenous leaders recognized that their children would need new knowledge to cope with the rapidly changing environment. With the depletion of natural resources and with increasing white settlement, these leaders saw that their traditional hunting and trapping lifestyles were going to be severely disrupted. They envisioned state schools that would be run in partnership with Indigenous peoples to preserve traditional Indigenous culture while preparing children for new times and non-traditional labour markets.

John Tootoosis (1899–1989), a prominent Cree leader, wrote the following in his biography:

> The Indians who at treaty time had asked that their children be educated were asking that they be taught to read and write, to learn to work with figures, to be trained into useful skills to enable them to compete on an equal basis for a way of making a living with the children of the white men. ... Poundmaker (chief at treaty time) had replied very clearly, "We want to be sure that life will be as good for them (our children) as it will be for your children." (Goodwill & Sluman, 1982, p. 113)

The federal government, however, had an altogether different vision for the schools. Canada viewed education as an efficient means of **subjugating** and **assimilating** the Indigenous people, a governmental ambition that we discussed in the previous chapter. While education in Canada has long been a provincial responsibility, the *British North America Act* gave the federal government jurisdiction over Indigenous people in this regard, a responsibility it bears to this day.

As early as 1830, four mission schools for Indigenous populations were established in Ontario, including the Shingwauk and the Mohawk institutes. A leader in this initiative was an Ojibwe man, Peter Jones, who was also a Methodist missionary. He had founded an agricultural settlement for the Mississaugas on the Credit River (near present-day Toronto), providing a reasonably successful education to young Indigenous people through the Credit River School. Jones wished to extend his education provisions to other Indigenous peoples by building residential schools that would provide manual training in addition to Christian teaching and English-language instruction.

The Mohawk Institute, which had been requested by the Indigenous leadership on the Six Nations of the Grand River, was established in 1833 by the New England Company and was dedicated to the Christianization, "civilization," and instruction of Indigenous people. The Mohawk

subjugation
forcing obedience to authority

assimilation
a process by which members of an ethnic minority group lose cultural characteristics that distinguish them from the dominant cultural group or take on the cultural characteristics of another group

Institute was a model for Jones. He asked four different bands in his area to help finance the schools by donating one-quarter of their treaty money. The Methodist church and the federal government also shared in the cost of establishing the schools. Jones envisioned that the schools would eventually be run by Christian Indigenous people. Neither the federal government nor the church shared his vision: both looked forward to using the school as an instrument of assimilation in keeping with the policies of the government of Canada.

Although Indigenous people supported the schools initially, they soon discovered that the goals of the church and the government were inconsistent with their own. Indigenous leaders recognized that schooling meant assimilation and a total rejection of all of their own values and traditions. They stopped financial support to the schools and withheld their children from them. The experiment was deemed a failure, but the precedent had been set—using partnerships with the church and missionaries in the education of Indigenous children (Grant, 1996).

When the question of education for Indigenous children arose again in 1870, the churches were recruited for the task for two main reasons. The first was that they could be expected to inculcate Indigenous children with the religious ideals of the day and have them reject all things associated with their own culture. The second reason was purely practical. The running of the schools and the instruction of the Indigenous children promised to be an expensive endeavour for the Indian department; the free labour of missionaries and priests would significantly reduce the cost. The federal government, in turn, would provide funding in the form of land grants drawn from reserved lands, per capita grants, and other material rewards to the four churches involved in Indian education. This partnership between church and state would last until 1969.

The decision to make education for Indigenous children "residential" rather than provide day schools on reserves was driven by similar motives. First, the cost of building a day school on each and every reserve, according to the Department of Indian Affairs, was too high (regardless of the wording within the treaty). Second, separating the children from the influence of their families and community was considered necessary if the children were to truly become "civilized" and internalize the religious teachings of the church. The "residential" component of Indian schools was considered critical to the achievement of their aims, as explained by Quebec politician Sir Hector-Louis Langevin, arguing before Parliament in 1883:

> Industrial schools have succeeded very well in the United States and it is quite likely they will succeed here as well. The fact is, that if you wish to educate the children you must separate them from their parents during the time they are being taught. If you leave them in the family, they may know how to read and write, but they will remain savages, whereas by separating them in the way proposed, they acquire the habits and tastes of civilized people. (Indian Tribes of Manitoba, 1971, p. 113)

Overview of the Residential School System

One of the first problems to surface in the residential school system was poor attendance. Parents opposed the curricula—the purpose of which, they saw, was assimilation—and rumours of abuse within the schools circulated quickly. In addition, health conditions were poor, and as many as 3,000 children died of diseases such as smallpox, tuberculosis, and polio. For these reasons, many Indigenous parents chose to withhold their children from residential schools.

Poor attendance resulted in a change to the *Indian Act* in 1894: school attendance became compulsory. Section 119 of the Act gave truant officers and Indian agents police authority to enforce attendance in day schools by removing children forcibly, if necessary, from their homes and families. In 1920, the Act was amended to give truant officers the same authority with respect to residential schools, and to make it an offence for parents to withhold their children from the schools.

In the following sections, we examine the general characteristics of residential schools and the many problems that existed within the system.

Age of Enrollment and Nature of Education

In addition to attendance, another problem that immediately surfaced concerned questions about what type of education should in fact be delivered, by whom, and to whom. The various agencies involved disagreed with one another about these matters.

Age of enrollment, for example, was a frequent source of dispute. Some Protestant ministers advocated enrolling students as young as three in residential schools, to "catch them early." Others argued that this would be a waste of money. Some argued the students should be kept until they were 14; some argued for 16, some 18, and some for 21. Enrollment ages did in fact change through the years. Bickering among the Catholic, Presbyterian, Anglican, and Methodist churches over who would get the students was common; each denomination viewed the contest for students as a battle for souls—or, in some instances, as a battle for per capita funding.

As far as curricula were concerned, some schools classed as "industrial schools" offered training in skilled trades such as carpentry, cabinet-making, and tailoring. Some of these schools produced a well-educated and literate group of graduates. However, these successes created two problems.

The first was that success in acquiring a skilled trade did not guarantee employment. In fact, there were no opportunities for employment for Indigenous people. One agent wrote to the department in December 1907, "Race prejudice is against them and I am afraid that it will take time, under the circumstances, before they can compete with their white brothers in the trades" (Malloy, 1999, p. 158). Critics of the system insisted that the more costly industrial school training was a waste of resources, since people in mainstream Canada were not prepared to accept working alongside Indigenous people. In response, the industrial schools were phased out.

The second problem with the early success of the schools was baldly expressed by the minister of the interior, Frank Oliver, in 1897: "We are educating these Indians to compete industrially with our own people, which seems to me a very undesirable use of public money" (Hall, 1983, p. 126). The attitudes expressed in these historical records may seem shocking to the average Canadian today, but they reflect the sentiments that were prevalent among many Canadians at the time. The status quo was being threatened by Indigenous people, who were showing that they could not only learn to read and write, but also become great craftsmen on par with non-Indigenous Canadians, and thus compete with the latter in the labour market for skilled jobs.

Staff and Quality of Instruction

As industrial schools were phased out and the number of residential schools increased, the quality of the education declined. By 1932, at the end of Duncan Campbell Scott's career as deputy superintendent general of Indian Affairs, there were 17,163 students enrolled in residential schools. Scott viewed this increase in attendance as proof of his success in the assimilation process. It was more likely due to the compulsory attendance legislation enforced by his government. The flipside of this statistic is that three-quarters of students enrolled were in grades 1 through 3. In 1932, only 100 students reached grade 6 (Malloy, 1999, p. 171).

In his autobiography, Indigenous scholar Basil Johnston (1989, p. 47) remembers having to repeat grades over and over in residential school and finally realizing, much to his dismay, that, as a matter of policy, Indigenous students' discharge from the school at the age of 16 had to coincide with their graduation from grade 8. In other words, no matter how they performed academically, Indigenous students were destined to repeat grades until they reached 16 and could be released from school.

Although there were some good and well-intentioned individuals among the staff at residential schools, it would be an understatement to say that the majority were unfit for the education of children. Bill Thomas (1991, p. 6), of the Peguis First Nation, described the staff in the school he attended as follows:

> The kooky clergy and even kookier staff make a shambles of any potential for effective development. … For the most part the "dedicated" staff I knew in the United Church school were old ladies trying to atone for earlier sins and mucking that up. Others were religious zealots or simply strange people who—under ordinary circumstances—could not get a job or fit in anywhere else.

Cree writer and lawyer Harold Cardinal (1969, p. 54) described his residential school experience as follows:

> In plain words, the system was lousy. The curriculum stank, and the teachers were misfits and second raters. Even my own elementary school days, in grade eight I found myself taking over the class because my teacher, a misfit, has-been or never-was sent out by his superiors from Quebec to teach savages in the wilderness school because he had failed utterly in civilization, couldn't speak English well enough to make himself understood. Naturally he knew no Cree. When we protested such inequities we were silenced as "ungrateful little savages who don't appreciate what is being done for you."

Complaints about the staff from residential school survivors are corroborated by studies conducted in the early 1960s. These studies indicate that, with few exceptions, staff fell into three categories:

1. relatively recent immigrants;
2. Canadians from lower socio-economic backgrounds; and
3. a small number of Indigenous people.

In 1967, researcher Richard King conducted a study of a Yukon Indian School at Mopass. King (1967) categorized staff as "generally deviant in the whiteman society." He found that many of the teachers lacked qualifications and many could not even speak English well. It seems that the reasonably generous pay in the residential schools—generous by comparison with other jobs such people would have been qualified for—attracted poorly educated and deficient personalities to work in them. As early as 1910, letters sent to school administrators by the Department of Indian Affairs addressed concerns over the quality of its teachers (Grant, 1996, p. 143).

Also damaging the academic standards of the residential schools was the requirement—based on the department's desire that the schools be self-sufficient—that students do long hours of manual labour. The students were supposed to spend half the day in class and half the day in manual labour, but the latter often took precedence. The records show that field workers and school inspectors were concerned from the first about this overemphasis on manual work. One letter, written in 1916, alerts the Department of Indian Affairs to the fact that the boys in one school had spent only 9 days out of 42 in class; the rest of their time was spent working on the farm to support the school (Malloy, 1999, p. 170). Poorly served by this regimen, many students left the school unable to read or even to converse well in English.

Health Conditions

The health of children in the schools was always a source of concern. Unsafe construction, overcrowding, inadequate food, and poor nutrition resulted in physical problems and a high death rate. In 2013, a report based on research of school documents estimated over 3,201 Indian children died in the schools. Nearly 500 of those children could not be identified.

At the time, the churches and the administrators at Indian Affairs were well aware of health problems associated with the schools, but funds were not readily available to provide more sanitary conditions in the schools through renovation. Dr. Peter Bryce was commissioned in 1903 to inspect residential schools and report on the health conditions. His report was scathing, indicating that some schools had a death rate of *50 percent*. He wrote as follows: "The sight of the ragged, ill-kempt and sickly looking children was enough to make me sick at heart" (Malloy, 1999).

Roger Cromarty said he had no memory of a doctor visiting the Sioux Lookout school during the seven years he spent there:

> Even though a lot of times once somebody caught something and it spread in the whole school like wildfire, and they would just more or less, we had to live out whatever it is that we caught, whether it's measles, mumps, sores, bedbugs, all that kind of stuff, we just had to live with it. We got some stuff from the matron. We used to have a matron that sort of acted as a nurse as well. So a medical doctor we never saw. (TRC, 2015b, p. 177)

In 1910, an Indian agent named MacArthur reported a 50 percent death rate at the Duck Lake residential school. S.H. Blake, a lawyer, conducted a review of the Anglican missions and reported as follows to Minister of Indian Affairs Frank Oliver: "The appalling number of deaths among the younger children appeals loudly to the guardians of our Indians. In doing nothing to obviate the preventable causes of death, brings the department within unpleasant nearness to the charge of manslaughter" (Malloy, 1999, p. 77).

Nutrition was lacking in many of the schools, and this left the children vulnerable to disease. In 1943, Dr. A.B. Simes conducted an inquiry into Elkhorn School in response to complaints from the Indians at The Pas, Manitoba. He reported (Malloy, 1999, p. 114) that the children were dirty, their clothes disgraceful, and that 28 percent of the girls and 69 percent of the boys were underweight. The menu he forwarded to the ministry had many omissions and few substitutions. Today, many residential school survivors remark about never having had enough to eat.

At File Hills Indian Residential School, Dr. Bryce found that 75 percent of the students on the discharge roll were dead. Of the 31 students on the roll, 15 had died in the school, and 7 had died at home within three years of discharge. At the time of first enrollment, all of these students had enjoyed good health. File Hills was certainly the worst case, but if its statistics are factored in with those of the other schools, the death rate in the 35 schools included in Dr. Bryce's study would be 42 percent. Those figures, projected throughout the 1907 school system, suggest that of the 3,755 children in the schools, 1,614—or 43 percent—would die prematurely (Malloy, 1999, p. 90).

This information was not restricted to government officials. Dr. Bryce's report made headlines in the newspapers; in other words, the Canadian public knew about the horrific conditions in the schools and about the unacceptable death rate. One reporter wrote that the death rate would be unacceptable even in war. Other efforts were made to attract public attention to the appalling conditions of the schools, but to no avail. It seems that the Canadian public was content to be complicit in the brutality of this process of forced assimilation. Up to 1922, Dr. Bryce continued to criticize the ministry for doing nothing to improve sanitation. Bryce was successful only in ensuring that he did not secure a position in Duncan Campbell Scott's administration as the department's minister of health.

Ultimately, modest measures were taken to improve conditions in the schools. But the communications between school administrators and Indian Affairs indicate that high death rates and poor sanitary conditions were constant problems throughout the decades the schools were in operation. Four decades after Dr. Bryce's first report, in 1948, Neil Walker, Indian Affairs superintendent, wrote as follows: "If I were appointed by the Dominion Government for the express purpose of spreading tuberculosis, there is nothing finer in existence than the average Indian residential school" (Malloy, 1999, p. 262).

Inhumane Conditions at Residential Schools

The following memo, dated October 21, 1953, was written by G.H. Marcoux, a regional inspector of Indian schools. It was addressed to the Indian Affairs Branch in Winnipeg, Manitoba.

I visited the school on October 19th and 20th and found the following situation:

From the front entrance to the corridor of the basement one was subjected to an unbearable odor. The floor of the boiler room was covered with liquid from the sewage system to a depth of 6 to 8 inches, some of the liquid was seeping into the boys' recreation room. At the other end of the building, in the girls' recreation room there are a number of trap openings on the floor. Upon opening these traps one could see the same kind of liquid containing raw sewage, direct from toilets, almost to the level of the floor.

It looks as if the entire sewage piping under the floor had collapsed and that the sewage piping leading to the outside has been blocked by some obstruction.

On Monday, October 19, the smell in the building was unbearable and no human being should be asked to live under such conditions. There is no doubt in my mind that such drastic action must be taken to remedy the situation and make sure it does not re-occur in the future. I, therefore, strongly recommend that the school be closed until such time as the necessary repairs are made. Should this condition continue or happen again at a later date, the health of the pupils and the members of the staff can be seriously affected. Furthermore, should there be an outbreak of disease in a school like this one, the Indian parents would blame the school and refuse to send their children there. This would be a ten year set back in the education plan.

This is respectfully submitted in the hope that the department be advised of the situation and that immediate appropriate action be taken.

Source: Indian and Northern Affairs Canada (1999).

EXERCISE 1

1. What value did mainstream society seem to place on Indigenous children? How did this change over time?
2. Consider the mandatory attendance legislation instituted by the government. How would you have felt about this legislation if you had been the parent of an Indigenous child in this era?

Abuse Within the Schools

Most people who write about abuse in residential schools divide the subject into four categories: sexual, physical, emotional, and spiritual and cultural. Here, we examine each category in turn, then look at the aftermath of the abuse and the efforts by the government and Indigenous communities to agree on liability and possible compensation.

Sexual Abuse

In 1964, 10-year-old Willie Blackwater was removed from his family home on Kispiox Reserve in British Columbia and taken to Alberni Indian Residential School on Vancouver Island, 1,600 kilometres away. Immediately, Blackwater was singled out by dorm supervisor Arthur Henry Plint, who sexually abused the boy during his years at the school. Blackwater revealed the abuse to several authorities, including a government official, none of whom believed him.

Furthermore, when news reached Plint that the boy had accused him of abuse, he beat the child so severely that Blackwater ended up in the infirmary.

After suffering greatly as an adult trying to cope with his childhood, Blackwater came forward again in the 1990s to initiate an investigation into his abuse at the school. Thirty other adult men also came forward in an attempt to make Plint accountable for his actions. After judgments against him in 1995 and 1997, Plint, at the age of 72, was convicted and sentenced to 12 years in prison; he showed no remorse. In his judgment, Supreme Court Justice Douglas Hogarth referred to Plint as a sexual predator and a sexual terrorist whose activities had been allowed to go on unchecked: "As far as the victims are concerned, the Indian residential school system was nothing more than institutionalized pedophilia" (Fournier & Crey, 1997, p. 72).

CLOSE-UP   George Clutesi

George Clutesi of the Tseshaht First Nation near Port Alberni, British Columbia was born in 1905 and died in 1988. He was widely acclaimed as an actor, artist, and writer. He exhibited his work in the 1940s with the support of Canadian artist Emily Carr. Expo 67 commissioned a mural of his work, and he received the British Columbia Centennial Award and the Canadian Centennial Medal. He appeared in nine feature films and the television series *The Beachcombers* and *Spirit Bay*. He attended the Alberni Indian Residential School.

The Alberni Indian Residential School operated as a day school when it opened in 1891 under Presbyterian management. The original school burned down in 1917 and was replaced by a new building funded by the government of

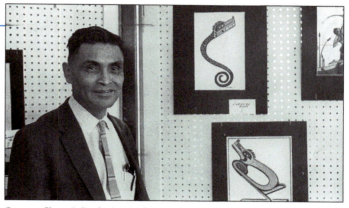

George Clutesi displaying Indigenous artwork, March 31, 1966.

Canada and operated by the United Church Women's Missionary Society in 1925. The school's survivors tell of suffering physical and sexual abuse and disease. The school closed in 1973.

This is only one of the thousands of incidents of sexual abuse in residential schools across Canada that came to light in the 1990s. In 1990, Phil Fontaine, who in 1991 was elected the Manitoba Grand Chief of the National Assembly of First Nations, talked publicly of his experience of sexual abuse while in residential schools in Manitoba. (See the Close-Up feature later in this chapter.) The Indigenous community was divided in its response to sudden public scrutiny. Some felt these experiences were so painful and shameful that they should not be brought forward, since they caused survivors to relive their pain. Others felt that the only way to begin the healing process was to openly face the harsh reality of what had been suffered.

The RCMP and other policing agencies became involved in uncovering information regarding past sexual assaults in the schools. They quickly uncovered thousands of victims. In 1994, the RCMP created a task force to deal with the many investigations required to address the complaints. Investigations were difficult because many of the perpetrators had died or could not be located. Many victims who made disclosures to police were unable to cope with dredging up the past; some committed suicide, and some turned to alcohol and drugs in order to deal with their pain.

No one can know for certain how widespread the sexual abuse was; we can count only those who have come forward voluntarily. In 1990, when residential school abuse became part of the political landscape, the *Globe and Mail* reported that Rix Rogers, who was then the special adviser to the minister of national health and welfare on child sexual abuse, indicated during a meeting of the Canadian Psychological Association that the abuse revealed to that date was believed to be just the tip of the iceberg. He believed that "a closer scrutiny of the past treatment of native children at Indian residential schools would show 100 percent of children at some schools were sexually abused" ("Reports of sexual abuse," 1990, p. A3).

Physical Abuse

Physical abuse, too, was rampant within the schools; the application of corporal punishment was difficult to monitor or contain. There are many stories of children being forced to eat their own vomit, having their faces rubbed in human feces, and being beaten for minor infractions of school rules. Many incidents of abuse are recorded in the Department of Indian Affairs files. Teachers who were sympathetic to the children and described or reported abuse by other teachers were dismissed for disloyalty.

One teacher described the physical abuse in a residential school as follows:

> Children's faces are slapped, [they are] hit on the head, struck across the nose causing nose bleeds. … One teacher said a boy in her classroom had a swollen face for two days from being slapped. Another teacher reported that one of her pupils was slapped because he couldn't read the small print in the hymn books. One of my grade 8 boys was slapped on the head until he was pale, he staggered, complained of feeling dizzy and his nose bled profusely. This was witnessed by most of the school boys. He fainted five days later in prayers and again in my classroom. (Malloy, 1999, p. 282)

Eventually, in response to the various allegations and to the reports of the children's injuries that were observed when the schools were inspected, the Department of Indian Affairs issued a number of regulations to address the use of corporal punishment. These regulations seem to have had little effect; school administrators continued on the old course of physical punishments, set as policy when the schools were first established.

In 1965, in response to the widespread allegations of physical abuse, the department solicited an evaluation of the residential school system, to be presented at the first Residential Principals' Conference. The department handpicked as witnesses six residential school graduates who were of "impeccable authority and character," each successful in public service, education, or church service. One respondent was a graduate of the Mohawk Institute in Brantford, Ontario and he described (Malloy, 1999, p. 284) the conditions there as follows: 90 percent of the children suffered from dietary deficiency, evidenced by boils, warts, and general ill health. He reported seeing children eating from the garbage and from the bin intended to feed the pigs. Lice infestations were common and so children's heads were frequently shaved. Captured runaways were brought back to run a gauntlet where they were hit with anything found on hand. He reported that he had "seen boys crying in the most abject misery and pain with not a soul to care—the dignity of man!" (Malloy, 1999, p. 284).

The appraisal of the schools resulted in some positive comments; overall, though, the comments were unfavourable and difficult to ignore.

Emotional Abuse

Emotional abuse is among the most damaging kinds of abuse, and it was constantly meted out in the residential schools. Students were made to endure humiliation and ridicule by staff. At one school, as a punishment for bedwetting, children were made to wear the wet sheet draped over their heads. In another school, female students were stripped of their underwear and struck on the bare buttocks in front of the class. This disclosure came from the principal of a northern school who believed the punishment to be reasonable.

Children reported being locked in a room in only their underwear and restricted to a bread-and-milk diet as a punishment for running away. Two female runaways were forced to attend meals in the dining room in only their underwear. Children were ridiculed and taunted by staff and called derogatory names that specifically targeted their race.

Doris Young recalled that runaways from the Anglican schools she attended in Manitoba and Saskatchewan were punished in front of the assembled students:

> They both were brought back into the dining room, where we witnessed them getting their head shaved. And, and then they had to remove their clothes, they'd remove their clothes, and they strapped them in front of all of us. And we all had to go into the dining room, where, where the, where usually the, the boys' and the girls' dining rooms were separated, and but we, we were all taken into the dining room, and we were, we had to witness this beating, and I thought, oh, I hope it's not one of my brothers, but, but it wasn't, and still they, they were boys and girls that, the boys and girls, and everybody, the, the supervisors were all standing there witnessing this, these horrible beatings that these boys were getting because they ran away from school. (TRC, 2015b, p. 147)

The department was aware of the persistent problem of children running away. Many died while trying to escape, mainly due to exposure. The department also had to deal with the problem of children attempting suicide within the schools. These two problems were further symptoms of real problems within the school itself and the system at large. In 1920, nine boys attempted suicide by eating water hemlock; one died. In 1981, at Muscowequan school, five girls between the ages of eight and ten tied socks and towels together with a view to hanging themselves (Malloy, 1999).

Spiritual and Cultural Abuse

Spiritual and cultural abuse were implicit in the very purpose of the schools: assimilation. The schools were meant to eliminate the Indigenous way of life and spiritual beliefs for the next generation. Duncan Campbell Scott believed and hoped that within three generations the "Indian race" would no longer exist, as a result of the government's assimilation policies; residential schools were seen as an effective means to this end. Ultimately, Scott was mistaken. Though several generations of Indigenous children—as many as five, in some cases—did attend residential schools, Indigenous nations are alive and persevering in Canada today.

Residential schools vigorously tackled the ambitious goal of eliminating Indigenous culture. Many survivors report that the most severe punishments meted out by school staff were reserved for children who spoke their original language or attempted to carry on any Indigenous tradition. As children arrived at the schools, their birth name was replaced with an identification number and a new Christian name. Many of them spoke little or no English and so could not communicate with staff. A few schools would assign an interpreter from the older student population, but most schools expected the child simply to stop speaking in his or her original tongue until he or she could acquire sufficient English to communicate.

The idea to eliminate Indigenous languages came from the United States. In 1867, President Ulysses S. Grant called strongly for linguistic genocide:

> Through sameness of language is produced sameness of sentiment, and thought. … In difference of language today lies two-thirds of our trouble. … Schools should be established, which children should be required to attend; their barbarous dialect should be blotted out and the English language substituted. (Reyhner & Eder, 2004)

For the children, the psychological effects of this linguistic suppression were severe. As we will see in Chapter 4, the continuation or retention of language is a factor in the well-being of individuals and communities, whereas loss of language has been linked to higher rates of youth suicide. Erasing the child's language meant erasing his or her identity, concept of self, and world view, as well as the child's sense of his or her place in the world.

That's where I had the most difficulty in school because I didn't understand English. My hand was hit because I wrote on my scribblers, the scribblers that were given on starting school, pencils, erasers, rulers and that, scribblers, and textbooks that were given. "Write your names," she said, "so they don't get lost." But I wrote on my scribblers in Cree syllabics. And so I got the nun really mad that I was writing in Cree. And then I only knew my name was Ministik from the first time I heard my name, my name was Ministik. So I was whipped again because I didn't know my name was Peter Nakogee.

Source: TRC (2015b, p. 48).

CALL TO ACTION

17. We call upon all levels of government to enable residential school Survivors and their families to reclaim names changed by the residential school system by waiving administrative costs for a period of five years for the name-change process and the revision of official identity documents, such as birth certificates, passports, driver's licences, health cards, status cards, and social insurance numbers.

A saying from this era expresses the non-Indigenous view of this erasure: "Kill the Indian and save the child/man." Once everything Indian in the child's life was destroyed, however, it was not replaced with any new values or world view. The original intention had been for Christianity to take the place of Indigenous culture and values, but the coercive way in which Christianity was taught belied its own values and detracted from its validity in the children's eyes, so that few of them internalized its ideals.

For many children, acquiring a new language under such stressful circumstances was difficult. Many children simply stopped speaking and ceased to express emotions such as frustration, fear, and anger; they learned to internalize emotion rather than express it. These self-protective barriers to communication remained in place after the child was discharged from the school. As the children returned to their home communities, the first generation of survivors could not communicate with any members of their community, even their own families. They had lost their language and now spoke only English, not widely spoken by members of their community. The emotional isolation thus continued.

We know that language is both the basis of culture and its conduit, and that if a language is forever lost, as is a risk for many Indigenous languages, the culture it conveys will be significantly diminished. Since the closure of the residential schools, various conditions have contributed to the decline of Indigenous languages. For example, there has been a significant influx of Indigenous people into large urban centres, where their original languages are inevitably eroded. The numbers are revealing (Statistics Canada, 2010):

- In 1941, less than 10 percent of Indigenous people claimed English as their first language.
- In 1971, by which point the schools had mostly been phased out after three generations of children had passed through them, 54 percent of Canadian Indigenous people reported English as their first language.
- By 1996, 75 percent of Canada's Indigenous population listed English as their mother tongue.
- According to the 2011 National Household Survey, there were 1,400,700 Indigenous people in Canada, but only 240,815 spoke an Indigenous language. (Indigenous and Northern Affairs Canada, 2011).

CLOSE-UP Rita Joe

Rita Joe was born on a Mi'kmaq reserve on Cape Breton Island in 1932. When she was 12 years old, she went to Shubenacadie Indian Residential School in Nova Scotia, the only Indian residential school in Atlantic Canada. Rita recalled being told at school that she was "no good." She began writing as an adult to challenge this message, eventually publishing six volumes of poetry and song. She has been referred to as the "poet laureate" of the Mi'kmaq people. In the prologue to her memoir (1996), she states, "My greatest wish is that there will be more writing from my people, and that our children will read it. I have said again and again that our history would be different if it had been expressed by us."

She was made a member of the Order of Canada in 1989 and of the Queen's Privy Council for Canada in 1992. She died in 2007 after suffering from Parkinson's disease.

Source: *Canadian Encyclopedia* (2007).

I Lost My Talk
by Rita Joe, Mi'kmaq

I lost my talk
The talk you took away.
When I was a little girl
At Shubenacadie school.

You snatched it away;
I speak like you
I think like you
I create like you
The scrambled ballad, about my word.

Two ways I talk
Both ways I say,
Your way is more powerful.

So gently I offer my hand and ask,
Let me find my talk
So I can teach you about me.

Source: Joe (1998).

CALL TO ACTION

13. We call upon the federal government to acknowledge that Aboriginal rights include Aboriginal language rights.

Aftermath of Residential Schools

In 1948, the federal government undertook a review of Indian residential schools. It found that the schools were a dismal failure, and proposed phasing them out and integrating Indigenous students into mainstream schools. According to the review, a graduate from the residential school system was less prepared for life than an Indigenous person who had never attended any formal education institution. The federal government began funding provincial schools on a per capita basis to include Indigenous children. Nevertheless, many of the residential schools were kept open until the 1960s. The last one, the Gordon Residential School in Saskatchewan, did not close until 1996.

Effects on Individuals, Families, and Communities

The effect of the schools on Indigenous communities has been devastating. As many psychological and sociological studies have shown, those who are abused often become abusers, particularly in cases of sexual abuse. Indigenous leaders report that sexual abuse is like a disease ripping through their communities, where its incidence is currently reported to be very high.

Families have also been torn apart by violence—another legacy of the residential school experience. This system taught students that adults exert power and control over children by physical punishment, and the survivors of the system have carried this conditioning into Indigenous communities where, traditionally, few would ever have thought to raise a hand against a child for punishment or for discipline. The cycle is difficult to break. Residential school survivors never experienced nurturing, respectful parenting, and many, as a result, have faced difficulties raising their own children. Until recently, these struggles were being passed from one generation to the next without intervention.

In 1990, a First Nations leader wrote to Minister of Indian Affairs Tom Siddon regarding the far-reaching effects of residential school experiences on survivors:

> Social maladjustment, abuse of self and others and family breakdown are some of the symptoms prevalent among First Nations baby boomers. The graduates of Ste. Anne's Residential school are now trying and often failing to come to grips with life as adults after being raised as children in an atmosphere of fear, loneliness and self loathing. Fear of caretakers. Loneliness in knowing that elders and family were far away. Loathing from learning to hate oneself, because of repeated physical, verbal or sexual abuse suffered at the hands of various adult caretakers. This is only a small part of the story. (Indian and Northern Affairs Canada, 1990)

On a reserve in British Columbia, research was conducted to determine the health status and quality of life of Indigenous residential school survivors compared with Indigenous members of the community who had not attended residential schools. There was little difference between the two populations, but both groups suffered from worse health and a lower quality of life than non-Indigenous people. Researchers concluded that the effects of residential schools were disseminated through Indigenous communities. In other words, the trauma of the residential school experience was a contagion, spreading to collateral victims and from generation to generation (Barton et al., 2005).

VOICES

Genine Paul-Dimitracopoulos's mother was placed in the Shubenacadie residential school in Nova Scotia at a very early age. Paul-Dimitracopoulos told the [Truth and Reconciliation] Commission that knowing this, and what the school was like, helped her understand "how we grew up because my mom never really showed us love when we were kids coming up. She, when I was hurt or cried, she was never there to console you or to hug you. If I hurt myself she would never give me a hug and tell me it would be okay. I didn't understand why."

Source: TRC (2015a, p. 136).

Indigenous leaders called for a public inquiry into the residential school system to determine the breadth and depth of the damage it had caused and to suggest resolutions for their communities regarding how to begin the healing process. Initially, the federal government did not agree to such an inquiry. In 1992, however, the Royal Commission on Aboriginal Peoples (RCAP) was established by the federal government in response to a land claims issue that erupted into violence.

The RCAP devoted considerable effort to the residential school issue. The final report, released in 1996, recommended (among other things) a full investigation into the residential school system in the form of a public inquiry in order to "bring light and begin to heal the grievous harms suffered by countless children, families, and communities" (RCAP, 1996, p. 338). Specifically, the RCAP recommended that:

- the inquiry hold hearings across the country;
- funding be sufficient to allow all of those who were affected to testify;
- the inquiry be allowed to commission research and analysis to help better understand the nature and effect of residential school policies; and

- the inquiry be authorized to recommend remedial actions that governments and churches can take to mitigate the damage done by the schools. These might include apologies from those responsible; compensation to help heal and rebuild communities; and funding to treat those affected by the schools and their families.

Although not all of its recommendations were followed, the RCAP's findings put several processes in motion. We examine these later in the chapter under the heading "Attempts at Resolution."

The Sixties Scoop

The government's past involvement with Indigenous children did not end with the residential school system. A discussion of the government's mistreatment of Indigenous people and the terrible legacy of the residential schools would not be complete without addressing a related phenomenon—something that occurred as the schools were being phased out between the 1960s and 1980s. It has been dubbed the "**Sixties Scoop**" by sociologists, and refers to the removal, by well-intentioned social workers, of thousands of Indigenous children from their communities. The children were placed in foster care or put up for adoption in non-Indigenous homes in the belief that they were being rescued from a life of poverty and despair—from conditions that were, in fact, a legacy of the residential school system. Despite its name, the "Scoop" continued until the late 1990s.

The "Scoop" began as the schools closed, and a question arose about what to do with the children of school age and younger. This emerged as a significant problem. After three or four generations of Indigenous people had been raised in schools rather than in family homes, the ability of residential school survivors to raise their own children was severely handicapped. The prevalence of poverty, alcoholism, and other social problems on reserves left many children in need of protection or, at the very least, of intervention. After generations of the schools' efforts to break and destroy family ties, the communities had difficulty rebuilding harmonious family lives.

In 1947, the Canadian Welfare Council and the Canadian Association of Social Workers presented a brief to a federal special committee asserting that, under provincial social legislation, Indigenous children suffering from neglect were not afforded the same protections as white children. This was true: Indigenous children fell under the authority of the federal government, which was in the process of dismantling the school system. Child welfare services were provided to the mainstream population through provincial funds and under provincial jurisdiction and legislation; these services were not available to Indigenous children.

Changes to the *Indian Act* in 1951 addressed the concerns expressed by social workers. These changes provided that all provincial laws respecting child welfare were now to apply to Indigenous children as well, effectively bringing Indigenous child welfare services under the authority of provincial child welfare workers. The following question then arose: Who would fund the provision of these services to the Indigenous reserves and Indigenous children? There was considerable debate over this issue, which resulted in the postponement of intervention for Indigenous children. When the federal and provincial governments finally agreed to a cost-sharing process to finance these services, well-intentioned social workers quickly sprang into action. Although only 1 percent of all children in care in 1959 were Indigenous, this number rose by the end of the 1960s to 30 to 40 percent, even though Indigenous people made up only 4 percent of the population.

Reasons cited for removing Indigenous children from their communities included inadequate housing, unsafe drinking water, no running water, no available school, and poor health conditions. Instead of addressing these conditions, the federal government chose to remove the children from their communities. Services such as counselling and child care were not made available to intact Indigenous families; these services could be funded only if the child became a ward of the state.

Sixties Scoop
the practice of removing Indigenous children from their communities and placing them in foster care or putting them up for adoption in non-Indigenous homes

The caseloads in social service agencies were so high that workers did not have time to properly screen homes, nor was monitoring of either foster or adoptive homes usually feasible. But most social workers, none of whom were aboriginal, felt little harm could befall an aboriginal child rescued from poverty and placed with a nice, middle-class, white family. Yet behind the closed doors of their foster and adoptive homes, aboriginal children were even more isolated and vulnerable than they had been in residential school. … In many cases, children were taken from parents whose only crime was poverty and being aboriginal. (Fournier & Crey, 1997, p. 85)

In a holdover from the residential school days, siblings were separated. This was due not only to the large sizes of Indigenous families but also to the belief that the individual children would adjust more quickly to their new homes and new environments without the influence of siblings.

Bridget Moran, a social worker in British Columbia at the height of the Sixties Scoop, writes in *A Little Rebellion* (2002) that social service workers had no resources available that might have helped keep Indigenous families together. They had no family support workers, treatment centres, or transitional housing. Moran reports that when they found a child at risk, they had no alternative but to place the child in foster care. Ernie Klassen, former district superintendent for Indian Affairs, recalls that on one weekend a social worker chartered a bus to apprehend 38 children on the Spallumcheen reserve in British Columbia and was asking for 38 different foster homes to accommodate them (Fournier & Crey, 1997).

One result of the apprehension of children was the intensification of social problems on reserves that were experiencing the loss of their young. Indigenous leaders spoke out against the practice with vehemence, but their voices were rarely heard.

By the end of the 1970s, one in every four status Indian children could expect to be separated from his or her parents for all or part of childhood. In British Columbia in 1997, one in three legal wards was of Indigenous heritage. Many Indigenous children were shipped out of province and many went to families in the United States. Some private adoption agencies, mostly of a religious nature, sprang up to secure Canadian Indigenous children for adoption to US families. In all, Manitoba lost the greatest number of Indigenous children, an estimated 20,000, of which 55 percent were sent out of province, in comparison with 7 percent of non-Indigenous adoptions going out of province.

Because of this history, there is a movement toward Indigenous-run child welfare services available on reserves. Those services recognize the importance of placing children in need with Indigenous families within the community and supporting family reunification if possible. However, on-reserve child welfare services are underfunded compared with those for the rest of Canada. In 2007, the Assembly of First Nations supported the First Nations Child and Family Caring Society in bringing a complaint to the Canadian Human Rights Tribunal to assert that First Nations children are subject to discrimination because of their race in terms of the funds available to assist them and their families. In January 2016, the tribunal ruled that this is in fact discrimination and that the Ministry of Indigenous and Northern Affairs must take immediate action to correct the inequities of service. The federal government announced that it would not appeal the tribunal's ruling but would work toward making the necessary changes.

VOICES

The [Truth and Reconciliation] Commission heard many stories of mistreatment in foster homes. One woman told us that her foster parents physically and sexually abused her. Her Aboriginal identity was constantly disparaged. She said, "[My foster parents were] adamant about Aboriginal culture being less than human, living as dirty bush people, eating rats. It made me not want to be one of those people. And for years, I didn't know how to be proud of who I was because I didn't know who I was."

Source: TRC (2015a, p. 140).

In 1982, Manitoba judge Edwin Kimelman, at the insistence of Indigenous leaders, was appointed to investigate the apprehension of Manitoba's Indigenous children. He concluded that the child welfare services were well-intentioned but misguided and were guilty of **cultural genocide**. In response to his findings, a moratorium was placed on out-of-province adoptions, and the wholesale removal of children was stopped in the mid-1980s.

Tragically, a large number of these adoptions failed: many of the children suffered from identity crises in their teens; many had to endure racism in school and from society at large without the support of the Indigenous community; and many had been subjected to abuse while in the foster system prior to adoption and were unable to overcome that legacy. Others suffered from health complications, such as fetal alcohol syndrome (FAS) and fetal alcohol effects (FAE), that had not been diagnosed prior to adoption, and many adoptive parents were unable to cope with the challenges of raising such a child. Today, our court system and our jails are filled with Indigenous people who are casualties of the mistakes of this era.

Today, Indigenous children are still apprehended at disproportionate rates. Statistics Canada reported that of the 30,000 children across Canada in 2011 in care of child welfare services 14 years and younger, 48 percent were Indigenous: 3.6 percent of Indigenous children opposed to 0.3 percent for the general population (Statistics Canada, 2013).

A number of class action lawsuits have been launched by adoptees from this era. The trial for *Brown v. Attorney General of Canada*, the class action launched in Ontario that represents approximately 16,000 Indigenous adoptees, began in June 2016. In February of 2017, Justice Belobaba issued a summary judgment, concluding that Canada breached a 1965 agreement to consult individual bands in relation to the application of child welfare services to their bands. The Justice also concluded that Canada had a common law duty of care to take reasonable steps to prevent on-reserve Indian children in Ontario, who had been placed in care of non-Indigenous foster or adoptive parents, from losing their Aboriginal identity. Canada breached this duty of care when it took no actions to assist these children in maintaining their Aboriginal identity. At the time of writing, the class action is in the stage of assessing damages or the amount that can be claimed by Ontario survivors of the Sixties Scoop. This has wide-ranging implications for the rest of Canada, as similar agreements were made in all provinces and territories. Shortly after the Ontario ruling, a class action was filed in British Columbia on a similar basis. The Ontario ruling will no doubt affect forthcoming rulings in other provinces.

cultural genocide
the destruction of those structures and practices that allow a group to continue as a group, such as language, spiritual practices, and cultural values

CALL TO ACTION

1. We call upon the federal, provincial, territorial, and Aboriginal governments to commit to reducing the number of Aboriginal children in care by:

    i. Monitoring and assessing neglect investigations.

    ii. Providing adequate resources to enable Aboriginal communities and child-welfare organizations to keep Aboriginal families together where it is safe to do so, and to keep children in culturally appropriate environments, regardless of where they reside.

    iii. Ensuring that social workers and others who conduct child-welfare investigations are properly educated and trained about the history and impacts of residential schools.

    iv. Ensuring that social workers and others who conduct child-welfare investigations are properly educated and trained about the potential for Aboriginal communities and families to provide more appropriate solutions to family healing.

    v. Requiring that all child-welfare decision makers consider the impact of the residential school experience on children and their caregivers.

Cultural Genocide

The term *cultural genocide* has been used widely by academics studying the history of the relationship between Canada and Indigenous peoples. *Cultural genocide* can be defined as the deliberate and systematic destruction of the culture, traditions, language, and ways of being of a specific cultural group. More recently, academics have applied this term to the experiences of Indigenous people in Canada and around the world.

In response to the discovery of the atrocities committed against Jews during the Second World War, the international community rallied together through the United Nations to create the *Convention on the Prevention and Punishment of the Crime of Genocide*. Canada participated in this Convention in 1948, more than 50 years after the establishment of residential schools and prior to the proposed closure of the schools. The Convention reads as follows:

> **Article 1:** The Contracting Parties confirm that genocide, whether committed in time of peace or in time of war, is a crime under international law which they undertake to prevent and to punish.
>
> **Article 2:** In the present Convention, genocide means any of the following acts committed with intent to destroy, in whole or in part, a national, ethnical, racial or religious group, as such:
>
> (a) Killing members of the group;
> (b) Causing serious bodily or mental harm to members of the group;
> (c) Deliberately inflicting on the group conditions of life calculated to bring about its physical destruction in whole or in part;
> (d) Imposing measures intended to prevent births within the group;
> (e) Forcibly transferring children of the group to another group.
>
> **Article 3:** The following acts shall be punishable:
>
> (a) Genocide;
> (b) Conspiracy to commit genocide;
> (c) Direct and public incitement to commit genocide;
> (d) Attempt to commit genocide;
> (e) Complicity in genocide.
>
> **Article 4:** Persons committing genocide or any of the other acts enumerated in Article 3 shall be punished, whether they are constitutionally responsible rulers, public officials or private individuals. (United Nations, 1948)

EXERCISE 2

Based on the articles of the Convention on Genocide quoted above and on what you have learned about the experiences of Indigenous people in Canada, do you think the UN Convention's definition of genocide applies?

If so, to what degree? Who should be held accountable, and how?

If not, why not?

Attempts at Resolution

Before discussing the attempts at resolution, it is important to note that Indigenous communities and leaders agree that no amount of money can ever compensate Indigenous people for the suffering they endured. The question, then, is how Canadians can reconcile themselves to their past and partner with Indigenous people to promote recovery. What is the fair and just thing to do, considering all that has taken place? Financial compensation should not be construed as a punishment to Canada and viewed in terms of a fine. Compensation could be perceived in appropriate terms—as a dedication of resources to help residential school survivors overcome their pain and move toward health and wellness.

Legal Proceedings and the Indian Residential Schools Settlement Agreement

As discussed earlier in the chapter, Arthur Henry Plint was convicted of sexually assaulting Willie Blackwater and many other boys at Alberni Indian Residential School during the 1960s. In 1995 and 1997, he was sentenced to 12 years in prison. In 1998, Blackwater and 30 other residential school survivors embarked on a civil suit against Plint. The suit also named the federal government, which organized the residential school system, and the United Church of Canada, which ran the Port Alberni school.

The trial was difficult for survivors to endure, since they faced hard questioning by government and church lawyers. In 2001, the complainants chose to take an out-of-court settlement for a reported $180,000 to $290,000 each in order to end the trial. But the questions remain: Who was responsible for these atrocities? Was it Plint alone or was it the entire Indian Affairs Department, which appears to have turned a blind eye to the abuse of children? Should the government be held fully responsible for setting up an education system with very few formal accountability processes, thereby creating a situation that was destined to foster abuse? The Indian Affairs Department records made available to date have now been extensively examined, and it is clear that the department attempted to document complaints of abuse. But its attempts to stop the abuse were modest, and they failed. Should churches share in the responsibility because they supplied the unqualified staff who were the abusers?

Survivors have tried a variety of methods of redressing the wrongs done them. The first method is the criminal prosecution of offenders. One problem with this method is that police are frequently unable to locate the offenders, many of whom are now deceased. The survivors' second method of seeking redress—and the one that has proved most popular—has been civil litigation.

As the Plint case showed, legal proceedings can be difficult for survivors, who are forced to relive their traumatic experiences during the investigation and trial. There are a number of reasons for choosing to pursue criminal charges or civil litigation, however, aside from the prospect of financial reparation inherent in the latter:

- *Public recognition*
  Victory in the public forum of the court system signifies acknowledgment on the part of Canada's mainstream judicial system that a legitimate wrong has occurred and that a victim deserves compensation. This type of public recognition satisfies those who seek vindication on a matter of principle.

- *Level playing field*
  The court system is perceived as levelling the playing field between the plaintiff or complainant and the accused. Of course, the playing field cannot be perfectly level, since one side—in this case, the defendants (government and churches)—often has more financial resources for the litigation process than the other side. Still, in the case of criminal proceedings, the complainant can be assured that there will be no back-door, high-pressure negotiation, with the powerful strong-arming the powerless, as sometimes occurs—or is perceived to occur—in the alternative dispute resolution (ADR) process. The justice system, although imperfect, aspires to be unaffected by unequal distributions of power.

- *Establishment of precedent*
  Another reason for survivors to choose to litigate is that a court decision may establish precedents that other courts are bound to follow, thereby helping to ensure that survivors will be treated equally.

- *Awareness and understanding*
  The final reason for survivors of the residential school system to seek redress through the civil litigation process is that they want their stories heard. This desire was clear in the findings of the RCAP, which recommended a cross-country inquiry into the damage done by the residential schools—a recommendation that the federal government originally refused to follow, but much later did implement in the form of the Truth and Reconciliation Commission (discussed further below). The survivors desired to be heard and understood, and they wanted their experience to register in the consciousness of mainstream Canadian society. At that time, this could happen only if a resolution was sought in a public forum such as the court system, where the transcripts and outcome are part of the public record.

For the Indigenous plaintiffs, there were drawbacks to the civil litigation process. The most obvious was the cost. Some survivors resolved this through the use of contingency fees, although they were sometimes charged up to half of their financial settlement in legal fees (Tibbetts, 2000). Another drawback to the civil litigation route was that the acknowledgment of harm was offered only to the individual survivor; there was no recognition of the harm done to the survivor's family, to subsequent generations, and to the community. This second kind of recognition is particularly important to Indigenous people and to their communities.

Despite the difficulties they faced in seeking restitution for past wrongs, a growing number of survivors came forward through the 1990s. As of July 2003, there had been 12,000 claims filed, very few of which had been resolved. Many prospective claimants waited to see what resolutions would be reached before filing their own claims. It was predicted at the time that the number of claims could reach 30,000. At its height, the residential school system included 88 schools across Canada, and the 1991 census reported that there were 105,000 residential school survivors alive at that time. It was estimated in 2003 that, if the number of cases continued to grow at the current pace, the pursuit of civil litigation could stretch the time frame for settlement to over 50 years, by which time almost all the plaintiffs would be dead.

In order to address these timing problems, the government embarked upon an alternative dispute resolution process. This process was slow because many matters had to be settled, not the least of which was the division of responsibility between church and state. The federal government announced, after negotiations stalled, that it would accept responsibility for 70 percent of the claim amount, leaving the churches responsible for the remaining 30 percent. The churches insisted that being made responsible for this amount could in fact leave them bankrupt. When the Indian Residential Schools Settlement Agreement was approved, the churches were responsible for contributing up to $100 million in cash and services toward healing initiatives.

Another issue that arose in this process was the government's refusal to address the loss of culture and language suffered by Indigenous people as a consequence of the residential school experience. The government insisted it would address those losses through government-funded initiatives for Indigenous language and cultural renewal, and would provide compensation to survivors only for sexual and physical abuse suffered in the schools.

A major shortcoming of the ADR process, at least where residential school survivors were concerned, is that it moved the negotiation of these matters from the public to the private forum, so that only those directly involved were aware of the negotiations. In this way, the process became less accountable to the public, which could not be sure whether justice had in fact been served. The ADR process began in June 2001. In 2003, a lawyer representing some residential school survivors pointed out that of the $1.2 billion dedicated to the ADR process, $540 million was earmarked for legal costs rather than compensation (Frank, 2003). The survivors of residential schools grow older each year, and many have passed away without closure to this most life-altering experience.

On May 10, 2006, through the ADR process, the **Indian Residential Schools Settlement Agreement (IRSSA)** was reached. In the following sections we examine two of its components, financial compensation for survivors and the Truth and Reconciliation Commission.

The Common Experience Payment

Under the IRSSA, Indigenous people who could prove their attendance in the schools became eligible to receive a "common experience payment" (CEP) of $10,000 for the first year of attendance and $3,000 for each subsequent year (known as the "10-plus-3" formula). As of June 2016, 79,309 applicants had been processed and paid, with an average payment of $20,457 per applicant (Indigenous and Northern Affairs Canada, 2016).

The IRSSA, which resulted from the largest lawsuit settled out of court in the history of Canada, began accepting applications in September 2007. The application process had a number of components. First, survivors applied to Indian Residential Schools Resolution Canada, whose role was to verify the applicant's years of attendance in one or more of the recognized schools. Following the verification, letters were mailed out and payment was made.

For those who were denied payment or were not happy with the results of their application, there was an appeal process. This process was put in place because the registration records of many students had been lost by the government, and the onus was on the survivor to prove his or her attendance. It is necessary to verify attendance and years of attendance in order to calculate entitlement. Attendance claims that could not be easily verified through archived records required additional research on the part of Indian Residential Schools Resolution Canada.

Another point of contention was that certain schools were not included on the list of residential schools. If we include the early mission schools and the final federally run schools, Indian education spanned 160 years and took many forms and had many partners. This meant that the survivors of these excluded schools did not qualify for the settlement process. Among the schools excluded were the Stirland Lake and Cristal Lake residential high schools in northern Ontario, which operated between 1971 and 1991. According to the Canadian government, these schools were private Mennonite schools and were not run with the direct involvement of the government of Canada (Residential Schools Settlement, 2012). A 2011 decision by the Ontario Superior Court confirmed that Stirland Lake must be added to the list and that all of the attendees must be considered for the CEP since the school met the definition of an Indian residential school (Nishnawbe Aski Nation, 2011).

The IRSSA included an independent assessment process (IAP) for certain kinds of survivors—those who identified themselves as survivors of sexual and physical abuse that had led to serious psychological trauma. In these cases, there was a hearing and an adjudicated judgment. This was done on a case-by-case basis; all records were to be fully disclosed by the government of Canada so that evidence could be collected to substantiate the alleged abuses in order to assess compensation. These records were intended to be kept as part of the TRC body of records for future archives. However, in 2014, the court had to clarify that the disclosure records for the IAP could be kept for the TRC records with permission of the survivor. In 2015, the court had to clarify for the federal government what "full disclosure" included, since police records were being withheld from those seeking settlement (Rennie, 2014).

Throughout this process, support services were put in place for the applicants, many of whom found that the application process triggered traumatic memories that led to depression, loneliness, fear, panic, and, in some cases, addictive behaviour and suicidal thoughts.

A further component of the IRSSA was the Aboriginal Healing Fund, administered by the Aboriginal Healing Foundation (AHF). The AHF had been created in 1998 following the apology issued by Cabinet minister Jane Stewart and was provided with a $350 million grant from the federal government for use over ten years for counselling programs and culture recovery

Indian Residential Schools Settlement Agreement (IRSSA) an agreement by which Indigenous people who could prove their attendance in the residential schools became eligible to receive a "common experience payment" (CEP)

initiatives. As part of the IRSSA, in 2007 the Aboriginal Healing Fund was assigned an additional $125 million over five years to operate healing initiatives and supports for survivors. The AHF closed in September 2014.

One of the AHF's initiatives was an evaluation of the common experience payment process. Its report was published in 2010, following interviews of 280 CEP recipients. The aim of these interviews was to determine whether the CEP had helped the survivors to heal and whether there were sufficient services in place to support them, practically and emotionally, in the application process.

The interviews conducted for this study produced many stories and reflections from survivors, some excerpts from which are included below. With regard to the application process, many found it straightforward enough, but some had difficulties on account of the poor education they had received in the residential schools. One survivor (AHF, 2010, p. 22) spoke as follows of his educational shortcomings:

> I didn't even get an education. I didn't go to a class or anything. … They made you work down there all the time. I didn't do any learning. I was on the farm, that's all I was doing. … There used to be rocks all over the fields, big boulders and they used horses and picked them all up. That's how they got that meadow there to make hay. We'd go out in the morning and first we'd clean the barn, pigs, chicken, we'd do that in the morning and then in the afternoon we'd go to the field. No time for the classroom. I can't even read or write, some of these heavy words [in the CEP application] I couldn't even understand.

A survivor in Nunavut (AHF, 2010, p. 29) spoke of the difficulty of finding school records to prove attendance at the schools, and of the skepticism with which their claims were often met:

> It was a waiting game, and you know, they don't believe you sometimes. They don't believe you went to the school. … Like us from before in the early 70's, we never keep all our records and our parents just threw them away. And that's what they want and that was hard. And then our school burnt down and all our records were in there and so for us around here it was kind of hard. I know there's still some people that are still waiting and trying.

Other survivors spoke about the long waiting times for the CEPs. Many of them—both for emotional reasons and for reasons of principle—were slow to apply, and then they had to wait a long time for the payment, sometimes for over a year. One survivor (AHF, 2010, p. 27) described this process as follows:

> I heard about [CEP] and it took me a long time. A lot of people applied for it right away but I didn't for a long time because I was angry, and I still am at the government because of what they have done to our Aboriginal people. I said, "they aren't going to buy me for what they have done to me." You know, it never replaces what we have lost … It took me quite a while and I thought about it for a long time. I wasn't going to apply for it in the beginning. No, I wasn't going to because I just felt that, "is that trying to replace what we lost?"

Another survivor described the emotional challenge of the application process, and the trauma of having to recall the details of his life in the school (AHF, 2010, p. 29):

> I waited a year and a half. It was a time consuming thing. They said to call back, asking the same questions over and over, and it was hard recalling names of people who died in school, who hung themselves, who died, who I grew up protecting. To bring it up again is kind of a hard thing to do.

The study asked participants whether the lump-sum CEP had had, overall, a positive or a negative impact on their lives. Of the 281 participants, 77 reported an overall positive experience,

38 a negative one, and 130 a mixed experience (AHF, 2010, p. 43). The remaining participants either did not respond or reported that their experience had been neither positive nor negative. Figure 3.1 lists the positive and negative effects of the CEP as described by the applicants.

A British Columbia survivor offered the following negative account of his CEP experience (AHF, 2010, p. 45):

> I want to mention about the negative experiences. I have lost about half a dozen cousins since we have gotten [CEP]. In my home community we are having funerals all the time. I have one cousin now who has wet brain and is in the hospital and he doesn't remember us. He drank and drank and drank and drank when the money came in. His younger brother died shortly after that money came in. He was young—he was 34 or 35 and he just drank and drank and drank. You know there is a lot more than just the half a dozen in my family and a lot of the people dying are younger than me. I'm 52 and many of them are my cohorts and were my cohorts in residential school and some of them are younger. There are Elders as well who passed away as a result. It is a common refrain in our territory. In our area there are three bands that speak the same language but culturally we are different. In the three bands, we were just having funerals and funerals and funerals. It is like the support people at the funerals just can't keep up. It has really done a lot of damage and destruction to our villages … Everyone keeps dying.

Those who saw the CEPs in symbolic terms—that is, as an official acknowledgment by the government of the wrong done the Indigenous people—had a more positive experience of the process. The following quotation (AHF, 2010, p. 50) reflects a perspective of this sort:

> My kids understand a little of what we went through. … The impact of being in that place [residential school], they didn't realize it. They put you in a strange place, they didn't see that. … My kids were helped in a lot of ways. In a lot of ways they understood where the money was coming from. Everyone thinks it's just money, all the pain you went through, that the CEP is just about money. It's not.

FIGURE 3.1   Positive and Negative Impact of CEP Experience on the Aboriginal Participants

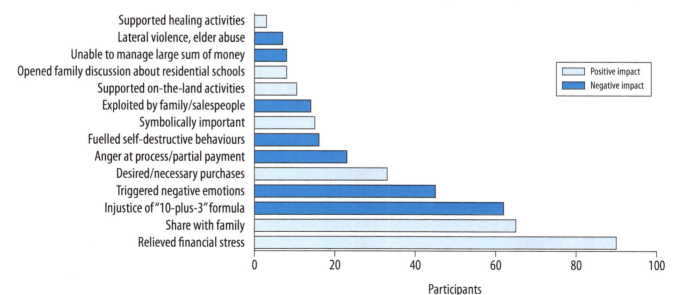

SOURCE: Aboriginal Healing Foundation (2010, p. 44).

Those who reported positive experiences tended to emphasize the benefits of sharing pain openly and of family healing, and they said the process gave them hope for future reconciliation with non-Indigenous Canada.

Survivors' efforts to heal themselves have taken various forms. Some have used Indigenous healing methods such as sweat lodges, traditional medicines, and other techniques for cultural reconnection. Some have adopted Western traditions of healing, such as therapy and counselling. Figure 3.2 shows the extent to which the recipients of the CEPs have been engaged in the healing process and—in cases where they have been engaged—how successful the process has been. Figure 3.3 shows the effects the CEPs have had on this process, according to the survivors themselves.

FIGURE 3.2   Residential School Survivors—Engagement in Healing

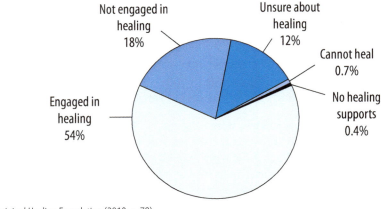

SOURCE: Aboriginal Healing Foundation (2010, p. 78).

FIGURE 3.3   Effects of CEPs on Healing and Well-Being

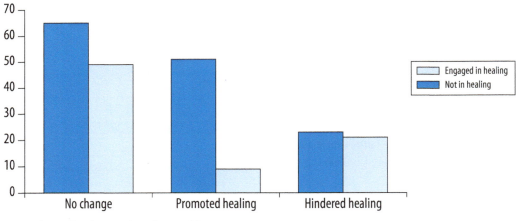

SOURCE: Aboriginal Healing Foundation (2010, p. 86).

The Truth and Reconciliation Commission

In addition to the CEP, part of the IRSSA's mandate was to create the Truth and Reconciliation Commission (TRC). The TRC had a five-year mandate (2008–2013) to accomplish the following, and to do so without holding any formal hearings, or acting as a public inquiry, or conducting any formal legal process:

1. Acknowledge residential school experiences, impacts, and consequences;
2. Provide a holistic, culturally appropriate, and safe setting for former students, their families and communities as they come forward to the commission;
3. Witness, support, promote, and facilitate truth and reconciliation events at both the national and community level;
4. Promote awareness and public education of Canadians about the Indian residential school system and its impacts;
5. Identify sources and create as complete an historical record as possible of the Indian residential school [IRS] system and its legacy. The record shall be preserved and made accessible to the public for future study and use;
6. Produce and submit to the parties of the agreement a report including recommendations to the Government of Canada concerning the IRS system and experience including: the history, purpose, operation and supervision of the IRS system, the effect and consequences of IRS (including systemic harms, intergenerational consequences and the impact on human dignity) and the ongoing legacy of the residential schools;
7. Support commemoration of former Indian residential school students and their families in accordance with the Commemoration Policy Directive. (TRC, 2011)

One of the TRC's tasks was to address concerns about the relative seclusion of the ADR negotiations—the fact that the records of abuse were not fully disclosed during this process. Canadians were not privy to the information that led to the various settlements. As mentioned, survivors want the rest of Canada to be aware of what they experienced in the residential schools. Only through a shared perspective—a common recognition of past and present—can Indigenous and non-Indigenous Canada be reconciled.

As part of its mission, the TRC travelled across Canada collecting statements from survivors of the residential schools. The commission received over 6,750 statements from survivors of residential schools, their families, and others who wished to share their stories. Seven major national events were held in Winnipeg, Inuvik, Halifax, Saskatoon, Montreal, Vancouver, and Edmonton between June 2010 and March 2014. As many as 155,000 people attended those events, in addition to 9,000 residential school survivors registered to attend them. These national events were also livestreamed to be accessible to Canadians everywhere. The TRC also held 238 days of local hearings in 77 communities across the country. Throughout its mandate the commission encouraged public participation in nearly 900 separate events.

The commission invited respected guests, both Indigenous and non-Indigenous, to the national events to represent all Canadians as "honorary witnesses" and partners in reconciliation. These witnesses included Michaëlle Jean, who was governor general of Canada at the start of the commission's mandate, and two former prime ministers, Paul Martin and Joe Clark.

Findings of the Truth and Reconciliation Commission

The TRC concluded its mandate in 2013 as scheduled and its final report, *Honouring the Truth, Reconciling for the Future*, was published in 2015. The report included 94 recommendations, or "calls to action," addressing, among other issues, the overrepresentation of Indigenous children in child welfare care; the overrepresentation of Indigenous people in the criminal justice system; jurisdictional disputes between provincial and federal governments over delivering health care for Indigenous people; discrepancies in the funding and delivery of education for Indigenous people; and strategies to maintain Indigenous languages and culture, and to recover what had been lost through the residential school era.

Concerning **reconciliation**, many recommendations aimed at healing the fractured relationship between Indigenous and non-Indigenous people in Canada. Many of these revolve around educating Canadians about the residential school era and commemorating the events so that we never forget this part of our history. One specific recommendation is the creation of mandatory, age-appropriate curricula on residential schools, treaties, and the contribution of Indigenous people, to be taught across Canada from kindergarten to grade 12, to ensure that all Canadians have a solid understanding of Indigenous history in Canada that includes Indigenous perspectives. Another recommendation calls for highly visible monuments to commemorate the residential school experience and the survivors of that era.

reconciliation
an ongoing process of establishing and maintaining respectful relations

The University of Manitoba will become the permanent home of all of the research done by the commission as it establishes the National Centre for Truth and Reconciliation (NCTR). This centre will be available to survivors and researchers as well as the general public. Its purpose is to ensure that survivors and their families have access to their own history, much of which has been hidden from them, as well as to ensure that educators can share the true history of the residential school era with new generations of Canadians. The NCTR will house all TRC records, including survivors' oral history statements, artworks, and expressions of reconciliation, and other materials gathered by the TRC such as government and church records. It will be a site of collective public memory and consciousness, bearing permanent witness to survivors' testimonies to shape how the residential school era is understood and remembered within Canada (TRC, 2015a, p. 314).

The Missing Children Project

Many Indigenous children died at their residential schools. As Figure 3.4 shows, the death rate in the residential school system was far greater than that for children in the general Canadian population. The TRC supported the Missing Children Project, which was launched in 2008 with the aim of determining the number and causes of deaths, illnesses, and disappearances of Indigenous children at residential schools, and the location of burial sites of children across the country who were not interred in their school graveyard. Once their bodies are found, they can be repatriated to their communities.

The TRC concluded that it is unlikely that the exact number of students who died in residential schools will ever be determined, due to incomplete historical records. School enrollment records could be destroyed after five years and records of accidents in schools were kept for only ten years. Health records, including dental records and records of medical treatment and admission to hospital, were kept for only two years. Some principals reported annually how many children had died at their schools but often did not report the names of the deceased. To the best of its ability, given the system's ill-kept records, the TRC established a National Residential School Student Death Register.

The register contains three sub-registers:

1. the Register of Confirmed Deaths of Named Residential School Students;
2. the Register of Confirmed Deaths of Unnamed Residential School Students; and
3. the Register of Deaths That Require Further Investigation (for example, to discover names) (TRC, 2015a, pp. 90–92).

Recognition of Wrong

Beginning in the 1990s, those responsible for the implementation and running of residential schools began to express their regret in various ways. Churches and the Canadian government

FIGURE 3.4   Comparative Death Rates per 1,000 Population, Combined Residential Schools and the General Canadian Population of School-Aged Children, Using Five-Year Averages, 1921 to 1965

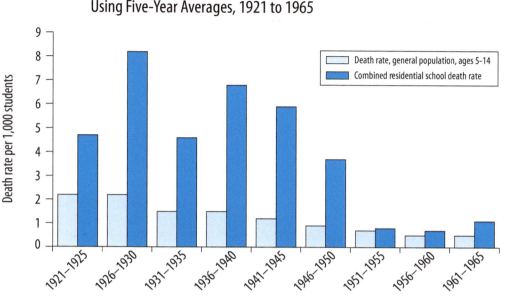

SOURCE: Truth and Reconciliation Commission of Canada (2015a, p. 91).

have both offered apologies. These differed in terms of the nature of the apology (that is, what was being apologized *for*) and in terms of the scope of the apology (that is, who was being apologized *to*). As with the CEP, individual reactions to the apologies have varied considerably.

Recognition by Churches

In 1994, the Roman Catholic Church recognized that terrible acts had been committed in the schools. The Catholic apology of 1994 was followed by an expression of "regret" for the Church and the "weaknesses of so many of her sons and daughters who sullied [the Church's] face." The acknowledgment of corrupted individuals acting on their own weaknesses implied no liability on the part of the Church. In reality, the Church apologized only to God for its agents' weaknesses—it neither apologized to former students, nor did it take responsibility for its larger role in the abuse in the schools. Individuals who were prosecuted would face secular civil proceedings, but the Church as an entity would not be held responsible. Survivors would be protected by the state.

Six years later, the Vatican issued a second apology, following a similar approach to that seen in the first. The "Day of Pardon" prayers of 2000 by Pope John Paul II included three prayers in his Mass that asked for the forgiveness of God for the weakness of the Church's clergy. Significantly, the Church did not ask for forgiveness from its victims. The Pontiff admitted that "Christians have often denied the Gospel; yielding to a mentality of power, they have violated the rights of ethnic groups and peoples, and shown contempt for their cultures and religious traditions." The Pope also acknowledged that "Christians have been guilty of attitudes of rejection and exclusion, consenting to acts of discrimination on the basis of racial and ethnic differences." Although not acknowledging sexual abuse committed by the Church's clergy, the Pope lamented "acts of injustice by trusting in wealth and power and showing contempt for the 'little ones'" (Pope John Paul II, 2000).

CALL TO ACTION

58. We call upon the Pope to issue an apology to Survivors, their families, and communities for the Roman Catholic Church's role in the spiritual, cultural, emotional, physical, and sexual abuse of First Nations, Inuit, and Métis children in Catholic-run residential schools. We call for that apology to be similar to the 2010 apology issued to Irish victims of abuse and to occur within one year of the issuing of this Report and to be delivered by the Pope in Canada.

In the years leading to the apology from the United Church of Canada in 1998, movement on the national political front included lobbying by national Indigenous lobby groups for the recognition of what had occurred in the schools. In 1998, the United Church's moderator, Bill Phipps, apologized to former students of United Church residential schools, their families, and communities:

> As Moderator of The United Church of Canada, I wish to speak the words that many people have wanted to hear for a very long time. On behalf of The United Church of Canada, I apologize for the pain and suffering that our church's involvement in the Indian Residential School system has caused. We are aware of some of the damage that this cruel and ill-conceived system of assimilation has perpetrated on Canada's First Nations peoples. For this we are truly and most humbly sorry. (Phipps, 1998)

Recognition by the Government of Canada

In 1998, the Canadian government issued a "statement of reconciliation," which included a carefully worded apology directed at those who had suffered physical and sexual abuse at the residential schools. The statement was delivered by Indian and Northern Affairs Minister Jane Stewart, working in cooperation with Assembly of First Nations (AFN) Grand Chief Phil Fontaine. Ms. Stewart signalled that the white population recognized the wrong that was committed in Canada, and expressed the profound regret of the government for its role:

> The government of Canada acknowledges the role it played in the development and administration of these schools. Particularly to those individuals who experienced the

CLOSE-UP   Robert Houle

Robert Houle, artist, art curator, intellectual, and arts educator, was born in 1947 and belongs to the Saulteaux First Nations in Manitoba. Houle earned a BA in art history from the University of Manitoba in 1972 and a degree in art education from McGill University in Montreal in 1975, and attended the Salzburg International Summer Academy. His work has been exhibited at the National Gallery of Canada in Ottawa, the Art Gallery of Ontario in Toronto, the Museum of Contemporary Art in Australia, the Canadian Cultural Centre in Paris, and the Stedelijk Museum in Amsterdam. He was featured in the 2011 film *Robert's Paintings*.

Houle attended the Sandy Bay Indian Residential School in Manitoba. The Sandy Bay Council had provided the Roman Catholic Church with 100 acres to build the school in 1905. In 1991, Reverend Doug Crosby of the Oblate Commission of Canada apologized for the way "children were usurped from their natural communities" and admitted that the school left a legacy of emotional and psychological chaos that has invaded entire communities. The school closed in 1970.

Source: Speaking My Truth (2012).

Robert Houle stands with his installation piece *Paris/Ojibwa*, which reimagines a performance by a troupe of Ojibwe dancers in Paris, France in 1845.

CLOSE-UP   Phil Fontaine

Born in 1944, Phil Fontaine was a victim of abuse in the residential school he was forced to attend. A member of the Sagkeeng First Nation of Manitoba and the longest-serving grand chief of the AFN, Fontaine worked closely with the Indian and Northern Affairs Canada officials for the first resolution and settlement agreement for Indian and Inuit residential schools.

Phil Fontaine speaks in the House of Commons on the event of Prime Minister Stephen Harper's 2008 apology for the residential school system.

tragedy of physical and sexual abuse at residential schools, and who have carried this burden believing that in some way they must be responsible, we wish to emphasize that what you experienced was not your fault and should never have happened. ... For those of you who suffered this tragedy, we are deeply sorry. (Stewart & Goodale, 1998)

The statement was accompanied by an announcement that a new initiative would support community-based healing for people affected by residential schools, including those suffering the intergenerational impacts. The Aboriginal Healing Foundation, mentioned above, was established and the Aboriginal Healing Fund was granted $350 million to this end.

Indigenous people were divided in their sentiment regarding both the apology and the Aboriginal Healing Fund initiative. Many felt that the apology was a step forward; others felt that the healing fund was incapable of even scratching the surface of the social problems inflicted on Indigenous peoples by the schools. Others believed that neither the healing fund nor the apology was sufficient.

Despite the mixed response from the Indigenous community, this was a historic occasion in Canada; it was the government's first public acknowledgment that its former policies had harmed Indigenous people.

The 1998 apology was a prelude to Canada's official apology ten years later. In 2008, Prime Minister Stephen Harper delivered a full apology in Parliament for Canada's role in the residential school system. He called on the government to partner with Indigenous people in the healing of the latter's communities. Many survivors made their way to Parliament Hill to hear the apology in person, and they reflected that this was the most significant movement toward healing to date.

In contrast to the church apologies described above, the government's apology contained a plea for forgiveness from victims. The governing Conservative party's apology was followed by statements from the Liberals, the Bloc Québécois, and the New Democratic Party. Prime Minister Harper thanked NDP leader Jack Layton for continuously leading the call for the apology. Harper's statement addressed 150,000 residential school **direct victims** (Harper, 2008, 6849-6851). **Collateral victims** also received recognition. The extension of the suffering from direct victims to collateral victims marks a significant turning point in the residential school narrative.

Prime Minister Harper asked forgiveness of Indigenous peoples on behalf of all Canadians. He said Canadians "recognize" the effect of attempts at assimilation and the residential schools on Indigenous peoples:

> Today, we recognize that this policy of assimilation was wrong, has caused great harm, and has no place in our country. One hundred and thirty-two federally supported schools were located in every province and territory, except Newfoundland, New Brunswick, and Prince Edward Island. ... The Government of Canada built an educational system in which very young children were often *forcibly removed* from their homes and often taken far

direct victim
a targeted victim of an act

collateral victim
an unintentional but expected victim of an act

from their communities. … All were deprived of the care and nurturing of their parents, grandparents, and communities. (Harper, 2008, 6850; emphasis added)

Harper admitted the government failed to protect children from this abuse. Indigenous parents were powerless, in turn, "to protect your own children from suffering the same experience."

Harper pledged Canada's help on the new road to healing and reconciliation. The apology created a new vision for Canada–Indigenous relations:

- Canada recognized that direct and collateral victims of residential schools faced physical, social, and mental harm through the transmission of intergenerational trauma. Canada recognized "their resilience as individuals" and pledged to work with Indigenous people to repair the harm.
- The admission that it was wrong to *forcibly remove children* from their homes has international law implications. The 1948 UN Convention on Genocide prohibits the forcible transfer of Indigenous children.
- Canada admitted its "final solution" Indigenous assimilation policy. "Our object is to continue," wrote Duncan Campbell Scott, chief architect of the policy, in the early 1900s, "until there is not a single Indian that has not been absorbed into the body politic of Canada and there is no more Indian question. That is the whole purpose of our legislation" (Dickason, 1992, p. 327). Harper said early in Canada's apology that "this policy of assimilation was wrong, has caused great harm, and has no place in our country."

The apology created a path where Canada would work with Indigenous people to heal the pain caused by Canada's Indian and Inuit residential school system.

EXERCISE 3

Read or listen to a survivor story from the website Where Are the Children? (http://wherearethe children.ca/en/stories/). Assess the apologies in this section and identify what each apology means to your selected survivor. Is an apology and the CEP enough? Why or why not?

CHAPTER SUMMARY

All aspects of the assimilation process have been devastating to Indigenous communities: the seizure of resources and territory, which forced economic dependence; the influence of missionaries in undermining traditional Indigenous values and forcing an agricultural way of life; the suppression of culture through provisions of the *Indian Act*. But nothing has been so devastating to Indigenous people as the residential school system, which targeted their youngest, most vulnerable members. Among its destructive consequences are broken families, violence, substance dependency, and ill health.

The Aboriginal Healing Foundation and the Truth and Reconciliation Commission have concluded their mandates and have submitted recommendations to chart the path forward to reconcile all Canadians with this dark history and move toward a brighter future. And there is finally a real hope that Indigenous and non-Indigenous Canadians may reconcile their shared history and move forward into a brighter future. This can only happen if this history, rather than being suppressed or ignored, becomes part of the national consciousness.

REFERENCES

Aboriginal Healing Foundation (AHF). (2010). *The Indian Residential Schools Settlement Agreement's common experience payment and healing: A qualitative study exploring impacts on recipients.* Aboriginal Healing Foundation research series. Ottawa: Author. http://www.ahf.ca/downloads/cep-2010-healing.pdf.

Barton, S., et al. (2005, August). Health and quality of life of Aboriginal residential school survivors, Bella Coola Valley, 2001. *Social Indicators Research, 73*(2), 295–312.

Brown v. Attorney General of Canada. (2014). 2014 ONSC 6967.

Canadian Encyclopedia. (2007). Rita Joe. http://www.thecanadianencyclopedia.com/articles/rita-joe.

Cardinal, H. (1969). *The unjust society: The tragedy of Canada's Indians.* Edmonton: Hurtig.

Dickason, O.P. (1992). *Canada's First Nations: A history of founding peoples from earliest times.* Toronto: McClelland & Stewart.

Fournier, S., & Crey, E. (1997). *Stolen from our embrace: The abduction of First Nations children and the restoration of Aboriginal communities.* Vancouver: Douglas & McIntyre.

Frank, S. (2003, July). *Time Canada, 162*(4), 30.

Goodwill, J., & Sluman, N. (1982). *John Tootoosis: A biography of a Cree leader.* Winnipeg: Pemmican.

Grant, A. (1996). *No end of grief: Indian residential schools in Canada.* Winnipeg: Pemmican.

Hall, D.J. (1983). Clifford Sifton and the Canadian Indian Administration 1896–1905. In I.A.L. Getty & A.S. Lussier (Eds.), *As long as the sun shines and the water flows: A reader in Canadian native studies.* Vancouver: University of British Columbia Press.

Harper, Rt. Hon. S. (2008, June 11). Apology to former students of Indian residential schools. Canada, Parliament, House of Commons. *Hansard, 142*(10). 39th Parliament, 2nd session.

Huck, N. (2015, February 9). Merchant law firm launches class-action lawsuit for "60s scoop" adoptees. *CBC News.* http://www.cbc.ca.

Indian Act. (1985). RSC 1985, c. I-5.

Indian and Northern Affairs Canada (INAC). (1990, November 15). Letter to Tom Siddon. File E6575-18-2, vol. 4.

Indian and Northern Affairs Canada (INAC). (1999). G.H. Marcoux memorandum to Mr. R.S. Davis, October 21, 1953. File 501/25-1-019, vol. 1. Reprinted in J. Malloy, *A national crime: The Canadian government and the residential school system 1879 to 1986* (pp. 259–260). Winnipeg: University of Manitoba Press.

Indian Tribes of Manitoba. (1971). *Wahbung: Our tomorrows.* Manitoba: Manitoba Indian Brotherhood.

Indigenous and Northern Affairs Canada. (2011). 2011 National Household Survey: Aboriginal language knowledge. https://www.aadnc-aandc.gc.ca/eng/1377004468898/1377004550980.

Indigenous and Northern Affairs Canada. (2016). Statistics on the implementation of the Indian Residential Schools Settlement Agreement. https://www.aadnc-aandc.gc.ca/eng/1315320539682/1315320692192.

Joe, Rita. (1996). *Song of Rita Joe: Autobiography of a Mi'kmaq poet.* Lincoln, NE: University of Nebraska Press.

Joe, Rita. (1998). I lost my talk. In D.D. Moses & T. Goldie (Eds.), *An anthology of Canadian Native literature in English.* Toronto: Oxford University Press.

Johnston, B.H. (1989). *Indian school days.* Norman, OK: University of Oklahoma Press.

King, A.R. (1967). Case study of a Yukon Indian school: How education fails. *The school at Mopass: A problem of identity.* New York: Holt, Rinehart, & Winston.

Malloy, J.S. (1999). *A national crime: The Canadian government and the residential school system 1879–1969.* Winnipeg: University of Manitoba Press.

Moran, B. (2002). *A little rebellion*. Vancouver: Arsenal Pulp Press.

Morris, A. (1971). *The treaties of Canada with the Indians of Manitoba and the North West Territories*. Toronto: Coles.

Nishnawbe Aski Nation. (2011). Windigo and Nan applaud landmark decision for Stirland and Cristal Lake Schools. http://www.nan.on.ca.

Phipps, B. (1998). Apology to former students of United Church Indian residential schools, and to their families and communities. *United Church Social Policy Positions*. United Church of Canada, Toronto, Canada.

Prime Minister of Canada Justin Trudeau. (2015). Statement by prime minister on release of the final report of the Truth and Reconciliation Commission. http://pm.gc.ca/eng/news/2015/12/15/statement-prime-minister-release-final-report-truth-and-reconciliation-commission.

Pope John Paul II. (2000). Confession of sins and asking forgiveness. *L'Osservatore Romano*. Vatican, Rome.

Rennie, S. (2014, January 15). Ottawa agrees to give residential-school survivors Ontario police records. *The Globe and Mail*. http://www.theglobeandmail.com.

Reports of sexual abuse may be low, expert says. (1990, June 1). *The Globe and Mail*, p. A3.

Residential Schools Settlement. (2012). Stirland Lake & Cristal Lake notice. http://www.residentialschoolsettlement.ca/English_Main%20Page.pdf.

Reyhner, J., & Eder, J. (2004). *American Indian education: A history*. Norman, OK: University of Oklahoma Press.

Royal Commission on Aboriginal Peoples (RCAP). (1996). *The report of the Royal Commission on Aboriginal Peoples* (Parliamentary Research Branch of the Library of Parliament No. 99-24E). http://www.parl.gc.ca/Content/LOP/ResearchPublications/prb9924-e.htm.

Sixties Scoop Class Action Lawsuit. (2015). Update—July 2015. http://sixtiesscoopclaim.com/2015/07/08/update-july-2015/.

Speaking My Truth. (2012). Learning from the past: Documents of reconciliation and apology from Canadian government and churches. http://speakingmytruth.ca/?page_id=955.

Statistics Canada. (2010). Family, community, and Aboriginal language among young First Nations children living off-reserve in Canada. http://www.statcan.gc.ca/pub/11-008-x/2010002/article/11336-eng.htm#a14.

Statistics Canada. (2013). *Aboriginal peoples in Canada: First Nations people, Métis and Inuit*. http://www12.statcan.gc.ca/nhs-enm/2011/as-sa/99-011-x/99-011-x2011001-eng.pdf.

Stewart, J., & Goodale, R. (1998). Statement of reconciliation. Government of Canada. Ottawa.

Thomas, W.C. (1991, January 7). Letter, *Western Report*, p. 6.

Tibbetts, J. (2000, August). Lawyers agree to stop swooping in on victims. *Ottawa Citizen*, p. A4.

Truth and Reconciliation Commission of Canada (TRC). (2011). Our mandate. http://www.trc.ca/websites/trcinstitution/index.php?p=7.

Truth and Reconciliation Commission of Canada. (2015a). *Honouring the truth, reconciling for the future: Summary of the final report of the Truth and Reconciliation Commission of Canada*. http://www.trc.ca/websites/trcinstitution/File/2015/Honouring_the_Truth_Reconciling_for_the_Future_July_23_2015.pdf.

Truth and Reconciliation Commission of Canada. (2015b). *The survivors speak: A report of the Truth and Reconciliation Commission of Canada*. http://www.trc.ca/websites/trcinstitution/File/2015/Findings/Survivors_Speak_2015_05_30_web_o.pdf.

United Nations. (1948, December 9). *Convention on the prevention and punishment of the crime of genocide*, adopted by Resolution 260(III) A of the United Nations General Assembly.

REVIEW QUESTIONS

True or False?

_____ 1. Schools for Indigenous children in Canada were originally wanted both by Indigenous people and by the government of Canada.

_____ 2. Indigenous education in Canada today is funded by the provincial and territorial governments.

_____ 3. Access to education for Indigenous people is a treaty responsibility of the federal government.

_____ 4. From 1867 to 1945, Indian children were not permitted to attend any school other than those designated for Indian education.

_____ 5. In 1920 the *Indian Act* was amended to make attendance at residential school mandatory for all Indian children and provided for Indian parents to be charged criminally for withholding their children from the schools.

_____ 6. Training schools called industrial schools were set up to teach Indian children more advanced skills such as carpentry and cabinet-making. These schools were phased out because the children were unable to learn those skills.

_____ 7. Under the leadership of Duncan Campbell Scott, more students voluntarily enrolled at residential schools.

_____ 8. The decision to use clergy as instructors in residential schools stemmed from the genuine belief that they were the most skilled teachers and could provide the highest-quality education available.

____ **9.** Dr. Peter Bryce was commissioned in 1903 to inspect residential schools and report on health conditions. He found that the death rate of the student population exceeded 50 percent in some schools.

____ **10.** Under article 4 of the United Nations *Convention on the Prevention and Punishment of the Crime of Genocide*, constitutionally responsible rulers or public officials cannot be charged under any of the acts of genocide mentioned in article 3 of the Convention.

Multiple Choice

1. Those who write about abuse within Indian residential schools generally divide the abuse into four categories. Which of the following is not one of those categories?

   a. physical

   b. sexual

   c. mental

   d. financial

2. In the struggle to redress the abuses suffered at the residential schools, the federal government has agreed to discuss compensation for which of the following forms of abuse?

   a. spiritual

   b. sexual/physical

   c. cultural

   d. emotional

3. The most popular method of seeking redress for individual victims of abuse prior to the IRSSA was

   a. police investigation

   b. criminal prosecution

   c. protesting

   d. civil litigation

4. The Truth and Reconciliation Commission's Missing Children Project believes that it is unlikely that all of the children will ever be accounted for. The primary reason is:

   a. The bodies were purposely hidden.

   b. The federal government refuses to disclose records.

   c. Too many children escaped.

   d. The record-keeping protocol at the schools was incomplete and allowed for destruction of records.

5. Which of the following was not involved in the set-up and administration of Indian schools?

   a. the provincial governments

   b. the federal government

   c. the Catholic Church

   d. the United Church

6. The ultimate purpose of residential schools was to

   a. provide quality education to Indigenous children

   b. forcibly assimilate Indigenous populations

   c. develop employment skills in Indigenous communities

   d. fulfill treaty obligations

7. There was a significant delay between the time that the need for child welfare services on reserves was recognized and the time that services became available. This delay was due to

   a. Indigenous people's refusal to allow service staff to help their children

   b. the remote location of the reserves

   c. the inability of the federal and provincial governments to agree on a cost-sharing process to provide services

   d. problems identifying children at risk on reserves

8. Which of these statements is most accurate regarding Indigenous languages in Canada?

   a. Most Indigenous people today speak their original Indigenous language.

   b. Many Indigenous people today speak their original Indigenous language.

   c. Few Indigenous people today speak their original Indigenous language.

   d. No Indigenous people today speak their original Indigenous language.

9. The alternative dispute resolution process set up to deal with compensation finally produced a resolution in 2006 called the Indian Residential Schools Settlement Agreement. If you were a survivor who experienced serious psychological trauma as a result of physical abuse, what avenues would be available to you?

   a. the individual assessment process

   b. the common experience payment alone

   c. the IRSSA legal prosecution department

   d. the common experience payment dispute resolution mediator

10. Article 2 of the 1948 United Nations Convention on Genocide identifies acts that, if committed with intent to destroy a national, ethnic, racial, or religious group, constitute genocide. Which of the following acts is not contained within the definition of genocide?

    a. causing serious bodily or mental harm to members of a group

    b. deliberately inflicting on a group conditions of life calculated to bring about its destruction in whole or in part

    c. failing to provide education in the language of choice

    d. forcibly transferring children of a group to another group

Discussion Questions

1. Do you think the Truth and Reconciliation Commission has met its mandate of informing all Canadians about this experience? Why or why not? Explain your answer.

2. Do you think that the settlement of the residential schools lawsuits would have been achieved better through private and class action lawsuits than through the ADR process? Explain.

3. If you were Dr. Bryce or Dr. Simes inspecting residential schools between 1903 and 1943, what actions would you take to advocate for the children?

4. Of the various kinds of damage that resulted from the residential school experience, which do you think was most harmful to Indigenous people? Explain.

APPENDIX 3.1

Apology to Former Students of Indian Residential Schools

Prime Minister Stephen Harper, June 11, 2008

I stand before you today to offer an apology to former students of Indian residential schools.

The treatment of children in Indian Residential Schools is a sad chapter in our history.

For more than a century, Indian Residential Schools separated over 150,000 Aboriginal children from their families and communities. In the 1870's, the federal government, partly in order to meet its obligation to educate Aboriginal children, began to play a role in the development and administration of these schools. Two primary objectives of the Residential Schools system were to remove and isolate children from the influence of their homes, families, traditions and cultures, and to assimilate them into the dominant culture. These objectives were based on the assumption Aboriginal cultures and spiritual beliefs were inferior and unequal. Indeed, some sought, as it was infamously said, "to kill the Indian in the child." Today, we recognize that this policy of assimilation was wrong, has caused great harm, and has no place in our country.

One hundred and thirty-two federally-supported schools were located in every province and territory, except Newfoundland, New Brunswick and Prince Edward Island. Most schools were operated as "joint ventures" with Anglican, Catholic, Presbyterian or United Churches. The Government of Canada built an educational system in which very young children were often forcibly removed from their homes, often taken far from their communities. Many were inadequately fed, clothed and housed. All were deprived of the care and nurturing of their parents, grandparents and communities. First Nations, Inuit and Métis languages and cultural practices were prohibited in these schools. Tragically, some of these children died while attending residential schools and others never returned home.

The government now recognizes that the consequences of the Indian Residential Schools policy were profoundly negative and that this policy has had a lasting and damaging impact on Aboriginal culture, heritage and language. While some former students have spoken positively about their experiences at residential schools, these stories are far overshadowed by tragic accounts of the emotional, physical and sexual abuse and neglect of helpless children, and their separation from powerless families and communities.

The legacy of Indian Residential Schools has contributed to social problems that continue to exist in many communities today.

It has taken extraordinary courage for the thousands of survivors that have come forward to speak publicly about the abuse they suffered. It is a testament to their resilience as individuals and to the strength of their cultures. Regrettably, many former students are not with us today and died never having received a full apology from the Government of Canada.

The government recognizes that the absence of an apology has been an impediment to healing and reconciliation. Therefore, on behalf of the Government of Canada and all Canadians, I stand before you, in this Chamber so central to our life as a country, to apologize to Aboriginal peoples for Canada's role in the Indian Residential Schools system.

To the approximately 80,000 living former students, and all family members and communities, the Government of Canada now recognizes that it was wrong to forcibly remove children from their homes and we apologize for having done this. We now recognize that it was wrong to separate children from rich and vibrant cultures and traditions, that it created a void in many lives and communities, and we apologize for having done this. We now recognize that, in separating children from their families, we undermined the ability of many to adequately parent their own children and sowed the seeds for generations to follow, and we apologize for having done this. We now recognize that, far too often, these institutions gave rise to abuse or neglect and were inadequately controlled, and we apologize for failing to protect you. Not only did you suffer these abuses as children, but as you became parents, you were powerless to protect your own children from suffering the same experience, and for this we are sorry.

The burden of this experience has been on your shoulders for far too long. The burden is properly ours as a Government, and as a country. There is no place in Canada for the attitudes that inspired the Indian Residential Schools system to ever prevail again. You have been working on recovering from this experience for a long time and in a very real sense, we are now joining you on this journey. The Government of Canada sincerely apologizes and asks the forgiveness of the Aboriginal peoples of this country for failing them so profoundly.

Nous le regrettons

We are sorry

Nimitataynan

Niminchinowesamin

Mamiattugut

In moving towards healing, reconciliation and resolution of the sad legacy of Indian Residential Schools, implementation of the Indian Residential Schools Settlement Agreement began on September 19, 2007. Years of work by survivors, communities, and Aboriginal organizations culminated in an agreement that gives us a new beginning and an opportunity to move forward together in partnership.

A cornerstone of the Settlement Agreement is the Indian Residential Schools Truth and Reconciliation Commission. This Commission presents a unique opportunity to educate all Canadians on the Indian Residential Schools system. It will be a positive step in forging a new relationship between Aboriginal peoples and other Canadians, a relationship based on the knowledge of our shared history, a respect for each other and a desire to move forward together with a renewed understanding that strong families, strong communities and vibrant cultures and traditions will contribute to a stronger Canada for all of us.

Questions

1. What can you, personally, do today that will contribute to the reconciliation of Canada and Indigenous people?

2. What actions could be taken in conjunction with this apology that would improve the relationship between residential school survivors and other Canadians?

3. How much of the information in this chapter is new to you? Assuming that you were relying only on your previous level of knowledge of these matters, reflect on how effective you would be in helping to renew and redefine the relationship between Indigenous and non-Indigenous people in Canada into the future.

4. Do you think the entire system of attempting to assimilate Indigenous children, from the inception of residential schools to the end of the Sixties Scoop, fits the UN's definition of genocide? Defend your position.

4 Current Socio-Economic Issues

A forester on Texada Island, BC shows wild pine mushrooms to participants in the University of British Columbia's Aboriginal Forestry Initiative. According to the Intertribal Forestry Association of British Columbia, Aboriginal peoples view forestry "as one of the main ways out of economic depression and as a vehicle for job creation, community stability, and environmental and cultural enhancement … . For these reasons, forestry in the broadest sense of economic, social and environmental development is especially important to Aboriginal people."

Introduction

The socio-economic issues facing Indigenous people today are a legacy of colonization and forced assimilation. We have journeyed here together as mainstream Canada and Indigenous people in a dynamic relationship with power structures shifting over our 500 plus years of connection. As one Indigenous speaker put it, "We were not standing on the shores of Eastern Canada waiting for the white man to arrive in his sailing ship carrying a welfare check" (Geddes, Doxtater, & Krepakevich, 1997). Indigenous populations are growing rapidly, but economic growth in their communities is slow. In this chapter, we look at obstacles to that growth and to the ultimate goal of self-sufficiency for Indigenous people. We examine their overall social and economic capacity, as well as the health and resilience of their communities. Our aim is to understand how they can achieve greater mental and physical health, positive economic growth, and increased community cohesion and strength.

Case Study: Grassy Narrows

Prior to discussing demographics, let us look closely at a northern Ontario reserve—the Asubpeeschoseewagong First Nation, also known as Grassy Narrows—and at how this community came to its current socio-economic condition. There are many Indigenous communities in Canada, each with a distinct individual history shaped by particular events and crises, and all deserve our attention. But space constraints prevent us from discussing more than one of them.

Grassy Narrows is located 80 kilometres north of Kenora, Ontario, near the Manitoba border. The Ojibwe community living on the reserve today consists of 639 people. Almost half of them are children or youth 19 years of age or under.

The reserved area was set aside for the Grassy Narrows people in 1873, with the signing of Treaty No. 3. By this treaty, the people of this area relinquished 14 million hectares to the government while retaining their right to pursue their traditional occupations, such as hunting and fishing, on the surrendered tract of land, except on such areas as may "from time to time" be required for settlement, mining, or forestry. The government was to maintain schools for instruction and pay annuities to the band in the amount of $5 per person per year.

Missionaries began work in the Grassy Narrows area in the 1840s, accessing the area by canoe. On their arrival, most of the Indigenous people were out of their reach, following a traditional hunting and trapping way of life. The people would return from the traplines in May to their summer grounds, where they would plant gardens and live in their spaciously distributed summer cabins. Those who were taken to the residential schools at McIntosh or Kenora were the ones most influenced by the missions.

Land development came with the building of a railway to access forestry products, but few Indigenous people left the community. There was no welfare or social services; the Indian agent came to the reserve once a year to distribute treaty money. Until 1963, the relative isolation allowed the Indigenous people of this area to preserve their culture, way of life, self-sufficiency, and freedom. In the summer of 1963, Indian Affairs began the process of relocating the people of Grassy Narrows to a new community on the Jones logging road, which was linked to both the railway and the city of Kenora. Indian Affairs intended to provide the Indigenous people with the benefits of modern life and to end the isolation that had helped them resist assimilation.

The new community was built 8 kilometres from the old one, on the English-Wabigoon river system. The rivers were to supply their water needs (the government's promise of running water was not initially fulfilled). The housing provided on the new reserve was crowded and of poor quality. The hunting and trapping way of life became difficult to maintain; the government insisted that the children remain on the reserve and attend school, and this made the parents reluctant to leave for the traplines through the fall and winter.

Prior to the move, the government had been systematically dismantling the traditional economic system of the Ojibwe people. Harvesting wild rice for sustenance had been an activity of Ojibwe people from time immemorial. In the 1950s, however, the government began to issue licences for that harvest; the price of wild rice had increased, making it a possible source of income for the Ojibwe. Initially, only the Ojibwe people were issued licences to harvest wild rice, but in the 1970s non-Indigenous wild rice farmers took over many of those licences. Their mechanical methods of harvesting were more efficient than the traditional Ojibwe methods.

Access to the new reserve from Kenora made it easier for government officials to impose fishing regulations on the Grassy Narrows people. Amendments to the *Indian Act* made all laws of the province applicable not just to non-Indigenous people but to Indigenous people, too; this made the Ojibwe subject to fishing regulations even though this restriction was in direct violation of their treaty rights. Commercial fishing licences were issued to some Grassy Narrows people, but sport fishing licences were given priority because they brought more revenue to the area, predominantly in white communities.

With limited access to paid employment and new constraints on their traditional means of sustenance, the community began to sink into despair. During this time of social upheaval and vulnerability, the Jones logging road, intended to bring the benefits of modern life to the people of Grassy Narrows, brought an unregulated flow of alcohol. Alcoholism, violence, and suicide spiralled out of control in the community.

Studies conducted at Grassy Narrows in 1977–1978 concluded that 70 percent of adults in their child-bearing years and 80 percent in their child-rearing years were heavy drinkers. Alcohol has been, and continues to be, a disruptive influence on Indigenous communities such as the one at Grassy Narrows, where the parents' drinking is largely responsible for the children's substance abuse and resulting failure to achieve academically. Gasoline sniffing, in particular, is a major problem among young people who live in these communities.

The federal government brought extensive development to the North, in the form of forestry and mining, and by doing so brought more hardship to the people of Grassy Narrows. In the early 1920s, a pulp and paper mill was opened in Dryden, Ontario, 130 kilometres upstream from the traditional Grassy Narrows area. Between 1962 and 1970, this mill, operated by Dryden Chemicals Limited, with the sanction of the Ontario government dumped over 20,000 pounds of mercury into the river system, poisoning it. The commercial fisheries on the reserve had to be shut down, and the people were advised not to eat fish caught in the rivers. Those who held fishing licences were issued $300 in compensation for the loss of their livelihood. In the 1970s and subsequently, health officials conducted tests on the population and found that their mercury levels were 40 to 150 times higher than the average Canadian's, likely due to their consumption not only of fish but also of animals that had ingested the mercury in some form.

The government's expenditures on Grassy Narrows skyrocketed. Within 15 years of relocating the Grassy Narrows Ojibwe, the Department of Indian Affairs and Northern Development was spending almost $1 million annually on health, food, and housing for a community formerly visited once a year by an Indian agent and requiring little in the way of health care.

There were disputes between the provincial government and the mill as to who was responsible for the environmental disaster; neither wished to accept accountability. Because the mill had followed environmental practices that were acceptable according to provincial law, the band was ultimately unable to hold any agency accountable.

The band continued to appeal to the government for assistance in alleviating its severe social problems. In 1977, the federal government held a Royal Commission on the Northern Environment. The commission cited the following reasons for the severe physical, mental, and spiritual breakdown in the Grassy Narrows community (Shkilnyk, 1985):

1. the intentional undermining of its religion and way of life;
2. the loss of income from trapping due to flooding and hydroelectric development;
3. the Jones logging road disrupting the community's isolation upon relocation;
4. new access to alcohol;
5. the introduction of a foreign value system;
6. the loss of commercial fishing due to mercury poisoning;
7. the availability of welfare but no work; and
8. the inability to hold any agency accountable for the mercury disaster.

It was not until 1985 that the Grassy Narrows community received a negotiated settlement for the poisoning of their environment. By then, the community had already hit rock bottom and was beginning to recover. The situation at Grassy Narrows improved through the 1990s, and today the people are moving forward and taking control over many aspects of their community life.

Currently, the community is addressing logging issues in its traditional territories with some success. In April 2011, Grassy Narrows signed a memorandum of agreement with the province of Ontario over the management of the Whiskey Jack Forest resources. This forest, traditionally used by the Grassy Narrows First Nation, was licensed by the Crown to Abitibi Lumber until 2009, by which point 50 percent of the area had been clearcut. For the ten years prior to 2009, the band had been blockading roadways in an effort to force a negotiation to preserve the forest and gain some control over timber access on their traditional territory. In a 2005 lawsuit against the province of Ontario, the band asserted that the province does not have the right to harvest timber on Treaty No. 3 territories. The Ontario Court of Appeal in 2013 disagreed and ruled that the province has the rights to timber in the area (*Keewatin v. Ontario*, 2013). While the band awaited a Supreme Court ruling in 2014, one of the largest timber companies in Ontario, EACOM Timber Corporation, which owns six sawmills, announced its solidarity with the people of Grassy Narrows, stating it would not purchase timber logged in that area (Aulakh, 2014).

The Supreme Court of Canada affirmed the Ontario Court of Appeal's decision in July 2014. It confirmed that the province of Ontario can open the area for mining, timber, and other resource extraction without the involvement of the federal government. The Supreme Court did assert that the province must consult and, if appropriate, accommodate the First Nations living in the area in a manner consistent with the duty of the Crown toward them. Ontario must therefore justify any resource extraction that limits or eliminates First Nations treaty rights in the area. Grassy Narrows has the distinction of running the longest-lasting blockade in Canada, from 2002 until 2015. Its ongoing legal battles with the province appear to have been a galvanizing force in the community, adding a level of unity and purpose that has sped its recovery (Mandell Pinder LLP, 2014).

The situation at Grassy Narrows has improved since the 1970s; however, in August 2015 the band declared a state of emergency after two years without access to safe drinking water. The installation of the reserve's water and sewer lines began in 1990 but remains incomplete. The chemicals used to remove the mercury from the water have been shown to cause cancer, and therefore the water is still unsafe. In June 2015, news broke that mercury levels were still rising near the community, which galvanized protests outside Queen's Park in Toronto. As a result, the Ontario government committed to testing the groundwater and cleaning up the mercury (Porter, 2015; Vendeville, 2016).

Indigenous peoples, many from Grassy Narrows, protested in front of Queen's Park in Toronto on April 7, 2010, demanding action from the provincial government on mercury cleanup in the English-Wabigoon river system.

Economically, the community is still struggling. The unemployment rate in 2011 in Grassy Narrows was 37 percent, compared with the provincial average of 8 percent. Annual average income in the same year was $21,641, compared with the provincial average of $43,833 (Statistics Canada, 2015c).

Conclusion

This has been a very brief look at the recent history of the Grassy Narrows people. You are encouraged to look into this history more deeply. This community is an extreme case, but its dealings with non-Indigenous Canada are typical in some respects of the Indigenous experience in Canada. Almost every First Nations community in Canada has been relocated at some point from its traditional territory, usually because the government or some private interest, such as a logging company, wanted readier access to the region's resources. Some Indigenous groups have been moved hundreds of kilometres from their traditional land. In almost all cases, relocation has brought severe social problems and economic hardship to the Indigenous group involved. The Canadian government has known about the negative consequences of relocation since it first began to impose it on Indigenous people in the 19th century. Until recently, however, the government continued this destructive practice. Some Indigenous communities are still suffering deeply from economic instability and social problems, but many are in the recovery phase, rebuilding their economic bases, healing from historic trauma, and building resilience in their young people for a brighter future.

EXERCISE 1

As mentioned in Chapter 2, the federal government of Canada, through the treaty process, undertook the fiduciary responsibility for Indigenous people. Do you think the government met that responsibility in the case of Grassy Narrows?

Indigenous Ancestry: Social and Legal Categories

Trying to describe Canada's Indigenous people in statistical terms can be very confusing; there are various categories of people with Indigenous ancestry. Another complicating factor is that statistical data in this area comes from three sources—Statistics Canada, Indigenous and Northern Affairs Canada, and the Aboriginal Peoples Survey. Each of these organizations uses a different classification system. Statistics Canada information is derived from the census survey, for which identification is voluntary. The census uses the umbrella term *Aboriginal identity*, which includes Métis, Inuit, and First Nations (status and non-status) people. Indigenous and Northern Affairs Canada, in its statistical surveys of the Indigenous population, includes only those Indians who are registered under the *Indian Act*. The Aboriginal Peoples Survey is different again, including in its statistical count only Inuit, Métis, and *off-reserve* First Nations populations. Because of these divergent accounting systems, statistics regarding Indigenous populations vary from source to source. This can be confusing to researchers and readers alike.

It is not surprising, then, that the number of registered Indians recorded by the Indigenous and Northern Affairs Indian Register differs from Statistics Canada's census counts of registered Indians; the two sources of data do not count registered Indians in the same way or for the same reason. The Indian Register is an administrative database, while the census is a statistical survey. To complicate matters further, although many registered Indians are members of one of the more than 600 bands in Canada, many others are not. Some band members are registered as Indians, but others are not. Some bands are connected to treaties and therefore sometimes are referred to as Treaty Indians, but some bands have never signed any treaty (as discussed in Chapter 2). See Figure 4.1 for an overview of these categories.

There have always been significant statistical differences between Indigenous people who live on reserve and those who live off reserve; therefore, Statistics Canada and Indigenous and Northern Affairs Canada collect information for both of these categories. However, because the Indigenous population tends to be more mobile than the non-Indigenous population, these numbers change regularly as the people move back and forth between reserved territories and cities.

FIGURE 4.1   Social–Legal Categories of Indigenous Peoples Residing in Canada

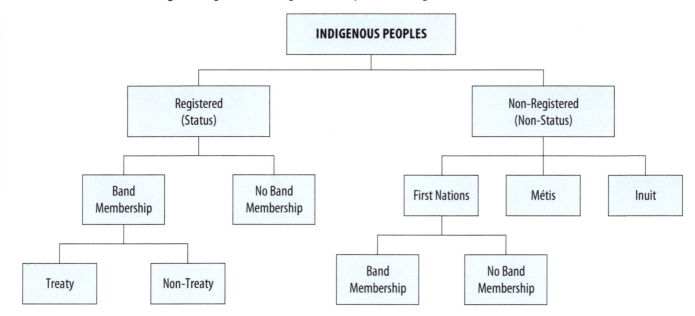

There is such diversity among Indigenous people that it is unwise to envision a homogeneous "Indigenous" population in Canada. A snapshot of census data covering all 600 bands, the Métis, and the Inuit cannot possibly capture the profound differences in all data areas among the various Indigenous groups. For example, there are profound differences between the Kanewake Mohawks of Quebec and the Lubicon Cree of Alberta, who differ from the Innu of Natuashish and the Cree Nation of Saskatchewan.

Size of the Indigenous Population

In the 2011 National Household Survey (NHS), 1,400,685 people identified themselves as having an Aboriginal identity, representing 4.3 percent of the total Canadian population. Of this number 851,560 or 60.8 percent report their identity as First Nations (North American Indian), 451,795 as Métis, and 59,445 as Inuit (see Tables 4.1 and 4.2).

The number of Canadians reporting Indigenous ancestry is growing rapidly; the growth rate between 2006 and 2011 was 20.1 percent, compared with only 5.2 percent for the non-Indigenous population. When the figures are broken down into categories of Indigenous identity types, First Nations' growth was 22.9 percent, Inuit growth was 18.1 percent, and Métis growth was 16.3 percent (see Table 4.1).

TABLE 4.1   Size and Growth Rate of Aboriginal Populations in Canada

Aboriginal identity population	2011 counts	Distribution (%) (2011)	Growth (%) (2001 to 2006)	Growth (%) (2006 to 2011)
Total population of Canada	**33,476,688**	**100.0**	**5.4**	**5.9**
Aboriginal identity population	1,400,685	4.3	20.1	20.1
Non-Aboriginal identity population	32,076,003	95.7	4.9	5.2
Total Aboriginal identity population	**1,400,685**	**100.0**	**20.1**	**20.1**
First Nations	851,560	60.8	14.6	22.9
Métis	451,795	32.3	33.3	16.3
Inuit	59,445	4.2	12.0	18.1

SOURCE: Statistics Canada (2013a).

TABLE 4.2   Size of the Indigenous Population, Canada, 2011

Aboriginal identity	Number	Percent
Total Aboriginal identity population	1,400,685	100.0
First Nations single identity	851,560	60.8
First Nations single identity (Registered or Treaty Indian)	637,660	45.5
First Nations single identity (not a Registered or Treaty Indian)	213,900	15.3
Métis single identity	451,795	32.3
Inuit single identity	59,445	4.2
Multiple Aboriginal identities	11,415	0.8
Aboriginal identities not included elsewhere	26,475	1.9

SOURCE: Statistics Canada (2013a, table 1).

It should be noted that the actual Indigenous population numbers may be higher than those reported in the NHS, because 36 Indian reserves and settlements did not participate in the 2011 census. In addition, some individuals may have chosen not to self-identify to government workers.

Factors Affecting Size

The growth rate of Canada's population is affected by three factors: the birth rate, the death rate, and the immigration rate. The growth rate of Indigenous populations is significantly affected by three factors: the birth rate, the death rate, and the rate at which individuals gain or lose status.

Status Loss and Gain

Canadian laws defining whom the government recognized as Indians pre-date the *Indian Act*. The earliest statutory definition of "Indian" did not discriminate on the basis of sex, but in 1869 provisions were introduced stating that women who "married out"—that is, who married non-Indians—would lose status, and their children would not be granted status. On the other hand, Indian men who married non-Indian women would not lose status. The 1876 *Indian Act* maintained these provisions; moreover, the 1876 Act also provided that an "Indian" included any woman who was married to "any male person of Indian blood reputed to belong to a particular band," whether or not the woman was Indian (Hurley & Simeone, 2010, p. 2).

The new *Indian Act*, enacted in 1951, established a national registry, with entitlement linked to band membership; it also maintained the provisions that discriminated, on the basis of sex, against women who married non-Indian men. Children born to an Indian mother and a non-Indian father were deemed non-Indian. However, the status of children born to an Indian father was determined by the "double-mother rule," which stated that if the child's mother and paternal grandmother had a right to Indian status only through having married an Indian man, the child had Indian status only up to the age of 21.

Prior to 1985, these provisions were strongly criticized by First Nations women's groups, human rights groups, and others, but these criticisms were ignored. However, when section 15 of the *Canadian Charter of Rights and Freedoms* came into force in 1985, the provisions were in clear violation of the new equality rights, which made it illegal to discriminate based on various categories, including sex. At this point, the government could not wait any longer to take action. In 1985, Bill C-31, *An Act to Amend the Indian Act*, was passed. Three principles guided the changes: (1) removing discriminatory clauses; (2) restoring status and membership rights; and (3) increasing control of Indian bands over their own membership (Aboriginal Affairs and Northern Development Canada, 2010).

With regard to entitlement to registration, sections 6(1) and 6(2) provided the following:

- Individuals entitled to registration prior to 1985 (including non-Indian women married to Indian men, and their children) retained full status (s. 6(1)(a)).
- Women who had lost status through marrying out or through an order of enfranchisement and persons who had lost status at 21 through the double-mother rule regained status (s. 6(1)(c)).
- Individuals with one parent entitled to registration under section 6(1) acquired status under section 6(2); persons with one parent registered under section 6(2) and one non-status parent were/are not entitled to registration.

Figure 4.2 shows the percentage change in Canada's registered Indian population from 1981 to 2015 and the effects of the 1985 amendments to the *Indian Act*.

The requirement that children registered under section 6(2) must partner with a registered Indian in order for their own children to be entitled to registration is often referred to as the

FIGURE 4.2   Percentage Change in Registered Indian Population, Canada, 1981 to 2015

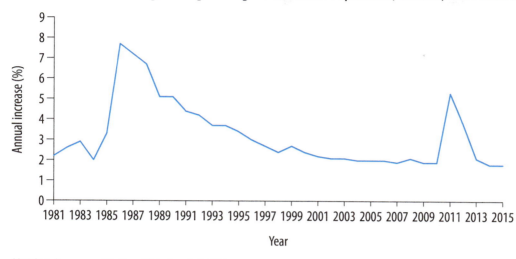

SOURCE: Indigenous and Northern Affairs Canada (2015a).

"second generation cut-off rule." This requirement was a primary target for charges that there was residual sex discrimination in the Act, and there were calls for the removal of this requirement (Hurley & Simeone, 2010, p. 4). In a 2005 statement, the Assembly of First Nations (AFN) commented that "[t]he Bill has not resolved any of the problems it was intended to fix … . Significant gender discrimination still remains, control over Indian status is still held by the Crown, and the population of Indians is declining as a direct result of Bill C-31" (Assembly of First Nations, 2005).

According to Indian and Northern Affairs Canada (2009, p. 3), between 1985, when Bill C-31 came into force, and 2007, over 117,000 persons who had lost status under discriminatory status provisions, as well as their descendants, had regained or acquired status. However, projections made several years ago warned of a "rapid decline" in the number of individuals entitled to registration. This decline would result from the section 6 rules and from marrying out, with one source predicting that sometime around the end of the fifth generation, the number of children born who would be entitled to Indian registration would fall to zero (Hurley & Simeone, 2010, p. 4).

Until recently, it was believed that applications for reinstatement had slowed to a trickle and that population growth in the future would no longer be affected by status reinstatement applications under Bill C-31. If this turns out to be the case, it will be largely owing to the 2009 BC Court of Appeal ruling in *McIvor v. Canada*, which has had a significant effect on the number of individuals who are eligible for registration.

To summarize the *McIvor* case, Sharon McIvor was not registered as an Indian prior to 1985. Had she been registered, she would have lost her registration because she married a non-Indian. McIvor became registered after 1985 under section 6(2), on the basis of having one parent registered under section 6(1) and one non-Indian parent. Her son, Jacob Grismer, has a child with a non-Indian woman. Because McIvor was registered under section 6(2) of the Act, her grandchild (Grismer's child) could not be registered as Indian.

The core of McIvor's argument on behalf of her grandson's registration was that if she had not been removed from status prior to 1985, she would have been registered as a section 6(1) Indian and thereby able to pass status on to her grandchild. If McIvor had been male (the court made use of a "hypothetical brother" of McIvor in considering this), she—or rather, "he"—

would have maintained status and been registered as a section 6(1) Indian once the changes to the Act took place in 1985. Any grandchildren of this hypothetical brother would be entitled to be registered. The BC Court of Appeal held that the "preferential treatment" enjoyed by Indian men who married prior to 1985—and whose grandchildren were afforded "enhanced status" as compared with those of a female who had married prior to 1985—was a violation of section 15 of the Charter. The court gave the government of Canada until April 2010 to amend the unconstitutional provisions in the Act.

In 2010, the government introduced amendments ensuring that eligible grandchildren of women who had lost status as a result of marrying non-Indian men would be entitled to registration under the Act. The current version of the Act, which came into force in January 2011, incorporates these amendments, in section 6(1)(c.1).

On January 8, 2013 the Federal Court of Appeal ruled in the case of *Daniels v. Canada*. The ruling in favour of Harry Daniels, a Métis, confirmed that non-status Indians and Métis are included as "Indians" within section 91(24) of the *Constitution Act*. This means they hold the rights accorded to Aboriginal people within the context of the Constitution and extends the federal government's fiduciary duty to non-status Indians and Métis. Prior to this ruling, neither the federal government nor any provincial government claimed jurisdiction over these groups. The government of Canada appealed the Federal Court's decision. The Supreme Court of Canada heard the case and on April 14, 2016 it affirmed the lower court ruling. The decision will open access to services to about 200,000 Métis and 400,000 non-status Indians that were previously available only to status Indians. It will also allow the federal government to amend its policy of interpreting "Indian" under the Constitution, and obligate the federal government to negotiate equal treatment under the Charter in the same manner as for status Indians. It is unclear at this point how and when services will be extended to Métis and non-status Indians, as the process of clarifying these rights unfolds over the next several years.

Prior to the 2009, 2013, and 2016 rulings, the determination of status under the *Indian Act* was both a complex topic and a live issue. Many Canadians may find the matter merely confusing, but for Indigenous people it is critical. Through the federal government and provincial agencies, a wide range of programs and services are available to status Indians that are not available to non-registered individuals; status determines eligibility for living on reserves, eligibility for tax exemption, and access to health care and education.

In addition to these tangible benefits, being officially registered is for many individuals with Indigenous ancestry an important part of identification with their family and with the larger community.

Birth and Death Rates

Like the birth rate for Canada as a whole, the birth rate for Indigenous populations is declining over time. Despite this, the Indigenous birth rate is still higher than that of the non-Indigenous population. As a result, the Indigenous population is younger on average than the non-Indigenous population. In fact, the median age (the point where exactly half the population is older and the other half younger) is 28 years for Indigenous people, compared with 41 years for the non-Indigenous population. The Inuit population is younger still, with a median age of 23 years. The Métis population has a median age of 31 years (Statistics Canada, 2013a, table 4).

Life expectancy for Indigenous people still lags behind that of the general population. This results in fewer seniors in the Indigenous population. Seniors represent only 5.9 percent of Indigenous populations, compared with 14.2 percent of the non-Indigenous population. Issues that affect the mortality rate of Indigenous people are discussed later in this chapter.

Population Distribution

Geographical Distribution

According to the 2011 census (Statistics Canada, 2013a, table 2), 80 percent of Indigenous people live in Ontario, Manitoba, Saskatchewan, Alberta, and British Columbia. The next greatest number live in Quebec. The Western provinces and the territories have the greatest ratio of Indigenous people to the total population. For example, the 27,360 Indigenous people (mostly Inuit) in Nunavut make up 86.3 percent of Nunavut's population. Table 4.3 shows the percentage of the total population that Indigenous people represent, in Canada and in the respective provinces and territories.

TABLE 4.3 Number and Distribution of the Population Reporting an Aboriginal Identity and Percentage of Aboriginal People in the Population, Canada, Provinces and Territories, 2011

Provinces and territories	Aboriginal identity population	Percentage distribution	Aboriginal identity population as a percentage of the total population
Canada	1,400,685	100.0	4.3
Newfoundland and Labrador	35,800	2.6	7.1
Prince Edward Island	2,230	0.2	1.6
Nova Scotia	33,845	2.4	3.7
New Brunswick	22,615	1.6	3.1
Quebec	141,915	10.1	1.8
Ontario	301,425	21.5	2.4
Manitoba	195,900	14.0	16.7
Saskatchewan	157,740	11.3	15.6
Alberta	220,695	15.8	6.2
British Columbia	232,290	16.6	5.4
Yukon	7,705	0.6	23.1
Northwest Territories	21,160	1.5	51.9
Nunavut	27,360	2.0	86.3

SOURCE: Statistics Canada (2013a, table 2).

EXERCISE 2

Consider the name of the branch of the federal government charged with responsibility for Indigenous people during the 1970s: Department of Indian Affairs and Northern Development. Separate that title into two distinct interests: "Indian Affairs" and "Northern Development." Think about what these two had in common and the conflicting interests between the two. Then consider the current name of the branch: Indigenous and Northern Affairs Canada. What do these names tell you about the interests and priorities of the federal government?

Urban/Rural Distribution

Another trend shown by the 2011 census is that the Indigenous population overall is becoming increasingly urban. The 2011 census figures separate the urban population of First Nations people into status and non-status, since non-status First Nations people account for 25.1 percent of the First Nations population (Statistics Canada, 2013a). Forty-nine percent of First Nations with registered Indian status live on reserves, which means that 51 percent live in urban centres, including large cities and smaller towns. Even though a large percentage of First Nations registered Indians live in urban centres, they do not make up a very large percentage of the populations in these places. For example, in Winnipeg, where more First Nations registered Indians (25,970) reside than in any other Canadian city, they account for only 3.6 percent of the population. The cities with the next largest registered Indian population are Edmonton (18,210, or 1.6 percent of the city's population) and Vancouver (15,000, or 0.7 percent).

The census metropolitan areas with the largest populations of First Nations people without registered Indian status are Toronto (14,505, or 0.3 percent of the population), Vancouver (13,635, or 0.6 percent), and Montreal (10,540, or 0.3 percent).

The majority of people who identified themselves as Métis live in either the Western provinces or Ontario. The largest population of Métis is in Alberta, where 21.4 percent of all Métis live. The next largest population is in Ontario with 19 percent, followed by Manitoba with 17.4 percent, British Columbia with 15.4 percent, and Saskatchewan with 11.6 percent. Winnipeg has the highest number of urban-dwelling Métis, with 46,325, followed by Edmonton with 31,780, and Vancouver with 18,485. There are 11,520 Métis in Saskatoon and 9,980 in Toronto.

According to the 2011 National Household Survey, 73.1 percent of Inuit in Canada live in the four regions of **Inuit Nunangat** (see Figure 4.3). There are 2,325 Inuit, or 3.9 percent of the total Inuit population, living in Nunatsiavut; they represent 89.1 percent of the total population of that region. Nunavik is home to 10,750 Inuit, or 18.1 percent of the Inuit population, and they too account for 89.1 percent of that region's population. The largest number of Inuit, 27,070, live in Nunavut and represent 45.5 percent of the Inuit population. Within Nunavut, the Inuit represent 85.4 percent of the total population. The Inuvialuit region is home to 3,310 Inuit or 5.6 percent of the total Inuit population, who account for 57.6 percent of the total population of this region. Inuit living outside these four regions predominantly dwell in Edmonton, Montreal, Ottawa, Yellowknife, and St. John's.

The trend toward urbanization among status Indians goes back over four decades. In 1966, only 19.5 percent of status Indians lived off reserve. By 1986, that figure had increased to 31.9 percent. By 2001, 42.5 percent of status Indians lived off reserve; by 2011, 51 percent lived off reserve. (Comparable data are not available for non-status Indians and Métis.)

A number of factors influence the decision to migrate to urban centres. Population increases on reserves can lead to overcrowding, lack of housing, and unemployment, which can cause individuals to look elsewhere for opportunity. Individuals may move to an urban centre to enter the labour market and/or to acquire education not readily available on a reserve. Individuals are more likely to migrate to an urban centre if there is one near their reserve.

Inuit Nunangat the four regions in which Inuit live, including land, water, and ice: Inuvialuit, Nunatsiavut, Nunavik, and Nunavut

Challenges for Urban Indigenous People

Among the challenges facing Indigenous migrants to urban centres are the ongoing jurisdictional disputes as to which level of government has legislative authority and responsibility for urban Indigenous people. The federal government acknowledges its responsibility for on-reserve registered First Nations people; however, the responsibility to provide services for other Indigenous people is often subject to disputes between provincial, municipal, and federal governments.

FIGURE 4.3 Inuit Nunangat (Inuit Regions of Canada)

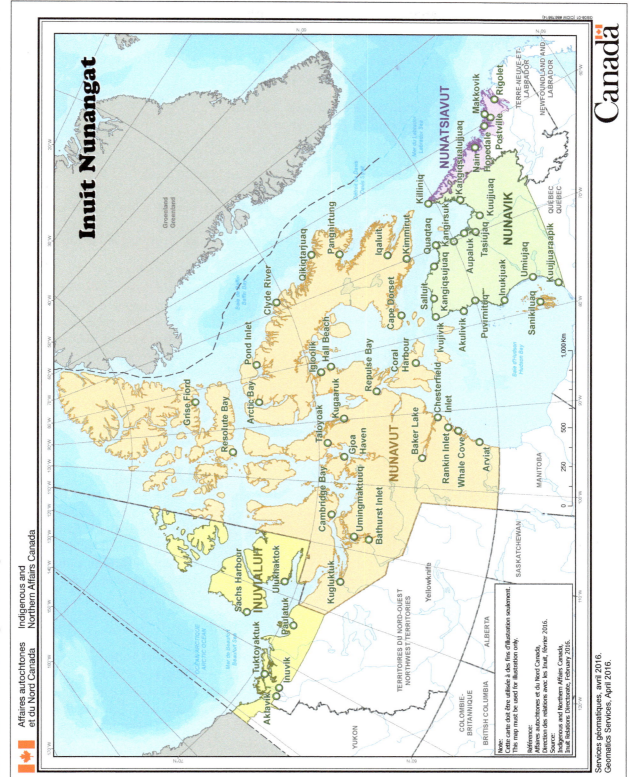

SOURCE: Indigenous and Northern Affairs Canada (2016a).

This situation often leads to a scarcity of services for Indigenous people living in urban areas. As a result of the *Daniels* case, however, improvements should begin to emerge over the next few years.

One analysis (Frideres & Gadacz, 2008, p. 170) has shown that urban Indigenous people, compared with their non-Indigenous counterparts,

- are more likely to have low levels of education;
- have low labour force participation rates;
- have high unemployment rates;
- have low income levels;
- have high rates of homelessness and greater housing needs;
- are overrepresented in the criminal justice system;
- have poor health status (particularly in the areas of mental health, suicide, HIV/AIDS, diabetes, and substance abuse); and
- are more than twice as likely to belong to lone-parent families and to experience domestic violence.

Currently in Canada, programs for urban-dwelling Indigenous people are offered through the National Association of Friendship Centres. There are 118 centres and seven provincial and territorial associations that provide services to urban Indigenous people, regardless of status. The Friendship Centres are funded federally through the Urban Aboriginal Strategy, which in 2014 implemented Community Capacity Support and Urban Partnerships programs. The programs offered at each centre depend on the specific needs of the communities they serve, but typically they focus on supporting education, economic development, cultural awareness, and youth initiatives. The goal is to encourage equal access to services and full participation in Canadian society for urban Indigenous people.

Education

The strong causal connection between education, participation in the labour market, and income has been well established by social science. Education is also connected to physical and mental health and to reduced criminal activity. There is also a generational spillover: the parents' educational level is connected to the educational attainment of their children. This is true for all Canadians, not just Indigenous populations. Indigenous people in Canada have had persistently low academic achievement relative to the general population, which has perpetuated their economic disadvantage.

Delivery and Funding

The history of Indigenous education in Canada is long and overshadowed by the residential school era. Since 2011 the federal government has been diligently working with First Nations people to overhaul the currently inadequate patchwork of First Nations education programming across the country. A panel was assembled in the fall of 2011, which, after extensive consultations with First Nations communities, submitted a report with recommendations for changes to the current system. The panel found that

> [i]n the early 1970s, following the dissolution of the residential school system, and the devolution of First Nation education to individual First Nations, virtually no thought was given to the necessary supporting structure for the delivery of First Nation education. There was no clear funding policy, no service provision and no legislation, standards or regulations to enshrine and protect the rights of a child to a quality education and to set

the education governance and accountability framework. (National Panel on First Nation Elementary and Secondary Education for Students on Reserve, 2013, p. 9)

The panel made five broad recommendations to improve First Nations education:

1. Co-create child-centred First Nations education legislation within 18 months of the panel's report, accompanied by an implementation plan and schedule that is consistent with the treaty and self-governing rights of First Nations people. The legislation was to include all necessary components of a high-quality education system, such as coordination of curriculum, standards, performance measures, and accountability.
2. Create a National Commission for First Nations Education to support education reform and improvement. The commission would take over the responsibility for First Nations education from Aboriginal Affairs and Northern Development Canada.
3. Facilitate and support the creation of a First Nation education system through the development of regional First Nation education organizations (FNEOs) to provide support services for First Nation schools and students. These FNEOs were seen as particularly necessary for northern or remote schools and those with needs unique to their area. Grouping schools under regional management would better provide for efficiencies and support.
4. Ensure adequate funding to support a First Nations education system that meets the needs of First Nations learners and communities, and of Canada as a whole. The panel found evidence of significant gaps in teacher compensation, a lack of equipment and supplies, inadequate supports for students with special needs, and school facilities in disrepair. Three recommendations address underfunding and were to be acted upon immediately:
   a. Increase education funding for 2012–13 to equal the funding increases in the provincial education system according to the location of each First Nations school.
   b. Increase teacher and administrator salaries to equal those in the provincial education system.
   c. Launch or expand early literacy programs with the goal of having all First Nations students reading by grade 3.
5. Establish an accountability and reporting framework to assess improvement in First Nations education by evaluating both the system and the students' progress. The panel found significant gaps in data tracking the progress of learners compared with that of provincial schools. These data are crucial to evaluating the progress and quality of education delivery. (National Panel on First Nation Elementary and Secondary Education for Students on Reserve, 2013, pp. 31–42)

By March 2012 the government of Canada had made a commitment to introduce a First Nations education act as part of its 2012 Economic Action Plan, and an intensive consultation process began in earnest in December 2012. In July 2013, the AFN passed a resolution to assert First Nations control over First Nations education. In October 2013 the government presented its proposal for a bill. The government and the AFN collaborated to produce Bill C-33, the *First Nations Control of First Nations Education Act*, which was introduced in April 2014. There was extensive debate in relation to Bill C-33 at both first and second reading; it was put on hold in May 2014. As we wait for a new national strategy to be agreed upon and implemented, we can review the current framework.

There are a number of paths to education for First Nations people in Canada. There are First Nations–managed (that is, band-operated) schools, funded by the federal government, which are predominantly on First Nations reserves across Canada and serve mostly First Nations students living on reserves. There are approximately 518 such schools, and approximately

61 percent of children who live on reserve attend band-operated schools. The band's degree of control over the education budget, curriculum, and staffing differs according to reserve and often depends on the numbers of students and staff involved. As well, the amount of funding per student allotted by the federal government is inconsistent region by region because it depends on the agreement between each First Nations group and the government, since a Canada-wide education strategy and legislation still do not exist. The goal for First Nations is and has always been to have the band exercise complete control over the education process, a goal that many bands have achieved (Laboucane, 2010, p. 18).

In 1988, the federal government created a Band Operated Funding Formula that sets out budgets for the operation of the schools. The formula, which was based on the number of students in the school multiplied by the cost of educational delivery, mirrored a similar funding formula in the provincial school systems throughout Canada. But there was tremendous growth in First Nations communities, and the federal government had not kept pace in funding either children who attended on-reserve schools or those who attended provincially run schools off reserve. In some cases provincial schools were paid more than double what on-reserve schools were paid for student tuition. In 2006–7, the support provided for First Nations students by the Elementary/Secondary Education Program was on average *$2,000 less per student* than the amount provided for provincial students (Laboucane, 2010, p. 18). Some estimates of the funding gap indicate the amount may in fact have been much greater (VanEvery-Albert, 2004, pp. 18–19). Teachers in band-operated schools were paid less than teachers in provincial schools. A Chiefs of Ontario report showed that the Ontario teacher's annual salary classed at year 5, level 5 on the grid was $54,079. First Nations teachers at the same level in band-operated schools had an average income of $46,179 (VanEvery-Albert, 2004, p. 7). This difference may have accounted for some of the funding shortfall, since salaries are a large part of education budgets. Robert Laboucane (2010, p. 21) paints a grim picture of reserve schools:

> There is no funding for on reserve school libraries or books. Schools are unable to provide competitive salaries for teachers on reserves. There is no funding for vocational training in secondary schools on reserves. There is no funding for extracurricular sports and recreation activities on reserves.

The failure of the federal government to adequately fund on-reserve K–12 schools, including a 2 percent cap on annual increases between 1990 and 2006, along with the increasing number of students attending First Nations on-reserve schools, has resulted in recent large increases in funding in order to catch up with provincial funding (see Figure 4.4).

These increases, however, have not managed to close the gap between First Nations schools and provincial schools, as is illustrated in Figure 4.5.

Of the 113,400 on-reserve students enrolled in K–12, 61 percent were in First Nations–managed schools, while 36 percent were in provincial schools and the remaining 3 percent in private schools (Bains, 2014). (These statistics exclude Nunavut, Northwest Territories, Atlantic Canada, and Quebec.) While many federally funded students attended band-operated schools from kindergarten through to grade 5, the number drops sharply by grade 12. This decrease is largely due to the fact that secondary schools are often unavailable in First Nations communities, so students transfer to the provincial system for secondary school, and the federal government transfers funds to the province to pay for the First Nations child's education.

In the past decades of neglect, many on-reserve school facilities had fallen into disrepair, many unsuitable for education. As part of Canada's Economic Action Plan in 2010, $200 million was committed over two years, with an additional $102 million over three years through the Building Canada Plan, toward renovating existing schools and to support new cost-efficient school projects. Funds have been allocated for construction of new schools and upgrades to current facilities. By March 2013, 110 school projects were in various states of completion (Indigenous and Northern Affairs Canada, 2016b).

FIGURE 4.4   AANDC Elementary/Secondary Education Expenditures, 2008–9 to 2013–14

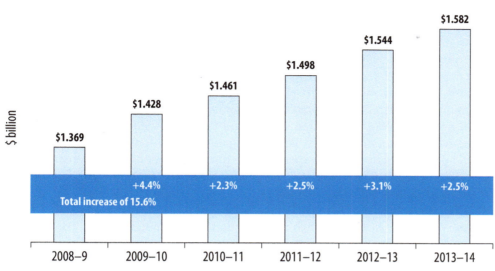

NOTE: INAC's investments in First Nations K–12 education on reserve, by fiscal year, from 2008–9 to 2013–14. It also outlines the year-over-year percentage increases to this funding over the same period.

SOURCE: Indigenous and Northern Affairs Canada (2016b).

FIGURE 4.5   Federal Funding for First Nations Schools

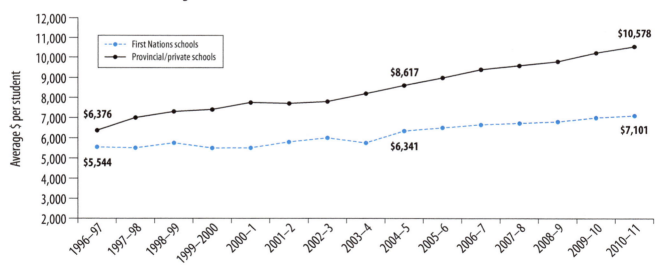

NOTE: Per-student funding is calculated using the following formula: Core funding allocated by the federal government for First Nations education (First Nations school or provincial/private school)/Nominal roll (First Nations school or provincial/private school).

SOURCE: Indian and Northern Affairs Canada, financial information (1996–2011); Indian and Northern Affairs Canada, nominal roll statistics (1996–2011).

Achievement Rates: A Comparison

Educational achievement rates for any population are strongly connected to the quality of education as well as to future labour participation and income rates. To examine the educational achievement rates of Indigenous people in Canada, we use the government data collected in both the 2011 National Household Survey (NHS) and the 2012 Aboriginal Peoples Survey (APS); however, the APS collects data from off-reserve Indigenous people only, so the statistics can be read differently. Off-reserve students attend provincial schools and thus are not surveyed within the First Nations school system. There are clear but less dramatic differences in educational achievement rates between First Nations students who are educated off reserve in provincial schools and non–First Nations children who attend the same schools. The differences in achievement rates are more dramatic when we compare First Nations students educated on reserve with non–First Nations students educated in provincial schools. Finally, there are differences among the achievement rates of First Nations, Métis, and Inuit students, both overall and when differences in location are factored in.

In 2012, 72 percent of First Nations people, 42 percent of Inuit, and 77 percent of Métis living off reserve aged 18 to 44 had a high school diploma. The figure for the non-Indigenous population in 2011 was 89 percent. Also in 2012, 43 percent of off-reserve First Nations people, 26 percent of Inuit, and 47 percent of Métis aged 18 to 44 had a post-secondary diploma or degree. The figure for the non-Indigenous population was 64 percent. Educational experiences correlate with employment experiences. According to the APS, in 2012, 72 percent of First Nations people who had completed high school were employed versus only 47 percent of those who had not. Of Inuit who had completed high school, 71 percent were employed versus 44 percent of those without a high school diploma; 80 percent of Métis who had finished high

FIGURE 4.6   Proportion of Aboriginal and Non-Aboriginal Identity Men and Women Aged 25 to 64 by Selected Levels of Educational Attainment, 2011

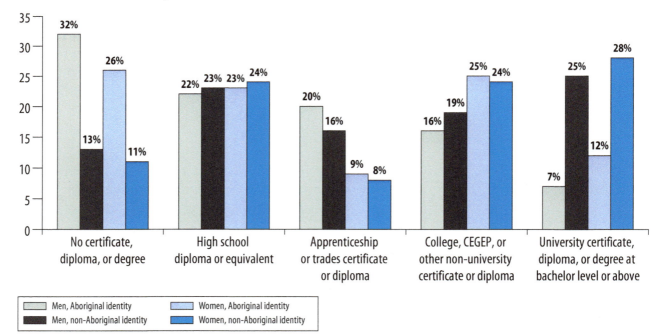

SOURCE: Employment and Social Development Canada (2013).

school were employed, versus 61 percent who had not. In addition, employed high school graduates were earning on average about $10,000 per year more than those who had not completed high school (Statistics Canada, 2013b).

The NHS collected statistics differently. The 2011 survey showed improved levels of educational achievement, with 68 percent of Indigenous people aged 35 to 44 having completed high school. In the same age category, 27 percent of Indigenous women and 18 percent of Indigenous men had a college diploma. Non-status Indigenous people generally have higher educational achievement rates than do status Indians (Bougie, Kelly-Scott, & Arriagada, 2015, Pt. A, s. 4).

FIGURE 4.7   Proportion of First Nations People Aged 25 to 64 Living On and Off Reserve by Selected Levels of Educational Attainment, 2011

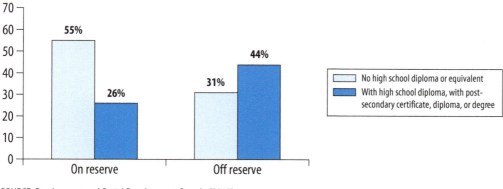

SOURCE: Employment and Social Development Canada (2013).

FIGURE 4.8   Proportion of Aboriginal People by Selected Levels of Educational Attainment and Age, 2011

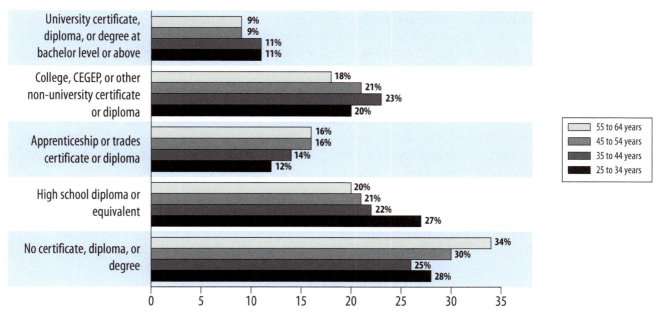

SOURCE: Employment and Social Development Canada (2013).

Factors Correlated with Success and Failure

A number of studies have been done to determine why Indigenous students perform as they do in the school system. These studies, along with more general research into the sources of academic achievement, confirm the role played by socio-economic status, parental education level, household living arrangements, and household income in determining student success.

The 2012 APS (Statistics Canada, 2012) identified a number of factors that are positively correlated with perceived academic achievement. (Recall that this survey considers only off-reserve status and non-status Indigenous people, Métis, and Inuit—in other words, those most likely to use provincial schools rather than band-operated schools.) These factors include:

- getting along with peers and having close friends with high educational aspirations;
- having parents with at least a high school education;
- having parents who spoke to and visited teachers and attended school events and activities;
- receiving support from school staff; and
- being involved in extracurricular activities.

The same survey identified a number of factors that correlated negatively with perceived academic achievement. These include:

- having close friends who missed school, smoked, or used drugs or alcohol;
- changing schools frequently;
- having parents who did not complete high school; and
- living away from home.

In Canada, British Columbia is the only province to publish standardized test results by various characteristics of schools and students, including Indigenous identity. In British Columbia, there are 60,000 self-identified Indigenous students in the provincial school system; they make up approximately 10 percent of the school population (Richards, Vining, & Weimer, 2010, p. 48). A study was conducted to examine Indigenous performance in the grades 4 and 7 standardized tests that assess the foundational skills of reading, writing, and numeracy. The study, focused on the period spanning the 2001–2 and 2005–6 school years, showed that a sizable gap exists by grade 4 between Indigenous and non-Indigenous student performance, and that this gap widens by grade 7 (Richards et al., 2010, p. 54).

In the BC study, the school catchment areas from which the results were drawn were measured in terms of socio-economic status. The improvement in test scores remained fairly constant for both Indigenous and non-Indigenous students when the catchment areas were in the highest income areas. Furthermore, the number of Indigenous students in each school was measured in relation to achievement levels, and it was found that a higher Indigenous student count in a school produced *lower* overall academic achievement for Indigenous students.

The BC study also looked for common denominators in the more successful districts, and it was found (Richards et al., 2010, p. 63) that these districts

- had school administrators and teachers who more consistently emphasized Indigenous educational success as a long-term priority;
- engaged Indigenous leaders from the broader community with greater success;
- made more consistent use of objective data on Indigenous student performance; and
- had a reputation for following through on policy implementation.

Clearly, this study has some implications for BC school system policy changes.

Generally speaking, the statistics indicate that the educational system is failing Indigenous students and failing Canada in the process. According to the Canadian Centre for the Study of Living Standards, Canada's economy would increase by $71.1 billion if Indigenous people achieved the same educational levels as other Canadians (Laboucane, 2010, p. 18). Among the various factors contributing to the underachievement of Indigenous students, an impoverished sense of identity is surely one. Certain factors contribute to such impoverishment: curricula that exclude Indigenous children's history, cultures, languages, and contributions to Canada, and educators' lack of knowledge about Indigenous culture and history.

Income and Labour Market Participation

According to the 2011 NHS, between 2006 and 2011, the number of Indigenous people of working age (that is, between the ages of 25 and 64) increased by 21 percent; for the general Canadian population, the increase was only 5 percent. The 2011 census enumerated 671,380 Indigenous people in this age group, of whom 481,325 participated in the labour force. Although the Indigenous employment rate (for individuals of working age) remained stable at 63 percent between 2006 and 2011, this rate is still much lower than the 76 percent employment rate for non-Indigenous people. The unemployment rate for Indigenous people of working age is more than twice the rate for other Canadians of the same age (13 percent versus 6 percent). The gap between the two groups narrowed by 8 percent between 2006 and 2011 (Bougie et al., 2015, Pt. A, s. 4).

There is also a difference in the employment rate between status and non-status Indigenous people. The employment rate for status Indians is only 55 percent, 20 percent lower than the rate for non-Indigenous Canadians. The overall unemployment rate for working-age status Indians is 17 percent; for those living on reserve the rate is 22 percent.

The Métis population has only a 9 percent unemployment rate; their lowest unemployment rates are in Manitoba and Alberta and the highest is in Newfoundland and Labrador.

For the Inuit population the employment rate is 59 percent, 17 percent lower than the rate for non-Indigenous Canadians. The overall unemployment rate for Inuit is 17 percent; for those living in Nunangat it is 20 percent.

Figure 4.9 shows the unemployment rate across several provinces for First Nations, Métis, all Aboriginal, and non-Aboriginal respondents for 2007. Figure 4.10 shows the employment rate of population aged 25 to 64, by Aboriginal identity and education, for 2011.

FIGURE 4.9   Unemployment Rate of Population Aged 25 to 54 by Province or Region and Aboriginal Identity, 2007

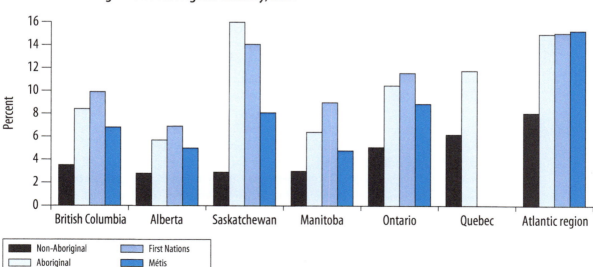

SOURCE: Statistics Canada (2008).

FIGURE 4.10 Employment Rate of Population Aged 25 to 64, by Aboriginal Identity and Education, Canada, 2011

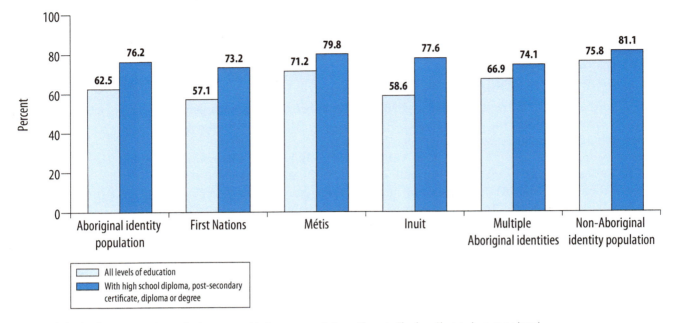

Legend:
- All levels of education
- With high school diploma, post-secondary certificate, diploma or degree

Category	All levels of education	With high school diploma, post-secondary certificate, diploma or degree
Aboriginal identity population	62.5	76.2
First Nations	57.1	73.2
Métis	71.2	79.8
Inuit	58.6	77.6
Multiple Aboriginal identities	66.9	74.1
Non-Aboriginal identity population	75.8	81.1

NOTE: Excludes data for one or more incompletely enumerated Indian reserves or Indian settlements. The three Aboriginal groups are based on the population reporting a single identity of "First Nations," "Métis," or "Inuit."

SOURCE: Statistics Canada (2015b, chart 15).

It appears that Indigenous people were hardest hit by the 2008 recession, with employment rates declining more steeply for the Indigenous population than for the non-Indigenous population (Statistics Canada, 2010). The unemployment rate in Canada for Indigenous people increased from 10.4 percent in 2008 to 13.9 percent in 2009, while the rate for non-Indigenous people rose from 6.0 percent to 8.1 percent. The manufacturing sector was hardest hit in this recession, with an 8 percent employment decline in 2009 from 2008; however, manufacturing employment fell for Indigenous people by 30 percent in the same year. In Alberta, the employment rate fell in 2008, at the start of the recession, from 75.1 percent to 65.1 percent, a steep decline for the province. The decline for Indigenous people was twice that.

As mentioned above, educational attainment is related to employability, and it is also related to income levels. This is true for all Canadians. The 2006 census (Statistics Canada, 2006) shows that Canadians who were employed full time and who had less than a high school education had an annual average income of $32,029. Canadians with a high school education made $37,403. Those with trades or apprenticeships made $39,996, and those with a college education earned $42,937. Canadians with some university education earned $47,253, while those with a bachelor's degree earned $56,048. The correlation between income and education levels is clear. Because Indigenous people's educational levels lag behind those of non-Indigenous people, so do their income levels—on average, by about $7,500 per year, according to the 2006 census (Statistics Canada, 2008). The gap between Indigenous and non-Indigenous education, employment, and income levels is closing, but slowly. Investment in Indigenous education will accelerate this process. Unfortunately, Statistics Canada's more frequent and detailed Labour Force Survey does not track on-reserve employment and unemployment; having these statistics gathered only in the census every five years makes the issue more difficult to address.

The labour force as a whole is important to Canada's economic future. Precisely because the Indigenous population is younger on average and its growth rate higher than the national average, it is an important resource for Canada's economic future. Key statistics in this regard include the following (Hull, 2008):

- Between 2001 and 2026, the number of Indigenous youth coming of age to enter the labour market will exceed 600,000.
- The 15–29 age group in the Indigenous population is projected to grow by 37 percent, compared with only 6 percent for this age group in the general Canadian population.
- By 2026, in Saskatchewan, 36 percent of the population between the ages of 15 and 29 is expected to be Indigenous; in Manitoba, the figure is expected to be 28 percent.

According to a medium growth rate projection, the Indigenous population will, by 2026, increase from its current 4 percent of Canada's population to 4.6 percent (Sharpe & Arsenault, 2010, p. 4). Because the Indigenous population is much younger than the rest of the population, it will be an increasing presence in the labour force as the aging population retires. If the current education (and, therefore, the employment) gap closes between the non-Indigenous and Indigenous populations, the latter will account for 19.9 percent of labour force growth between 2006 and 2026 (Sharpe & Arsenault, 2010, p. 4). Conversely, if the education gap remains as it is or becomes wider, given the projected increase in the Indigenous population, the result will be a higher social assistance dependency rate for that population and a negative economic effect for Canada as a whole.

The increased Indigenous population will have the greatest effect in the Western provinces. In Manitoba, Indigenous people are expected to account for 50 percent of the labour force growth and employment growth between 2006 and 2026 (Richards et al., 2010; Sharpe & Arsenault, 2010, p. 23). In Saskatchewan, the decrease in the non-Indigenous labour force (due to the aging population) between 2006 and 2026 means that Indigenous people are expected to account for more than 100 percent of all labour force and employment growth (Sharpe & Arsenault, 2010, p. 16). Clearly, investing in an educated and skilled Indigenous workforce is of paramount importance, in these two provinces and across the country.

Health

As with education and employment, Indigenous people suffer from a health gap; they are afflicted by certain illnesses more than the general population is, and overall life expectancy for Métis and status Indian populations is three years less than the general population's; the Inuit life expectancy is 10 years less for women and 14 years less for men. The causes of death differ by age category.

Delivery of Services

Before discussing Indigenous people's health issues, we need to discuss how health services are provided to Indigenous people. Health care is generally a provincial responsibility, but for status Indians living on reserve and for the Inuit in the North, it is a federal responsibility covered by Health Canada. For the rest of the Indigenous population—those living off reserve, whether status or non-status—health care is provided by the province. Federal funding for health services on reserves flows through the band. The federal funding formula for health care services and the itemized list of what is covered differ substantially from the provincial system.

Because hospitals and doctors bill the province for services, there has to be a way for the province to recoup from Health Canada the expenses it incurs for treating on-reserve status Indians. Different provinces have different policies concerning how this is done. Often, where the hospital or doctor prescribes or recommends a service that Health Canada does not ordinarily cover, Health Canada must pre-approve the expenditure. The levels of coverage differ between the provincial and federal systems; Health Canada does not fund all of the services the provinces do. As with education, there is a funding gap for the services provided to Indigenous people.

Because the provincial and federal systems are funded differently and have different operating budgets, disagreements sometimes arise over the financial obligations of service delivery. One such disagreement, central to events surrounding the death of five-year-old Jordan River Anderson in 2005, led to the passing of a private member's bill in the House of Commons known as Jordan's Principle. Jordan's story is about the inability of the federal and provincial governments to agree on who would cover the cost of his home care. While disagreements continued, Jordan remained in hospital, where he died while his family waited for a decision to be made. Jordan's story, and the tragic repercussions for his family, is the subject of Appendix 4.1.

The private member's bill, which passed in the House of Commons in 2007, proposed that, in the case of an on-reserve child who requires medical care, the level of government first contacted by the family, whether federal or provincial, should immediately pay to meet the child's medical needs, with the financial details to be worked out later.

Today formal agreements exist with each province on the administration of Jordan's Principle. These agreements and implementation protocols have not been without criticism. One complaint is that children's different identity categories influence whether Jordan's Principle is invoked. This may have the effect of creating disparities between different groups of Indigenous children in their access to health resources under Jordan's Principle. Furthermore, families have found navigating the formal case conferencing process lengthy and confusing (Blumenthal & Sinha, 2015). Figure 4.11 shows the process for New Brunswick's Jordan's Principle Agreement as summarized by the Assembly of First Nations.

In order to be covered for health benefits provided by Health Canada under the Non-Insured Health Benefits (NIHB) Program, an individual must be either a registered Indian according to the *Indian Act*, an Inuk recognized by an Inuit land agreement, or the infant of a qualified parent. As well, he or she must have no access to any other public or private health plan. In 2014, 808,686 people of Indigenous ancestry met these requirements (Health Canada, 2016). Although medical services are provided by all levels of government—municipal, provincial, and federal—the federal government, generally speaking, reimburses the other levels for services delivered to Indigenous people recognized under the NIHB program. All other people of Indigenous ancestry are covered under their respective provincial or private systems. The number of Indigenous clients served by Health Canada fluctuates depending on population and status, and will fluctuate into the future as the health services it provides go through the devolution process. For example, in 2014 responsibility for health services in British Columbia for Indigenous people was transferred to the First Nations Health Authority in that province (Health Canada, 2016; First Nations Health Authority, n.d.). Across the country, however, as a result of the creation of the Qalipu Mi'kmaq First Nation band and the *Gender Equity in Indian Registration Act*, an additional 51,267 registered Indians became eligible to receive benefits under the NIHB program. Of the clients served by Health Canada in 2014, 94.6 percent were First Nations people and 5.4 percent were Inuit (Health Canada, 2016).

On reserves, Health Canada also provides health promotion, nursing stations, transportation for health services, mental health and general health treatment, and many other services. Many First Nations and Inuit communities are taking more control over their own health services and programming; Health Canada is promoting the devolution—that is, the return—of administrative control over health care responsibilities to the respective communities.

FIGURE 4.11   Jordan's Principle: The 8 Steps to Get There

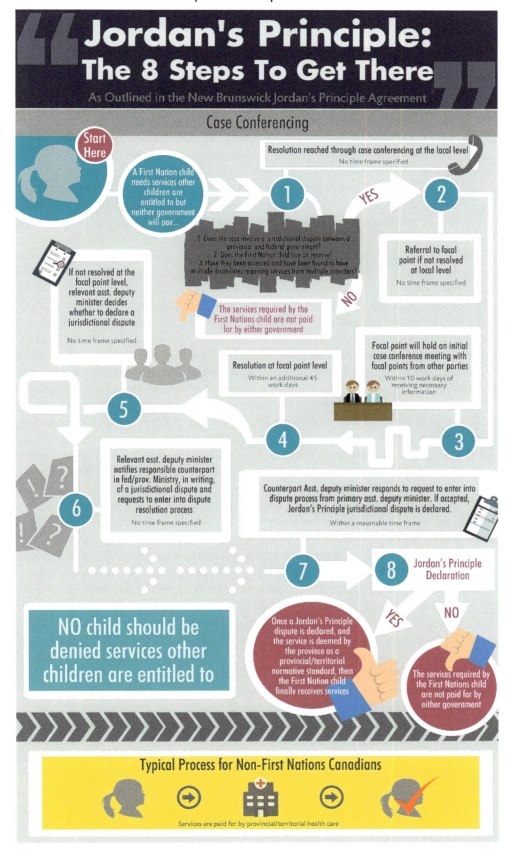

Physical Health

Currently, the major health concerns facing Indigenous people are diabetes, HIV/AIDS, heart disease, tuberculosis, mental health issues, and suicide. All of these problems are significantly more prevalent among the Indigenous population than among the general Canadian population.

Diabetes

The body of a person with diabetes, which is a chronic disease, either does not produce insulin (type 1 diabetes) or cannot properly use insulin (type 2 diabetes). Insulin is an essential hormone that regulates the amount of glucose in the blood. Those at greatest risk for developing type 2 diabetes are seniors, Indigenous people, baby boomers, and people who are prone to obesity, such as those who lead a sedentary lifestyle.

Indigenous people living on reserve have a prevalence rate of 17.2 percent of diabetes compared with 5 percent in the general public. The rate for the Indigenous population off reserve is lower at 10 percent but still double that of the general public. The prevalence rate for Métis is 7.3 percent. Indigenous people are generally diagnosed at a younger age, and the rate of gestational diabetes is also higher in Indigenous communities (Public Health Agency of Canada, 2011, "Report highlights").

In 2002, it was noted that rates of diabetes among the Inuit were lower than among the general population (Health Canada, 2002, p. 1). Since then, this statistic has changed dramatically. More recent research (Egeland, 2010, p. 17) has determined that Inuit are now diagnosed with diabetes at twice the rate of non-Indigenous Canadians. This same report indicates that 75 percent of Northern Labrador Inuit are overweight or obese—conditions linked to diabetes and other diseases. Forty percent of those surveyed who were over 40 had high blood pressure, compared with 20 percent of non-Indigenous Canadians in the same age category (Egeland, 2010, p. 17). It is interesting to note that food insecurity—that is, concern about the affordability or availability of food—was highest among the Inuit, with 13 percent of families reporting severe food insecurity and 34 percent reporting moderate food insecurity, compared with only 2.9 percent in the general population of Canada. Food insecurity among the Inuit is mostly a consequence of low incomes and the high cost of food in the regions where they live (Egeland, 2010, p. 20).

To address the diabetes epidemic, Health Canada implemented the Aboriginal Diabetes Initiative (ADI) in 1999. The ADI's primary purpose was to reduce the prevalence of type 2 diabetes by supporting health-promotion and disease-prevention activities and services, delivered by trained community diabetes workers and health service providers (Health Canada, 2011). The ADI comprised three phases. The first phase, from 1999 to 2004, focused on measuring the scope of the problem and developing strategies to increase awareness and health promotion to prevent diabetes; it received funding of $115 million. The second phase, from 2005 to 2010, included health promotion, primary prevention, screening and treatment, capacity building and training, and research surveillance evaluation and monitoring; it received funding of $190 million. The third and final phase, from 2011 to 2015, which received funding of $275 million, focused on initiatives for children and during pregnancy and pre-pregnancy, food security, and enhanced training for health practitioners. It included both on-reserve populations and off-reserve First Nations, Inuit, and Métis through partnerships with provinces. Now that all phases of the ADI are complete, Health Canada will assess its success over the next few years and provide statistics on its results.

It is now generally accepted that the increase in diabetes among Indigenous people is related to their rapid transition from traditional lifestyles of hunting and fishing to the more sedentary lifestyles and diet of the general population. The ADI partnered with tribal councils, First Nations organizations, Inuit community groups, and provincial and territorial governments to deliver a range of primary prevention, screening, and treatment programs for Indigenous people. The

ADI's aim was to implement strategies that were community-based and culturally appropriate. The programs that ADI promoted varied by community and included walking clubs, weight-loss groups, diabetes workshops, fitness classes, community kitchens, community gardens, and healthier food policies in schools. For example, vending machines that sell sugar-sweetened soft drinks and high-sugar, high-fat snacks were removed from many schools. The ADI also supported traditional activities such as drumming and dancing, canoeing, traditional food harvesting and preparation, and traditional games.

HIV/AIDS

As with many other health concerns, Indigenous people are overrepresented in the Canadian HIV/AIDS epidemic. They have

- a lower onset age for HIV/AIDS than other ethnicities do;
- a higher rate of new HIV infections than the general population has, and a high percentage of infections related to injection drug use; and
- much higher rates of infection among women than is the case in the general population.

It has been reported (Public Health Agency of Canada, 2010) that Indigenous people, who represented 3.8 percent of the Canadian population in the 2006 census, contracted 8.0 percent of all HIV infections in Canada—an estimated 4,300 to 6,100 cases. This represents a 24 percent increase over the 2005 numbers. With respect to new HIV infection rates, Indigenous people accounted for approximately 12.5 percent of new infections in 2008, an increase of 10.5 percent over the 2005 figure. In 2014, 10.8 percent of new HIV infections were in Indigenous people, bringing the number of Indigenous people living with HIV to 6,850—9.1 percent of all HIV cases in Canada in 2014. Due to the increase in Indigenous population, to 4.3 percent of the population total, Indigenous people's risk of contracting HIV in 2014 dropped; it is now only 2.7 times higher than that of the non-Indigenous Canadian population (Public Health Agency of Canada, 2015).

Figure 4.12 tracks the proportion of reported cases of HIV by race and ethnicity. Figure 4.13 shows the proportion of reported HIV cases among Indigenous subgroups (Public Health Agency of Canada, 2015).

Injection drug use (IDU) represents a significant exposure category for the HIV epidemic in Canada. "Exposure category" refers to the way in which individuals who test positive for HIV have acquired the virus—for example, through sexual activity or through injecting drugs. Statistics concerning exposure categories reveal that the HIV epidemic in Canada is complex in its sources, with different ethnicities acquiring the virus via different modes of transmission. For Indigenous people, IDU is a particularly important risk factor for HIV/AIDS. In 2014, the proportion of new HIV infections among those who inject drugs in the Indigenous population was 50.6 percent, while the rate among the non-Indigenous IDU population was 49.4 percent (Public Health Agency of Canada, 2014). IDU accounted for more HIV infections and cases of AIDS among Indigenous women than it did among Indigenous men—from 1979 to 2008, approximately double the number (Public Health Agency of Canada, 2010). This breakdown of statistics between men and women, however, was not repeated in the 2014 study.

The incidence of HIV/AIDS among young Indigenous people was a growing concern; positive HIV test reports and reported AIDS diagnoses were, in general, seen in the Indigenous population at younger ages than was the case with the general population. From 1998 to the end of 2008, nearly a third of the positive HIV test results among Indigenous people were for individuals aged 15–29 (32.6 percent of people diagnosed). Among other ethnicities, the rate was 20.5 percent (Public Health Agency of Canada, 2010). Age categories were not broken down by ethnicity in the 2014 study and therefore no comparison is possible.

FIGURE 4.12   Reported Cases of HIV, by Race and Ethnicity, by Year, Canada, 2009 to 2014

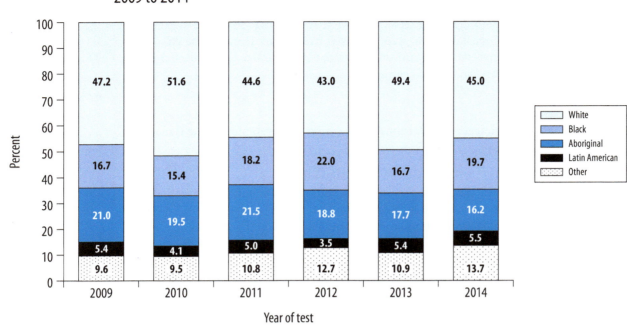

SOURCE: Public Health Agency of Canada (2015).

FIGURE 4.13   Proportion of Reported Cases of HIV/AIDS Among Aboriginal Subgroups, 2009 to 2014

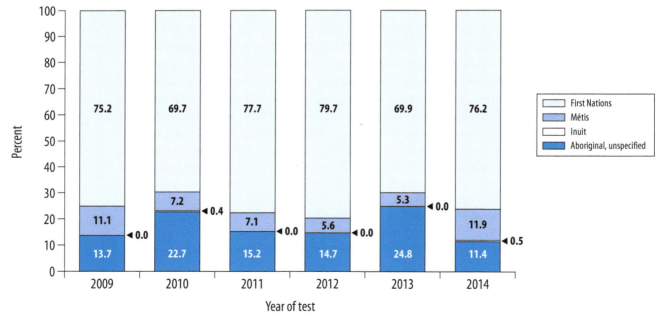

SOURCE: Public Health Agency of Canada (2015).

CLOSE-UP   Dr. Stanley Vollant

Dr. Stanley Vollant is a surgeon and First Nations coordinator in the Faculty of Medicine of the University of Montreal. Vollant is Innu, from Pessamit, Quebec. In 2010 he began a 6,000-kilometre series of treks on foot and by canoe through the Indigenous communities in Eastern Canada from Labrador to James Bay. The journey, called Innu Meshkenu (Innu Road), is meant to encourage young Indigenous people to excel and to stay in school, and to encourage healthy lifestyles and physical activity. Vollant experienced both poverty and racism as a child but had a passion for healing that he says comes from his grandparents, who raised him in the woods of Innu territory. He believes that obesity, diabetes, and school dropout rates are the most serious threats to Indigenous people in Canada. Vollant appeared in Ottawa in 2014 in support of an inquiry into missing and murdered Indigenous women in Canada.

Females are disproportionately represented in the HIV/AIDS epidemic among Indigenous people. Between 2009 and 2014, the percentage of females among the reported cases of Indigenous people with AIDS was 35.6 percent; in the non-Indigenous population for this same period, the percentage of women was 24.2 percent. In every year between 2001 and 2008, females have represented over 30 percent of reported AIDS cases among Indigenous people (Public Health Agency of Canada, 2015).

Tuberculosis

Tuberculosis (TB) is an infectious disease that affects the lungs. It is contagious, since it spreads through the air as a result of coughing and sneezing. TB is treatable through rounds of antibiotics and is most effectively treated when caught early. In Canada, TB has made a resurgence as a disease associated with poverty, easily spread in close living quarters and through neglect of treatment. The rates of TB infection for First Nations people were 8–10 times higher than for the non-Indigenous population (Health Canada, 2006). It was most prevalent among individuals aged 15 to 44. The rates of infection varied by community, but the highest rates were in British Columbia, Saskatchewan, Manitoba, Alberta, and northwestern Ontario. In 2013, Indigenous people made up 19 percent of all TB cases in Canada; they represented more than 65 percent of all cases in Manitoba and Saskatchewan, and 98 percent of all cases in the Northwest Territories, Nunavut, and Yukon. The rates broken down into Indigenous identity per 100,000 population are 3.3 for Métis, 21.8 for First Nations, and a shocking 154.2 for Inuit. The rate for the non-Indigenous Canadian-born population is 4.7 per 100,000. Risk factors associated with the contraction of TB include HIV and diabetes, as well as substance abuse, poor nutrition, and other factors that may weaken the immune system.

Overcrowded living conditions increase the rate of person-to-person transmission of TB. Living density among the general population of Canada is 0.4 persons per room (Health Canada, 2006). For First Nations people who live on reserve, the living density is, on average, 0.7 persons per room (Health Canada, 2006), but in many on-reserve communities the number is much higher. The First Nations communities that between 1996 and 2000 had the highest incidence of TB also had the highest living densities. TB is also more common in remote reserves, probably because these communities have restricted access to health professionals who can diagnose the disease early and restrict its spread.

Tuberculosis was an even more pressing issue for the Inuit, whose infection rate was 32 times the national average in 2008 (Zarate, 2010). This statistic is related to severe overcrowding in Inuit communities due to housing shortages.

Mental Health: Depression and Suicide

To be understood fully, Indigenous people's mental health issues must be considered in the light of the collective trauma through colonization that is part of their history, as well as the history of dispossession and oppression and the current state of struggle against poverty and the weakened social fabric of their communities. Indigenous populations in Canada face unique challenges in the area of mental health. Studies show that First Nations people experience depression at twice the rate of the average Canadian and that they more frequently report that the depression interferes with the activities of daily life (Kahn, 2008, pp. 6–7). The levels of reported depression among the Inuit are very low, but their suicide rate is very high. Indigenous people seek professional help in the form of treatment or counselling at twice the rate of the general Canadian population.

First Nations and Inuit communities experience higher rates of suicide, overall, than other communities in Canada do (see Figure 4.14). The rate varies from community to community, with some First Nations communities reporting no suicides or suicide attempts for years at a time, while others have annual suicide rates that are 11 times the national average. Suicide rates are highest for young Indigenous people aged 15–24; the rates for this age group are five to seven times what they are for people of this age group in the general population. Because of the relative youth of suicide victims in the Indigenous community, suicide accounts for the greatest number of potential years of life lost in Indigenous populations in Canada. As with the non-Indigenous population, rates of completed suicide are higher among Indigenous males than among Indigenous females (Kahn, 2008, p. 7).

Research (Statistics Canada, 2012) indicates that 24 percent of First Nations living off-reserve, 23.5 percent of Inuit, and 19.6 percent of Métis reported having suicidal thoughts. Thirty-nine percent of girls aged 12–17 and 17 percent of boys in the same age bracket have considered suicide. Young people with a close family member who had committed suicide in the last 12 months were more than twice as likely to report having had suicidal thoughts. A 2004 health survey (Anctil, 2008, p. 5) suggested that 20 percent of Inuit respondents had made a suicide attempt in their lifetime and that almost 7 percent had done so in the previous year. Having a parent who had attended a residential school increased the odds from 18 percent to 26 percent that a youth would have thoughts about suicide (Public Health Agency of Canada, 2006, p. 166).

FIGURE 4.14   Suicide Rates for First Nations, Inuit, and the General Population

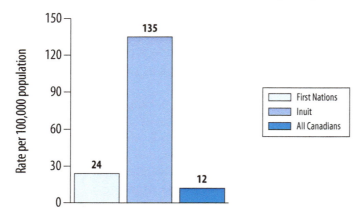

SOURCE: Public Health Agency of Canada (2006, p. 167).

Studies have identified suicide risk factors and protective factors at both the individual and the community levels (see Table 4.4). Anything that contributes to the risk of suicide is called a risk factor; any process that reduces the risk is referred to as a protective factor. Examining individual First Nations or Inuit communities with a view to these factors helps us to understand their suicide rates. Not all Indigenous communities experience high levels of suicide; some experience very few suicides or none at all. These healthy communities often have high protective factors, such as a strong sense of community and deep cultural connection. A study of bands in British Columbia found that those with a higher level of Indigenous language knowledge had fewer suicides. These features of a community are referred to as cultural continuity (Centre for Suicide Prevention, 2013, p. 5).

In January 2015, Health Canada introduced the First Nations Mental Wellness Continuum Framework (Figure 4.15). This was developed in partnership with Health Canada's First Nations and Inuit Health Branch, the Assembly of First Nations, and Indigenous mental health leaders. The centre of the model is the core of hope, belonging, meaning, and purpose, surrounded by a ring representing kinship, clan, elders, and community. The model is built and layered with elements foundational to supporting First Nations mental wellness. It recognizes cultural values such as sacred knowledge, language, and spiritual practices as foundations of strength and resilience. There are five key themes:

1. culture as foundation;
2. community development, ownership, and capacity building;
3. quality care systems and competent service delivery;
4. collaboration with partners; and
5. enhanced flexible funding.

TABLE 4.4   Suicide: Risk Factors and Protective Factors at the Community and Individual Levels

Community/social risk factors	Individual risk factors
• Historical trauma and loss	• Mood or other psychiatric disorder, including depression
• Lack of meaningful activity or work available in the community	• History of abuse (physical or sexual)
• Interpersonal conflict and crisis within the community	• Family history of suicide
• Suicide common in community (clusters)	• Hopelessness and pessimism
• Use/abuse of alcohol and other substances prevalent in the community	• Poor coping skills
• Community social isolation	• Impulsivity
• Poverty	• Influence of alcohol or other substances
• Lack of community control over social services and finances	• Access to lethal means

Protective factors
- Perception of family connectedness
- Intergenerational connectedness throughout the community
- Emotional well-being
- School/community involvement
- Academic success or meaningful work
- Spiritual connection and cultural continuity

SOURCE: Kirmayer, Fraser, Fauras, & Whitley (2010).

FIGURE 4.15   First Nations Mental Wellness Continuum Framework

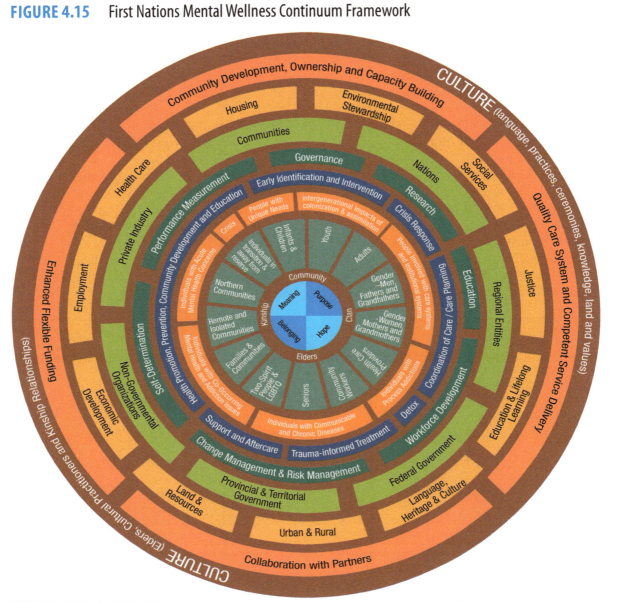

SOURCE: Health Canada (2014, p. 3).

The summary report recognizes the need for a full spectrum of culturally competent supports and services to support mental wellness, including health promotion, illness prevention, community development, and education as well as early identification and intervention, crisis response, and coordination of care and care planning. It recognizes the need for detox centres and for treatment that is informed by the trauma common in Indigenous communities and culturally appropriate, as well as the need for support and aftercare. It is hoped that the framework can help reduce suicides as well as substance abuse and addiction (Health Canada, 2014).

Substance Abuse and Addiction

The rate of alcohol-related deaths in the Indigenous population is twice that in the non-Indigenous population, and death due to illicit drugs is three times the rate in Indigenous populations. In a survey, one in five Indigenous youths reported having used solvents. Of those, one in three were under the age of 15. The rate of incarceration for Indigenous youth is eight times that of non-Indigenous youth in Canada. Of those incarcerated youth, eight in ten have a substance abuse problem (Chansonneuve, 2007, p. 25).

According to a survey conducted by Health Canada in 2003, 73 percent of First Nations and Inuit people consider alcohol a problem in their community, and 59 percent also report drug abuse as a problem (Kahn, 2008). Thirty-three percent indicate alcohol is a problem in their own family and 25 percent indicate that they have a personal problem with alcohol (Kahn, 2008). This is interesting, because fewer First Nations and Inuit people actually drink alcohol than do people in the general population: 66 percent of those living on reserve report consuming alcohol, compared with 76 percent of the general population. What is clear is that many of those First Nations and Inuit who do consume alcohol do so in quantities that present problems for themselves and their communities (Kahn, 2008).

Health Canada has funded the National Native Alcohol and Drug Abuse Program since the 1970s. In recent years, Indigenous people themselves have taken control of much of this program. There are 52 residential treatment centres across the country, equipped to treat Indigenous people in culturally appropriate programs. This program also focuses on prevention, intervention, and aftercare.

Once again, it is important to remember that all Indigenous communities are different. Some have few problems with alcohol and substance abuse, while others have severe problems. Communities that are in crisis need to be given culturally appropriate assistance and treatments. The First Nations Mental Wellness Continuum Framework will inform the delivery of assistance and treatment into the future.

Housing and Infrastructure Conditions

The 2006 census demonstrated that 25 percent of First Nations people on reserve were living in overcrowded conditions and 44 percent of the houses were in major need of repairs. The extent of the housing shortage differs, but all parties agree that it exists. The Assembly of First Nations reports the shortage as approximately 85,000 units across the country, while Aboriginal Affairs and Northern Development Canada estimates the shortage at only 35,000 to 40,000 units (Standing Senate Committee on Aboriginal Peoples, 2015, p. 6). The housing shortage leads to overcrowding and the use of inadequate shelter (such as people living in condemned units), which in turn leads to health problems. The type of housing can also interfere with cultural activities of the population, particularly if the population maintains traditional lifestyles such as hunting and preparing meat and hides. Housing that is considered appropriate for southern communities, city dwellers, or nuclear families may not provide the best opportunity for Indigenous peoples to maintain cultural continuity.

The housing shortage is difficult to address since the infrastructure must be in place to support the building of homes. Sewage systems, roads, and utilities must be available to develop serviceable lots on which to place new homes. There are major deficits in these areas on reserves, some of which have been under boil-water advisories for years because of inadequate water treatment or well systems.

As to the adequacy of the housing, the report of the Standing Senate Committee on Aboriginal Peoples (2015, p. 19) indicates that 37 percent of the 108,000 units on reserve need major repairs and 34 percent need minor repairs. Mould has been a significant problem in on-reserve housing. Many of the structures were poorly built out of materials inappropriate for the climate or environment.

In 2004 the government of Nunavut presented a 10-year action plan to address the housing crisis in its communities. The plan called for the immediate construction of 3,000 housing units and renovation of 1,000 existing units. It proposed an additional 2,730 new units by 2016 to address the projected population growth. It is unknown how many housing units have been built through this plan, since the program is completed but is yet to be reviewed. In 2010, however, the Nunavut Housing Needs Survey reported that 1,220 people in Nunavut were homeless (Nunavut Housing Corporation, 2010). The Conference Board of Canada in its 2011 map *Sleeping on the Couch* showed that Nunavut had the highest overcrowding rates in Canada. In March 2010, it was reported that 49 percent of people in Nunavik were living in overcrowded conditions (CBC News, 2010). The problem is made worse by the short lifespan of government housing, which is built to last only 15 years, in a region where weather conditions are extremely hard on the existing structures. Building costs are high due to the difficulty of transporting construction materials to areas accessible by road only at certain times in the year or not at all. In 2015, CBC News reported that 2,313 households in 25 communities in Nunavut were on social housing waiting lists, although the need is estimated as closer to 3,000 (Van Dusen, 2015).

Landownership in First Nations communities differs from the rest of Canada in important ways that complicate financial access to capital. Under the *Indian Act*, the lands of Indigenous people are held by the Crown. Section 89 of the Act restricts the use of Indian land as collateral against financing loans through traditional sources. As a result, many financial institutions are reluctant to grant traditional mortgages or loans to fund infrastructure on reserve territory. The Act also prohibits transfer of lands to any entity other than the band or another band member, which in effect limits any traditional for-profit housing on reserve.

The federal government's Ministerial Loan Guarantee (MLG) program backs loans up to a stated dollar limit for construction of on-reserve housing. Indigenous people taking advantage of these types of loans must demonstrate enough income to repay the loans. The diverse economic conditions on reserves means that home ownership is common in areas where unemployment rates are low and economic development provides sufficient income, but on remote reserves, where unemployment can be as high as 85 percent, home ownership and loan repayment are simply not feasible. The Canada Mortgage and Housing Corporation (CMHC) funds housing programs to provide social housing on reserve for those who require housing and cannot own their home; many of these people rent housing from the band through shelter allowances in their social assistance incomes. This funding also has limits set by the federal government.

In 2008, the federal government began the $300 million First Nations Market Housing Fund to promote private ownership of market housing on reserve. The fund secures mortgages for Indigenous people living on reserve to purchase or construct homes. CMHC is a financial partner in the fund with other lending institutions. One hundred First Nations communities have qualified for the program by demonstrating fiscal responsibility. The fund's goal was to help build 25,000 privately owned homes by 2018. As of May 2015, only 99 had been built. On-reserve housing has long been seen as a treaty responsibility of the federal government, and the new concept of market-based privately owned housing has not been immediately embraced by First Nations communities. The fund-backed mortgages still require a credit history from applicants and a demonstrated steady income, which many band members lack. Furthermore, in many remote communities there is no market history of housing prices and therefore no guarantee of a return on investment for a band member to personally finance the construction of a new home.

The Standing Senate Committee on Aboriginal Peoples began an investigation into the state of on-reserve First Nations housing in Canada in 2013. It released its report in February 2015. The introduction states:

> There was unanimous agreement among witnesses, including departmental officials, that there is a significant housing shortage in First Nation communities, and that the existing stock of housing in many communities is in deplorable condition. It is not an exaggeration to suggest that, in many First Nation communities, the housing situation is in a state of crisis. (Standing Senate Committee on Aboriginal Peoples, 2015, p. 3)

This report made a number of recommendations to address the housing and infrastructure problem on reserves. Here are just a few:

1. Indigenous and Northern Affairs should remove the 2 percent cap on annual increases in all department funding beginning in the 2016–17 budget.
2. CMHC should allocate sufficient funds to the On-Reserve Non-Profit Housing program to address the shortage of on-reserve housing and allow multi-year funding so that there is adequate time to organize construction and plan ahead.
3. The annual Band Support Program at Indigenous and Northern Affairs should fund the hiring of a qualified housing manager if a band finds it necessary.
4. Indigenous and Northern Affairs in consultation with First Nations should explore the implementation and enforcement of building codes.
5. Indigenous and Northern Affairs should assess whether the shelter allowance component of the Income Assistance Program is adequate to cover shelter costs, including rent and heating, and ensure consistency in funding across regions.
6. Indigenous and Northern Affairs and CMHC should collaborate to develop a housing strategy for remote and isolated communities that reflects the challenges and costs of building in remote areas.

The housing crisis in on-reserve housing has been decades in the making; it will not be resolved inexpensively or overnight. With community consultation, new plans are being developed that are consistent with the diversity in geography and social capacity across communities.

Social Assistance and Economic Renewal

Social Assistance

Income assistance is common for First Nations people, particularly those living on reserve, where there are few economic opportunities. It provides income for families to meet their basic needs such as housing and food and clothing if they cannot provide these for themselves through employment. According to Indigenous and Northern Affairs, in the 2012–13 fiscal year the government invested approximately $861 million in income assistance payments to 86,798 clients and their families living on reserve. In some communities the income assistance dependency rate is more than 80 percent. Across all communities the rate was 33.6 percent, compared with a little over 5 percent for the rest of the Canadian population (Indigenous and Northern Affairs Canada, 2012). Indigenous and Northern Affairs is currently working with 130 First Nations communities to fund projects aimed at reforming income assistance. As of January 2015, youth from 88 First Nations across the country were participating in skills training and job readiness programs to increase their employability (Indigenous and Northern Affairs Canada, 2015b).

Once again, it is important to realize that every Indigenous community is unique. Needs for income assistance vary tremendously between communities. For example, Indian and Northern Affairs Canada data for the Far North, including Yukon, Northwest Territories, and Nunavut, show that only about 50 percent of the Indigenous population had employment in 2001 compared with up to 90 percent of non-Indigenous people in the same regions (Indian and Northern Affairs Canada, 2005, p. 92, figure 7.5). In this case, the need for income assistance and government services is very high. In other areas of the country, such as southern Ontario, Indigenous people have had relative success in education and in the labour market, and this reduces the need for assistance.

Ultimately, economic development on reserves is one of the best methods of addressing the social ills that exist there. However, there are barriers to such development.

Land and Resource Management

Under legislation such as the *Indian Act*, the *Indian Oil and Gas Act*, and the *First Nations Land Management Act*, federal organizations still have considerable responsibility and control over First Nations' economic development, particularly when it comes to reserved land. There is no single land management regime that applies to all reserves in Canada. Each First Nations territory is governed by one of three types of land management: the *Indian Act* land management framework, the First Nations Land Management (FNLM) Regime, or a self-government arrangement as a stand-alone agreement or as part of a modern treaty. Of the 617 recognized First Nations bands, 550 adhere to the original *Indian Act* framework, which many find cumbersome, complicated, uncertain, and slow. This system does not inspire confidence in outside investors. The FNLM Regime gives bands greater control over their lands and resources. First Nations under this framework can pass laws for development and protection of lands, and issue licences and leases with community approval; ministerial involvement and approval are reduced. As of March 2014, 77 First Nations bands had joined the FNLM Regime and 48 were on a waiting list; of the 77, 36 had enacted land codes and 30 were preparing codes (Standing Committee on Aboriginal Affairs and Northern Development, 2014, p. 9). First Nations with stand-alone self-government agreements under modern, constitutionally protected treaties enjoy extensive land management and law-making authority, further reducing ministerial approval processes. There were 18 such agreements as of March 2014 (Standing Committee on Aboriginal Affairs and Northern Development, 2014, p. 8).

Under the *Indian Act*, by which most bands currently operate, there are different land tenure arrangements. Customary land holdings are the most common, in which individuals or families acquire tracts of land allotted by the band council. That individual or family can build a home or a farm or start a business on that land. The land cannot be sold in any formally documented manner since it belongs to the band. Land can also be held under a certificate of possession, which closely resembles **fee simple ownership**. These certificates are issued under the authority of the minister of Indigenous and Northern Affairs after the band council grants its permission. Such land can be leased to third parties, including non-band members, but land ownership is retained by the band. Finally, there are leasehold interests that can be leased to third parties for development purposes. These leases are completed by the minister as well, and income is managed by the minister on behalf of the band.

fee simple ownership
the right to exclusive use, possession, and disposal of a piece of land

First Nations are currently seeking to develop modern professionally managed land management systems that will allow their communities to tap into outside investments as well as develop the land's resources. Because of the complexity of the *Indian Act* land management framework, and to a lesser extent the FNLM Regime, simple on-reserve transactions can take up to five times longer than for off-reserve lands, which discourages outside investors. The procedure for leasing lands to outside third parties takes two to three years to pass through all the levels of approval. Investors are not usually prepared to wait so long, and First Nations are losing out on economic opportunities.

First Nations communities report difficulty in meeting the criteria of the federal government's business-development programs and thus obtaining program funding. These communities see access to natural resources as an important part of economic development, but they are having difficulty gaining that access. Many resources are on lands that are currently under claim and are therefore inaccessible until a resolution is reached.

First Nations people have difficulty accessing capital to invest in economic development. Many do not have large investment funds, and, owing to the nature of communal ownership and to the *Indian Act*, they cannot use reserved land to secure loans for capital ventures. In the past, banks and other capital lending institutions have been reluctant to learn about and accommodate their policies to First Nations organizations, which have unique legal status. First Nations people have found that their funding proposals are often rejected by federal officials, who view these proposals as high-risk. First Nations people have pointed out that approval for the funding of prospective Indigenous businesses moves more slowly than that for non-Indigenous businesses. At times, gaining funding approval can take years.

The *Indian Act* processes can be cumbersome, and the processes required by resource management are complex. For example, royalty payments from resource development on reserved lands are not paid to the band; they go to Indigenous and Northern Affairs, to be held in trust accounts. To access the money, the band must apply to the minister and detail how the money will be spent. This requirement, intended to ensure that the Crown meets its fiduciary duty to First Nations, is a complex system that can cause delays in accessing capital. To bypass the red tape involved in accessing government economic development programs, some First Nations seek partnerships with non-Indigenous business communities.

One of the greatest obstacles to the economic development of Indigenous society is the lack of land. Indigenous people are trying to boost their economies; however, in a country whose economy is based on natural resources, it is difficult for First Nations people to enter that economy when, until 2004, they had less than half of 1 percent of Canada's land mass. As a result of treaty entitlement and specific and comprehensive land claims, particularly in British Columbia and undeveloped northern regions, First Nations–held land mass has increased to 3.8 million hectares and is expected to increase by another 1.1 million hectares over the next decade. This will triple the 2004 level of First Nations landholdings. It is crucial that First Nations develop sustainable land management strategies consistent with their own values and traditions to make the most of the land and resources to boost their economies and provide hope for the future.

Access to Natural Resources

Resources that had supported First Nations people for thousands of years are now in the control and possession of private industry and governments that are not willing to allow First Nations to share in them; recall the Mi'kmaq lobster fishing dispute discussed in Chapter 2. Forestry and timber harvesting rights are another particular area of contention. First Nations have privileges for logging on only 3 percent of Crown land, with the remainder leased by the Crown to private industry. In 2005, a decision by the Supreme Court of Canada denied Indigenous people in Eastern Canada the right to access Crown land for logging to increase their presence in the logging industry (*R v. Marshall*; *R v. Bernard*, 2005). The Supreme Court ruled that logging for profit was not part of the pre-contact Indigenous economy and that therefore the Indigenous people concerned had no right to access the industry. In 2014, however, the Supreme Court of Canada unanimously ruled that the Tsilhqot'in Nation in BC had rights over ancestral lands outside of their reserve, including the right to use them for modern economic purposes, such as forestry, without destroying them for future generations (*Tsilhqot'in Nation v. British Columbia*, 2014). The right to access natural resources is conditional on establishing Indigenous title over the land, so as claims move forward, the landscape of Indigenous access to industry in natural resources may change.

Separating Indigenous people from their land and its resources has demoralized them and entrenched them in Canada's economy as wage labourers for the dominant culture and for Canada's private business interests. Major changes have recently occurred that will alter the trajectory of First Nations economies and their futures. Access to land and resources is the primary focus of Chapter 2.

EXERCISE 3

Casinos are one common opportunity for economic development on reserves. What do you think the potential benefits and possible pitfalls are of building casinos on reserves?

Language

In the 2011 census, over 60 different Indigenous languages grouped into 12 distinct language families were recorded as being spoken by First Nations people in Canada. Many of the 60 languages, those that are spoken by fewer than 500 people, are considered endangered for long-term survival. In 2011, according to the National Household Survey, only 17.2 percent of people who reported an Indigenous identity could conduct a conversation in an Indigenous language; this is a decrease from 21 percent in the 2006 census. The proportion of people who could speak an Indigenous language was highest among the Inuit, at 67 percent. The proportion among First Nations was 22.4 percent (5.6 percent lower than in the 2006 census) and 2.5 percent among the Métis. Many Indigenous people who speak an Indigenous language have learned it as a second language, since they did not report it as their mother tongue on the survey. However, of those who did report an Indigenous language as their mother tongue, 6.9 percent could no longer conduct a conversation in that language.

These figures represent a significant decrease overall since the 1940s. In 1941, English was the first language of less than 10 percent of Indigenous people; in 1971, it was the first language of approximately 54 percent; in 1991, of 60.4 percent.

According to the 2011 census, the ten most-reported languages account for almost 90 percent of the population who can speak an Indigenous language. Also, the number of people who speak an Indigenous language at home varies depending on where they live, with most Indigenous language speakers residing on reserve or in other areas with high proportions of Indigenous people.

A 2007 study shows that the continuation or retention of language is a factor in the well-being of individuals and communities (Hallett, Chandler, & Lalonde, 2007). This study tracked youth suicide rates in Indigenous communities in British Columbia, and found that bands in which a majority of members could converse in an Indigenous language experienced few youth

FIGURE 4.16   Proportion of the Population Whose Mother Tongue Is One of the Ten Most Reported Aboriginal Languages Who Speak Their Language Most Often or on a Regular Basis, Canada, 2011

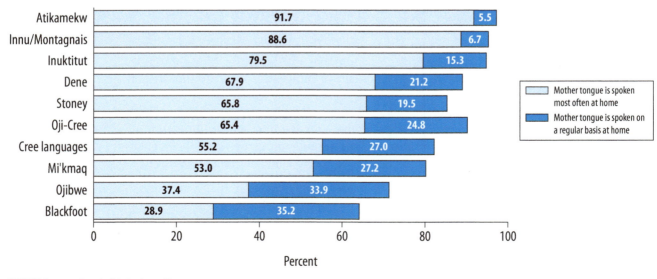

SOURCE: Statistics Canada (2015a, figure 3).

suicides. Youth suicide rates were *six times greater* for bands in which fewer than half of the members could converse in an Indigenous language. In sum, the study shows that "indigenous language use, as a marker of cultural persistence, is a strong predictor of health and wellbeing in Canada's Aboriginal communities" (Hallett et al., 2007, p. 398).

It is for these reasons that Heritage Canada has initiated the Aboriginal Languages Initiative to provide funds for programs that work for the preservation and revitalization of Indigenous languages for the benefit of Indigenous peoples and all Canadians.

Aboriginal Languages Initiative

One of the many programs financed by Heritage Canada's Aboriginal Languages Initiative is the Pre-School Language Nest Program in British Columbia. This program provides cultural immersion environments for pre-school children and their parents with the goal of creating new fluent speakers in their respective traditional languages. Indigenous communities across Canada can apply to the Aboriginal Languages Initiative for funding as they create their own language initiatives.

EXERCISE 4

In *Surviving as Indians*, Professor Menno Boldt (1993, p. i) defines *justice* in terms of "the survival and well-being of Indians as *Indians*, that is, defined by their traditional principles and philosophies." Boldt highlights the following five imperatives:

1. Moral justice for Indians.
2. Canadian policies that treat the needs, aspirations, interests, and rights of Indians as equal to those of Canadians.
3. Indian leadership committed to returning Indian government to the people.
4. The revitalization of Indian cultures, languages, and social systems within a framework of traditional philosophies and principles.
5. Economic self-sufficiency and independence through employment in the Canadian labour force.

Based on what you have read in this chapter, how does the reality of Indigenous people in Canada correspond to Boldt's imperatives? Do you see positive developments in certain areas? Where does Canada currently stand in relation to Boldt's definition of "justice"?

CHAPTER SUMMARY

In the case study that opened the chapter, we saw how the Grassy Narrows First Nations community lost control over its traditional territory. Its treaty with the federal government, the influence of nearby industry, and its relocation all contributed to serious and persistent socio-economic problems. But through activism and new agreements with government, the community has regained some control over its circumstances.

Counting the Indigenous populations in Canada and determining their needs are complicated by different categories of Indigenous ancestry and various survey methods used by government agencies. Legal changes in 1985 and 2009 allowed many Indigenous people who had lost or been denied registered Indian status to regain or acquire it. In 2016, the *Daniels* ruling extended the rights of status Indians to non-status Indians and Métis; it remains to be seen how this ruling will be put into practice.

While it is difficult to generalize about diverse Indigenous populations, it can be said that on the whole, they are younger than the non-Indigenous Canadian population and are becoming increasingly urban; both of these trends present socio-economic challenges.

Education is the chief means by which Indigenous people can improve their economic prospects. The fact that the federal government's funding of First Nations education has lagged behind that of the provincial education systems has led to a generally lower quality of education for First Nations children. Various federal programs and initiatives are attempting to improve the standards of First Nations schooling.

Statistics on the health of Indigenous people are cause for concern, since they show that several serious diseases disproportionately afflict Indigenous populations, as do mental health issues, addictions, and suicide. Again, the fact that the federal government funds and manages health care for many status Indians and Inuit leads to a different level of care from that available in the provincial health care systems, and sometimes to disputes about which level of government is responsible for care, as in the case of Jordan Anderson in 2005.

Housing on First Nations reserves and in Inuit communities is often substandard or in short supply, which contributes to health and social problems. Related infrastructure such as the water supply is often deficient as well. Land management on First Nations reserves, long under the control of the federal government, is being reformed so that the communities can benefit from the value of the land and its resources.

Language is key to culture and a sense of belonging. The Indigenous heritage of Canada includes over 60 languages, many of which are little spoken today and in danger of being lost forever. Various programs are encouraging Indigenous communities to learn, speak, and teach the languages of their people.

REFERENCES

Aboriginal Affairs and Northern Development Canada. (2010). How do the new legislative changes to the *Indian Act* affect me? http://www.aadnc-aandc.gc.ca/eng/1100100032501.

Anctil, M. (2008). Survey highlights. *Nunavik Inuit health survey 2004: Qanuippitaa? How are we?* Quebec: Institut national de santé publique du Québec (INSPQ) and Nunavik Regional Board of Health and Social Services (NRBHSS). http://www.inspq.qc.ca/pdf/publications/774_ESISurveyHighlights.pdf.

Assembly of First Nations. (2005, June 28). Bill C-31 twenty years later: AFN national chief calls for First Nations control of First Nations citizenship [Press release]. http://www.turtleisland.org/news/news-c31.htm.

Assembly of First Nations. (2012). Chiefs Assembly on Education: Information package—Federal funding for First Nations schools. http://www.treatysix.org/pdf/AFN Education Assembly Information Package_ENG.pdf.

Assembly of First Nations. (2015, February 10). Jordan's principle. http://www.afn.ca/en/jordans-principle-feb10.

Aulakh, R. (2014, March 25). Grassy Narrows First Nation greets Ontario lumber firm's decision. *The Toronto Star*. http://www.thestar.com.

Bains, R. (2014). *Myths and realities of First Nations education*. Centre for Aboriginal Policy Studies. Vancouver: Fraser Institute. https://www.fraserinstitute.org/sites/default/files/myths-and-realities-of-first-nations-education.pdf.

Blackstock, C. (2009). Jordan's story: How one boy inspired a world of change. *Canadian supplement to The state of the world's children 2009: Aboriginal children's health: Leaving no child behind*. Toronto: UNICEF Canada.

Blumenthal, A., & Sinha, V. (2015). No Jordan's Principle cases in Canada? A review of the administrative response to Jordan's Principle. *The International Indigenous Policy Journal, 6*(1), art. 6. http://ir.lib.uwo.ca/cgi/viewcontent.cgi?article=1206&context=iipj.

Boldt, M. (1993). *Surviving as Indians: The challenge of self-government*. Toronto: University of Toronto Press.

Bougie, E., Kelly-Scott, K., & Arriagada, P. (2015). *The education and employment experiences of First Nations people living off reserve, Inuit, and Métis: Selected findings from the 2012 Aboriginal Peoples Survey*. Statistics Canada catalogue no. 89-653-X. http://www.statcan.gc.ca/pub/89-653-x/89-653-x2013001-eng.htm.

Canadian Charter of Rights and Freedoms. (1982). Part I of the *Constitution Act, 1982*, being Schedule B to the *Canada Act 1982* (UK), 1982, c. 11.

CBC News. (2010, March 18). Nunavik housing shortage a "crisis": Inuit. *CBC News*. http://www.cbc.ca/news.

CBC News. (2013, November 1). Nunavut hamlet overcrowding nears breaking point. *CBC News*. http://www.cbc.ca.

Centre for Suicide Prevention. (2013). *Suicide prevention resource toolkit*. https://suicideinfo.ca/LinkClick.aspx?fileticket=MVIyGo2V4YY%3D&tabid=563.

Chansonneuve, D. (2007). *Addictive behaviours among Aboriginal people in Canada*. Ottawa: Aboriginal Healing Foundation. http://www.ahf.ca/downloads/addictive-behaviours.pdf.

Conference Board of Canada. (2011). *Sleeping on the couch* [Map]. Centre for the North Research Centre. Ottawa: Author.

Constitution Act, 1982. (1982). Being Schedule B to the *Canada Act 1982* (UK), 1982, c. 11.

Daniels v. Canada. (2013). 2013 FC 6, aff'd. 2016 SCC 12.

Egeland, G. (2010). *Inuit health survey 2007–2008: Inuvialuit settlement region*. Ste-Anne-de-Bellevue, QC: Centre for Indigenous Peoples' Nutrition and Environment, McGill University.

Employment and Social Development Canada. (2013, Fall). *Aboriginal Labour Market Bulletin*. http://www.esdc.gc.ca/eng/jobs/aboriginal/bulletins/fall2013.shtml#h2.4-h3.2.

First Nations Health Authority. (n.d.). About us. http://www.fnha.ca/about.

First Nations Land Management Act. (1999). SC 1999, c. 24.

Frideres, J.S., & Gadacz, R.R. (2008). *Aboriginal peoples in Canada: Contemporary conflicts* (8th ed.). Toronto: Pearson.

Geddes, C., Doxtater, M., & Krepakevich, M. (1997). *No turning back: The Royal Commission on Aboriginal Peoples*. Montreal: National Film Board of Canada.

Gender Equity in Indian Registration Act. (2010). SC 2010, c. 18.

Hallett, D., Chandler, M.J., & Lalonde, C.E. (2007). Aboriginal language knowledge and youth suicide. *Cognitive Development, 22*, 392–399. http://web.uvic.ca/psyc/lalonde/manuscripts/2007CogDevt.pdf.

Health Canada. (2002). First Nations, Inuit and Aboriginal health: Aboriginal diabetes initiative (ADI) evaluation framework. http://www.hc-sc.gc.ca.

Health Canada. (2006). First Nations, Inuit and Aboriginal health: Tuberculosis in First Nations communities. http://www.hc-sc.gc.ca.

Health Canada. (2011). First Nations, Inuit and Aboriginal health: Diabetes. http://www.hc-sc.gc.ca/fniah-spnia/diseases-maladies/diabete/index-eng.php.

Health Canada. (2013). First Nations and Inuit health. http://www.hc-sc.gc.ca/fniah-spnia/pubs/services/tripartite/framework-accord-cadre-eng.php.

Health Canada. (2014). First Nation mental wellness continuum framework—Summary report. http://www.hc-sc.gc.ca/fniah-spnia/pubs/promotion/_mental/2014-sum-rpt-continuum/index-eng.php.

Health Canada. (2016). *Non-insured health benefits program: First Nations and Inuit Health Branch—Annual report 2014–2015*. Ottawa: Author. http://healthycanadians.gc.ca/publications/health-system-systeme-sante/non-insured-health-benefits-annual-report-2014-2015-rapport-annuel-services-sante-non-assures/alt/nihb-ar-2014-2015-ra-ssna-eng.pdf.

Hull, J. (2008). Aboriginal youth in the Canadian labour market. *Horizons, 10*(1), 40–44.

Hurley, M.C., & Simeone, T. (2010, March 18; November 15). Bill C-3: Gender Equity in Indian Registration Act [Legislative summary]. Ottawa: Parliamentary Information and Research Service, Library of Parliament. http://www.lop.parl.gc.ca/Content/LOP/LegislativeSummaries/40/3/c3-e.pdf.

Indian Act. (1985). RSC 1985, c. I-5.

Indian and Northern Affairs Canada. (2005). *Basic departmental data 2004*. Ottawa: Minister of Public Works and Government Services Canada. http://dsp-psd.pwgsc.gc.ca/collection_2008/inac-ainc/R12-7-2004E.pdf.

Indian and Northern Affairs Canada. (2009). Discussion paper: Changes to the *Indian Act* affecting Indian registration and band membership—*McIvor v. Canada*. http://www.aadnc-aandc.gc.ca/DAM/DAM-INTER-HQ/STAGING/texte-text/mci_1100100032488_eng.pdf.

Indian Oil and Gas Act. (1985). RSC 1985, c. I-7.

Indigenous and Northern Affairs Canada. (2012). Income assistance program: Background. https://www.aadnc-aandc.gc.ca/eng/1334589796211/1334589859785.

Indigenous and Northern Affairs Canada. (2015a). Percentage change in registered Indian population, Canada, 1981 to 2015. http://www.aadnc-aandc.gc.ca.

Indigenous and Northern Affairs Canada. (2015b). Skills and job training: Income assistance program. https://www.aadnc-aandc.gc.ca/eng/1100100035256/1100100035257.

Indigenous and Northern Affairs Canada. (2016a). Inuit Nunangat map. http://www.aadnc-aandc.gc.ca/Map/irs/mp/index-en.html.

Indigenous and Northern Affairs Canada. (2016b). Kindergarten to grade 12 operating expenditures 2013–2014 overview. http://www.aadnc-aandc.gc.ca/eng/1349140116208/1349140158945.

Intertribal Forestry Association of British Columbia. (1990). *Lands, revenues and trusts forestry review.* Kelowna, BC: Author.

Kahn, S. (2008). Aboriginal mental health: The statistical reality. *Visions: BC's Mental Health and Addictions Journal, 5*(1), 6–7. http://heretohelp.bc.ca/publications/aboriginal-people/bck/3.

Keewatin v. Ontario (Natural Resources). (2013). 2013 ONCA 158, aff'd. (*sub nom. Grassy Narrows First Nation v. Ontario (Natural Resources)*), 2014 SCC 48, [2014] 2 SCR 447.

Kirmayer, L.J., Fraser, S.-L., Fauras, V., & Whitley, R. (2010). Current approaches to Aboriginal youth suicide prevention. Canadian Mental Health Research Unit working paper no. 14. Montreal: Jewish General Hospital. http://www.namhr.ca/pdfs/Suicide-Prevention.pdf.

Laboucane, R. (2010, October). Canada's Aboriginal education crisis. *Windspeaker, 28*(7), 18–19. http://www.ammsa.com/publications/windspeaker/canada%E2%80%99s-aboriginal-education-crisis-column.

Mandell Pinder LLP. (2014, July 21). *Grassy Narrows First Nation v. Ontario (Natural Resources) 2014 SCC 48—Case summary.* http://www.mandellpinder.com/grassy-narrows-first-nation-v-ontario-natural-resources-2014-scc-48-case-summary/.

Marshall, R. v; R v. Bernard. (2005). 2005 SCC 43, [2005] 2 SCR 220.

McIvor v. Canada (Registrar of Indian and Northern Affairs). (2009). 2009 BCCA 153.

National Panel on First Nation Elementary and Secondary Education for Students on Reserve. (2013). *Nurturing the learning spirit of First Nation students: The report of the National Panel on First Nation Elementary and Secondary Education for Students on Reserve.* Ottawa: Aboriginal Affairs and Northern Development Canada. https://www.aadnc-aandc.gc.ca/DAM/DAM-INTER-HQ-EDU/STAGING/texte-text/nat_panel_final_report_1373997803969_eng.pdf.

Nunavut Housing Corporation. (2010, October 29). *An analysis of the housing needs in Nunavut: Nunavut Housing Needs Survey 2009–2010* [Working paper prepared by Income Statistics Division, Statistics Canada]. http://www.stats.gov.nu.ca/Publications/Housing/NHNS Pubs/Analysis of the Housing Needs in Nunavut, 2009-2010.pdf.

Porter, J. (2015, June 15). Mercury levels still rising near Grassy Narrows First Nation, report says. *CBC News.* http://www.cbc.ca.

Public Health Agency of Canada. (2006). *The human face of mental health and mental illness in Canada 2006.* Ottawa: Minister of Public Works and Government Services Canada. http://www.phac-aspc.gc.ca/publicat/human-humain06/pdf/human_face_e.pdf.

Public Health Agency of Canada. (2010). HIV/AIDS among Aboriginal people in Canada. In *HIV/AIDS epi updates—July 2010.* http://www.phac-aspc.gc.ca/aids-sida/publication/epi/2010/pdf/EN_Chapter8_Web.pdf.

Public Health Agency of Canada. (2011). *Diabetes in Canada: Facts and figures from a public health perspective.* Ottawa: Author. http://www.phac-aspc.gc.ca/cd-mc/publications/diabetes-diabete/facts-figures-faits-chiffres-2011/index-eng.php.

Public Health Agency of Canada. (2014). Chapter 8: HIV/AIDS among Aboriginal people in Canada. In *HIV/AIDS epi updates.* Ottawa: Author. http://www.phac-aspc.gc.ca/aids-sida/publication/epi/2010/8-eng.php.

Public Health Agency of Canada. (2015). HIV and AIDS in Canada: Surveillance report to December 31, 2014. http://healthycanadians.gc.ca/publications/diseases-conditions-maladies-affections/hiv-aids-surveillance-2014-vih-sida/index-eng.php.

Richards, J.G., Vining, A.R., & Weimer, D.L. (2010, February). Aboriginal performance on standardized tests: Evidence and analysis from provincial schools in British Columbia. *Policy Studies Journal, 38*(1), 47–67.

Sharpe, A., & Arsenault, J.-F. (2010, December). Investing in Aboriginal education in Canada: An economic perspective. *CPRN research report.* Ottawa: Canadian Policy Research Networks. http://www.cprn.org/documents/51980_EN.pdf.

Shkilnyk, A. (1985). *A poison stronger than love: The destruction of an Ojibwa community.* New Haven, CT: Yale University Press.

Standing Committee on Aboriginal Affairs and Northern Development. (2014). *Study of land management and sustainable economic development on First Nations reserve lands.* http://www.parl.gc.ca/content/hoc/Committee/412/AANO/Reports/RP6482573/AANOrp04/aanorp04-e.pdf.

Standing Senate Committee on Aboriginal Peoples. (2015). *Housing on First Nations reserves: Challenges and successes.* http://www.parl.gc.ca/Content/SEN/Committee/412/appa/rms/08feb15/home-e.htm.

Statistics Canada. (2006). Earnings and incomes of Canadians over the past quarter century, 2006 census: earnings. Higher education: Gateway to higher earnings. http://www12.statcan.gc.ca/census-recensement/2006/as-sa/97-563/p8-eng.cfm.

Statistics Canada. (2008). Aboriginal people living off-reserve and the labour market: Estimates from the Labour Force Survey, 2007. http://www.statcan.gc.ca/pub/71-588-x/71-588-x2008001-eng.htm.

Statistics Canada. (2010, May 13). Study: Aboriginal labour market update. *The Daily.* http://www.statcan.gc.ca/daily-quotidien/100513/dq100513b-eng.htm.

Statistics Canada. (2012). Aboriginal peoples survey (APS). Catalogue no. 89-653-X. http://www5.statcan.gc.ca/olc-cel/olc.action?objId=89-653-X&objType=2&lang=en&limit=0.

Statistics Canada. (2013a). *Aboriginal peoples in Canada: First Nations people, Métis and Inuit*. http://www12.statcan.gc.ca/nhs-enm/2011/as-sa/99-011-x/99-011-x2011001-eng.pdf.

Statistics Canada. (2013b). The education and employment experiences of First Nations people living off reserve, Inuit, and Métis: Selected findings from the 2012 Aboriginal Peoples Survey. http://www.statcan.gc.ca/daily-quotidien/131125/dq131125b-eng.htm.

Statistics Canada. (2015a). Aboriginal languages in Canada. https://www12.statcan.gc.ca/census-recensement/2011/as-sa/98-314-x/2011003/fig/fig3_3-2-eng.cfm.

Statistics Canada. (2015b). Employment. In *Aboriginal statistics at a glance* (2nd ed.). Catalogue no. 89-645-X. http://www.statcan.gc.ca/pub/89-645-x/2015001/employment-emploi-eng.htm.

Statistics Canada. (2015c). NHS Aboriginal population profile, 2011. https://www12.statcan.gc.ca/nhs-enm/2011/dp-pd/aprof/index.cfm?Lang=E.

Tsilhqot'in Nation v. British Columbia. (2014). 2014 SCC 44, [2014] 2 SCR 257.

Van Dusen, J. (2015, September 30). Nunavut housing crisis: "Dire straits" in Igloolik. *CBC News*. http://www.cbc.ca.

VanEvery-Albert, C. (2004). A review of the band operated funding formula. http://chiefs-of-ontario.org.

Vendeville, G. (2016, July 7). Protesters march on Queen's Park over mercury poisoning in Grassy Narrows First Nation. *The Toronto Star*. https://www.thestar.com.

Zarate, G. (2010, March 10). Inuit TB infection rate 32 times above national average in 2008. *Nunatsiaq Online*. http://www.nunatsiaqonline.ca/stories/article/9879_inuit_org_wants_tuberculosis_strategy/.

REVIEW QUESTIONS
True or False?

____ 1. The federal government relocated the Ojibwe of Grassy Narrows in 1963 because it wanted to end the isolation that had helped this community resist assimilation.

____ 2. Most Indigenous communities have been relocated from their original territories.

____ 3. With the 1951 changes to the *Indian Act*, Indian women who "married out" no longer lost their Indian status.

____ 4. The *Canadian Charter of Rights and Freedoms* has had little effect on Canada's registered Indian population.

____ 5. Government funding of on-reserve schools has kept pace with the rapid growth in Indigenous communities.

____ 6. By 2026, over one-third of Saskatchewan's population between the ages of 15 and 29 is expected to be Indigenous.

____ 7. The passing of Jordan's Principle in the House of Commons in 2007 put an end to jurisdictional disputes over the funding of government services to on-reserve Indigenous children.

____ 8. The increase in diabetes among Indigenous people is related to their rapid transition from traditional lifestyles of hunting and fishing to a more sedentary lifestyle.

____ 9. The proportion of people in the Indigenous population who drink alcohol is smaller than the proportion of people in the general population who do so.

____10. All Indigenous languages are in sharp decline and will soon be lost.

Multiple Choice

1. Which of the following calamities came to the people of Grassy Narrows in the 1960s?
   a. HIV/AIDS
   b. competition in the wild rice market from non-Indigenous farmers
   c. the *Indian Act*
   d. mercury poisoning from a pulp and paper mill

2. Among the people in Canada reporting Indigenous ancestry, the fastest growing population is
   a. Cree
   b. Inuit
   c. Métis
   d. Indian

3. The growth rate of Canada's Indigenous population is significantly affected by which of the following factors?
   a. the birth rate
   b. the death rate
   c. the rate at which individuals lose or gain status
   d. all of the above

4. Which of the following Canadian cities has the largest population of Indigenous people?
   a. Kenora
   b. Montreal
   c. Winnipeg
   d. Vancouver

5. Which of the following factors is negatively correlated with academic achievement?
   a. playing sports every day
   b. living in a household with a high income
   c. strong social skills
   d. none of the above

6. For status Indigenous people living on reserve and for the Inuit, health care is
   a. a provincial responsibility
   b. a community responsibility
   c. a federal responsibility covered by Health Canada
   d. none of the above

7. Compared with people in the general population, how likely are Indigenous people to be diagnosed with type 2 diabetes?
   a. no more likely
   b. twice as likely
   c. less likely
   d. three times as likely

8. Which of the following Indigenous populations has an infection rate for tuberculosis that is 32 times the national average?
   a. the Métis
   b. those who live in cities
   c. the Inuit
   d. the Ojibwe of Grassy Narrows

9. One path to economic development for Indigenous communities is to access the natural resources in the land, but they are having trouble doing so because
   a. the equipment required is expensive
   b. the resources are on lands that are currently under claim
   c. the resources have been used up
   d. it goes against their conservationist beliefs

10. Which of the following is thought to contribute to Indigenous communities' sense of continuity and their ultimate well-being?
    a. facilities for preserving cultural artifacts and traditions
    b. a degree of self-governance
    c. secure access to traditional lands
    d. all of the above

APPENDIX 4.1

Jordan's Story: How One Boy Inspired a World of Change

Jurisdictional Disputes and the Denial of Government Services

Jordan was born in 1999 to a large family in Norway House Cree Nation, Manitoba. ... He was born with complex medical needs and remained in a Winnipeg hospital for the first two years of his life while his medical condition stabilized. While Jordan's mother, Virginia, stayed with him in Winnipeg, his father, Ernest, returned to Norway House First Nation in northern Manitoba to look after the couple's other children. ... Shortly after Jordan's second birthday, his doctors agreed that he was ready to go home. But Jordan never made it. ...

Provincial and federal governments do not always agree on which level of government is responsible for the payment of government services for First Nations children living on reserve, services that are routinely available to other children. When one of these jurisdictional disputes occurred, the typical practice of both levels of government was to deny or delay the provision of services to the child until the payment issue could be sorted out. ...

For Jordan, this amounted to provincial and federal bureaucrats arguing over every item related to his at-home care—while he stayed in hospital at about twice the cost. ...

Jordan died while waiting for a resolution. He was only five, and he had never spent a day in his family's home.

We can say that two lives were lost as a result of this jurisdictional dispute. Jordan's mother, Virginia, did not have a history of substance abuse prior to Jordan's hospitalization, but the heartbreak of seeing her young son remain needlessly in hospital, and enduring the long separation from her husband and other children, likely contributed to Virginia's subsequent slide into substance abuse. Just months after Jordan passed away, Virginia died in a Winnipeg bus shelter. ...

A Groundswell of Advocacy for Change

Buoyed by the strength of his son's spirit, Ernest Anderson vowed this type of discrimination would never happen to another First Nations child in Canada. Those touched by Jordan and the Anderson family were galvanized by the compelling need for change, but uncertain about how to address federal and provincial government policies to make Ernest's dream come true. There was no money and only a small group of Jordan's Principle supporters at the beginning, but all knew Ernest was right, and they were determined to succeed.

When Jordan passed away in 2005, the First Nations Child and Family Caring Society of Canada was conducting a research project on First Nations child welfare, which provided a platform to study the incidence of jurisdictional disputes affecting First Nations children. This study ... suggested that each year, thousands of First Nations children were being denied on the basis of their race and residency the government services that are routinely available to other children.

Just as these findings were coming to light in June 2005, UNICEF Canada hosted the North American consultation on violence against children, during which Jordan's Principle to resolve jurisdictional disputes was announced for the first time. Simply put, Jordan's Principle puts the child's interests first in any jurisdictional dispute within and between federal and provincial/territorial governments. When a dispute arises around the provision or payment of government services (such as health care, education, child welfare, recreation, and other services normally enjoyed by all Canadian children) to a status Indian or Inuit child, Jordan's Principle requires that the government of first contact pays the bill immediately—and then resolves the payment issue later. ...

In 2005, all of the provinces/territories and the federal government were notified of Jordan's Principle and asked to take immediate steps to implement it. ...

Although the federal government and provinces/territories were slow to act, hundreds of Canadians and Canadian organizations stepped forward to support an online declaration for Jordan's Principle, calling on governments to move quickly to adopt and implement the principle. ... By the time Jordan's Principle came for a vote in the House of Commons, more than 1,400 Canadians and organizations had officially registered their support.

Ernest Anderson and his daughter Jerlene, along with other families from Norway House Cree Nation who were also affected by jurisdictional disputes, flew to Ottawa to watch the vote take place. At 5:30 p.m. on December 12, 2007, members of Parliament stood in unanimous support of Private Members' Motion-296 supporting Jordan's Principle and followed with a standing ovation for the Anderson family and all those who supported Jordan's message. It was, by all accounts, a wonderful day, but, as Ernest Anderson warned, the good that was accomplished in Jordan's name that day would be little more than a victory in name only if Canada and the provinces/territories did not immediately move to implement Jordan's Principle. The result? The federal government decided to strike a working committee to discuss implementation.

Gathering Provincial/Territorial Government Support for Jordan's Principle

On January 24, 2008, British Columbia Premier Gordon Campbell announced that B.C. could become the first province to endorse Jordan's Principle. ... More recently, the government of Ontario announced its support for Jordan's Principle and although it plans to begin implementation for children with special needs, it has acknowledged the need to apply Jordan's Principle across health and social programmes in the province.

Meanwhile, jurisdictional disputes continue to negatively affect the lives and health of First Nations children. As of May 2008, as the governments of Manitoba and Canada engaged in a jurisdictional dispute concerning payment for children's special-needs care, 37 children in Norway House Cree Nation faced unnecessary placement in foster care. Norway House Cree Nation used their own revenue to provide the life-saving and wellness services these children needed, while the governments continued to argue that they lacked sufficient funds. ...

Jordan's Lasting Legacy

Jordan's Principle is now the most widely supported child policy movement in recent Canadian history. It is an example of what can be accomplished when a group of committed people stand up against injustice for the best interests of children, leveraging their networks and talents to bring about change, even without financial resources. However, the question remains: Why won't Canada vigorously and fully implement Jordan's Principle without delay? We must have an immediate answer: First Nations children are dying, and their best interests and safety are being jeopardized while waiting for governments to do the right thing.

Source: Blackstock, C. (2009). Jordan's story: How one boy inspired a world of change. *Canadian supplement to The state of the world's children 2009: Aboriginal children's health: Leaving no child behind.* Toronto: UNICEF Canada.

5 Indigenous People and the Criminal Justice System

The Okimaw Ohci Healing Lodge provides a safe and empowering environment where Aboriginal women can begin their individual healing journeys, while being supported and encouraged through daily interaction with Aboriginal spiritual leaders, community representatives, and Healing Lodge staff. Healing for Aboriginal women means the opportunity, through Aboriginal teachings, programs, spirituality, and culture, to recover from histories of abuse, regain a sense of self-worth, gain skills, and rebuild families. Through healing, Aboriginal women are able to change or release negative behaviours such as addictions and criminal behaviour. Delving deep into issues allows for an intensive healing experience, which improves their ability to re-establish themselves in their community.

LEARNING OUTCOMES

After completing this chapter, you should be able to:

- Distinguish between Indigenous and non-Indigenous concepts of justice.
- Identify reasons for Indigenous people's overrepresentation in the criminal justice system, as both victims and offenders.
- Recognize that Indigenous communities have different needs with regard to policing and justice.
- Identify the internal changes that have been made to the justice system to address the unique challenges faced by Indigenous people in that system.

Introduction

The incarceration rate for Indigenous people in Canada is high, as is their victimization rate. Both statistics have been linked to socio-economic issues and institutionalized discrimination. In this chapter, we will examine the relationship between the criminal justice system and Indigenous people in Canada, the advent of Indigenous policing and alternative justice, the role of Correctional Service Canada in delivering services to Indigenous people, and the unique challenges that Indigenous people face within the justice system. This chapter addresses a variety of issues and should prompt discussion on how to improve the relationship between Indigenous people and the criminal justice system.

Case Study: Hobbema (Maskwacis)

Like Chapter 4, this chapter begins with a case study—in this instance, a description of the Maskwacis reserve (formerly known as Hobbema reserve), taken from a CBC News article (2008, pp. 31–32). Just as Grassy Narrows is not representative of all Indigenous communities, Hobbema is not typical of all reserves; it is an extreme case.

A Community Fights Gangs and Guns

Two-year-old Asia Saddleback was eating a bowl of soup at her family's kitchen table when a bullet ripped through the side of her house, striking her in the stomach. Asia was taken by air ambulance to an Edmonton hospital. The bullet hit her kidney and her spine, but the resilient girl survived—despite the fact that doctors were unable to remove the bullet. Within days, two teenage boys, one 15 and one 18, were charged in the drive-by attack. While it was clear the boys didn't intend to shoot Asia, police struggled to find out why they fired on the house in the first place. The incident horrified people living in Hobbema, and soon all of Canada would learn of the serious gang problem in the small Alberta town.

Descent into Chaos

The descent of Hobbema into chaos can be traced to a number of factors: substance abuse, shattered families, poverty, unemployment, and the erosion of Aboriginal traditions to name a few. Couple these socio-economic factors with evidence of systemic racism (much of which was revealed in the now defunct residential school system that openly tried to destroy Aboriginal culture over its 100-year history) and it becomes clear why First Nations communities are in what seems to be a state of perpetual crisis. Hobbema appears to be the current epicentre of this crisis, as an array of troubles have hit the town.

Hobbema, Alberta

Hobbema is a town of about 12,000 people located within a one-hour drive south of Edmonton. It is the home of four First Nations communities, including the Samson Cree reserve where Asia lives with her family. What might come as a surprise to most Canadians is that the RCMP office in Hobbema is arguably the busiest police detachment in all of Canada. They are dealing with a high volume of violent crime brought on by Hobbema's 13 gangs, who are fighting for drug turf in the town. In fact, Hobbema has the highest ratio of gang members in Canada, with 18.75 members for every 1,000 people living in the town (compared with Toronto's 1.15 members for every 1,000 people). Of all calls received by the RCMP, two-thirds of them come from the Samson Cree reserve. How did a town of 12,000 become a gang hub, producing so much violence in such a concentrated area?

Squandered Cash

One would think that Hobbema would be sitting pretty. Located on prime Alberta oil land, local residents have historically been the beneficiaries of royalty money collected by the federal government and redistributed to each citizen of the town. Instead of saving the money, most residents squandered the cash, going on shopping sprees—with more than a few spending their money on drugs, drinking, and gambling. Despite the fact that oil revenues on the reserve have been steadily declining, Aboriginal youth still manage to receive a large, lump sum royalty payment when they turn 18. Candace Saddleback, Asia's mother, received a cheque for $234,000 when she turned 18 and she has nothing left to show for it. This is common in Hobbema.

Gang Formation

The royalty cheques are one way that gangs are putting Hobbema's youth under their control. Drug dealers give kids under 18 free drugs for years on condition that they pay for the drugs when they get their royalty cheque when they turn 18. By the time the dealers come to collect, many of the youth are fully fledged gang members who willingly turn over their mountain of cash. With over half of Hobbema's population under the age of 18, gangs have no shortage of targets on which to set their sights. The gang life inevitably draws the attention of the police, and many of Hobbema's youth find themselves in young offenders' institutions or, after they turn 18, provincial and federal prisons. It is in prison that gang members get their real education. Surrounded by other professional criminals, novices enter incarceration ignorant and leave with skills that will serve them in their later criminal endeavours.

Once released, gang members return to their surrogate families—the gang itself—and Hobbema has no shortage of places for gang members to find a safe haven. With 13 known gangs in the town, many of which are on the Samson Cree reserve, the RCMP have their hands full keeping a lid on the high level of violence brought on by the gangs. Whether it's Redd Alert, the Alberta Warriors, the Indian Posse, or one of the up-and-coming gangs, Hobbema is a community held on the ropes by the two-punch combination of violence and intimidation.

Community Activism

In the meantime, the citizens of Hobbema have rallied together in response to the shooting of little Asia Saddleback. Abandoned homes are being torn down to prevent the gangs from turning them into crack houses. Graffiti, one of the main ways that gangs use to mark their turf and communicate their messages, is being painted over almost as soon as it goes up. In the summer of 2008, the RCMP declared a four-month gun amnesty, allowing gang members to turn in their weapons and ammunition without being charged with weapons offences. Despite these measures, Hobbema is still mired in gang violence, with almost daily reports of shots being fired and three gang-related shooting deaths in the summer of 2008.

Conclusion

Hobbema has become the flashpoint for communities rallying to keep gangs from taking over their neighbourhoods. The gangs didn't just show up one day and declare Hobbema to be their own. They established themselves over time, feeding on the general state of decay on the reserves and capitalizing on the oil money that many people were happy to party away. While lessons can be learned from Hobbema, it will be interesting to see if anyone is taking note.

Since the shooting of Asia Saddleback, violence has continued to haunt Hobbema. A four-month gun amnesty was introduced in August 2008 in response to Asia Saddleback's shooting, but two homicides occurred that month. One of those homicides, the death of Delena Lefthand, was a result of a gang-related shooting. In 2011, five-year-old Ethan Yellowbird was killed as he slept by shots fired outside his house; two months later, his aunt, Chelsea Yellowbird, was shot in the back yard of the house next door.

In January 2014, Hobbema changed its name to Maskwacis to reflect the heritage of the community, since Hobbema is not a Cree name. However, the name change did not change the cycle of tragedy in the community; the same month, teenager Jacob Soosay was shot and killed by a 16-year-old shooter. RCMP reported that the shooting was gang-related. In 2014, the federal government announced that it would put $2 million toward an existing anti-gang violence program in the community. The program's strategy includes the promotion of community involvement, education, employment skills training, and counselling programs. Case workers assigned to the community each mentor 25 youth for school, family, and social issues. The funding meant that the program could continue for another five years. As of this writing, it is too early to assess its effect on the community.

EXERCISE 1

Consider the case of Maskwacis in light of what you have learned so far in this text about the Indigenous experience in Canada. Explain, in broad terms, how the community has reached its current condition. What possible strategies could be used to intervene? How would you design a new anti-gang violence program with $2 million in funding?

Indigenous Overrepresentation in the Criminal Justice System

Indigenous people are overrepresented in the criminal justice system, both as perpetrators and as victims of crime. In 2012 the Office of the Correctional Investigator released a report announcing that 21.5 percent of federally incarcerated individuals are Indigenous. The Indigenous proportion of federally incarcerated females dropped slightly to 31.9 percent from 33 percent in 2009. However, in the period from 2002 to 2012, the increase in Indigenous incarcerated women was 85.7 percent, while the increase for all incarcerated Indigenous people was 43 percent (Office of the Correctional Investigator, 2012).

In addition to higher rates of incarceration, Mann (2009) notes that, compared with non-Indigenous inmates, Indigenous inmates

- are released later in their sentences,
- are overrepresented in solitary confinement,
- are more likely to have previous sentences, and
- are classified as higher risk and are more likely to reoffend.

CALL TO ACTION

30. We call upon federal, provincial, and territorial governments to commit to eliminating the overrepresentation of Indigenous people in custody over the next decade, and to issue detailed annual reports that monitor and evaluate progress in doing so.

Just as Indigenous people are overrepresented among the accused in the justice system, they are also overrepresented among victims, especially victims of violent crime. The best measure of victimization comes from Statistics Canada's General Social Survey—Victimization (GSS), which collects information from a sample of Canadians in the provinces regarding their victimization in eight categories of crime in the last 12 months: sexual assault, robbery, assault, break and enter, theft of motor vehicle, theft of household property, vandalism, and theft of personal property (Statistics Canada, 2015b). The GSS also rates opinions and satisfaction with the criminal justice system in its various forms.

The GSS reports that, in 2015, 30 percent of Indigenous people living in the provinces had been a victim of one of the identified eight types of crime in the past 12 months. This is 11 percent higher than the figure for the non-Indigenous population.

Violent crime is divided into two areas: spousal violence and non-spousal violence. In 2009, 12 percent of Indigenous people reported being the victim of non-spousal violence in the past 12 months. This is more than double the rate of the non-Indigenous population. The most commonly reported violent crime was assault, where Indigenous people were twice as likely to be victimized; however, for sexual assault, Indigenous people were three times more likely to be victimized (see Figure 5.1).

FIGURE 5.1   Self-Reported Non-Spousal Violent Victimizations, Canada's Ten Provinces, 2009

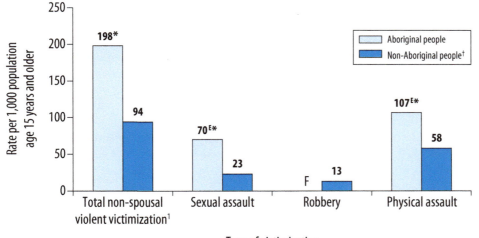

NOTES:
†   reference category
*   significantly different from reference category (p < 0.05)
E   use with caution
F   too unreliable to be published
1.   Includes robbery and excludes all incidents of spousal sexual and physical assault. Includes incidents that occurred during the 12 months preceding the survey.

SOURCE: Perreault (2011, p. 8).

CALL TO ACTION

39. We call upon the federal government to develop a national plan to collect and publish data on the criminal victimization of Aboriginal people, including data related to homicide and family violence victimization.

The Homicide Survey collects data on all reported homicides in Canada (Statistics Canada, 2015c). In 50 percent of cases, the cultural identity of the accused is unknown. Nonetheless, in 2014, police reported that Indigenous people made up 23 percent of homicide victims and 32 percent of persons accused of homicide. While no relevant data were available in the 2014 Homicide Survey, earlier reports indicated that most homicides involved the use of alcohol or drugs. In 73 percent of these cases, the victim was under the influence of drugs or alcohol, as was the accused in 91 percent of these cases (Perreault, 2011, p. 8). Eighty-six percent of the accused were young males, with an average age of 34.

The GSS also collects data regarding socio-demographic factors in connection with violent victimization, such as age, marital status, and the lifestyle characteristics of victims (for example, alcohol and recreational drug use). A number of factors associated with a high risk of victimization were reported more frequently by Indigenous people than by others. It was concluded that, with these risk factors taken into account, Indigenous people are three times more likely to be victimized than are non-Indigenous people (Statistics Canada, 2015b).

Missing and Murdered Indigenous Women

Helen Betty Osborne was born in Norway House Cree Nation, in northern Manitoba in 1952. Helen Betty left her reserve to attend school in the town of The Pas, Manitoba with dreams of becoming a teacher. On November 13, 1971 she was brutally murdered by four young men. It took 18 years to bring the perpetrators to trial, and only one was convicted of the abduction and brutal murder. The matter was reviewed in the Aboriginal Justice Inquiry in 1992. The inquiry revealed that her death and the barriers to justice that followed her death were the direct result of racism, sexism, and indifference, which took the form of sloppy police work and the disinterest of citizens toward resolution of the case. The government of Manitoba apologized to the Osborne family for the failure of the justice system, and in 2001 a foundation was created to honour her memory and her educational dreams.

Helen Betty Osborne came to symbolize hope for all families of missing and murdered Indigenous women in Canada—hope that the justice system would evolve to equally serve all Indigenous women in Canada through the elimination of racism and sexism within the system. Helen Betty's story has been told in the film *A Conspiracy of Silence* as well as in a graphic novel.

In late 2013 the commissioner of the RCMP led a study of reported incidents of missing and murdered Indigenous women across all police jurisdictions throughout Canada. This was a response to the Native Women's Association of Canada Sisters in Spirit initiative (2010), which asserted that 600 Indigenous women in Canada had been murdered or reported missing in the previous three decades. The RCMP study used a similar time frame as the Sisters in Spirit initiative, 1980 to 2012, in order to compare or corroborate its findings. The RCMP found that, in fact, 1,017 Indigenous women had been murdered over that period. Overall, Canadian women in general accounted for 32 percent of all homicide victims in that 33-year span; of that number,

16 percent were Indigenous. This is a serious overrepresentation, since Indigenous women made up only 4.3 percent of the total female population during this time. The RCMP also reported 120 unsolved cases of murdered Indigenous women and 105 unsolved cases of missing Indigenous women. The report did, however, conclude that the solve rates for Indigenous and non-Indigenous female homicides were equal at 90 percent (Royal Canadian Mounted Police, 2014).

The 2012 Missing Women Commission of Inquiry in British Columbia, led by Justice Wally Oppal, was established in light of the serial slayings of Downtown Eastside Vancouver sex-trade workers. Robert Pickton was convicted of the deaths of six of the missing women in 2007, but the DNA of 33 missing women were found on his pig farm outside the city. Pickton was recorded by police during an undercover sting asserting that he had killed up to 50 women over the years. Many of Pickton's victims were Indigenous women, as confirmed through DNA. The inquiry did not address exclusively Indigenous women, but many of the 63 recommendations produced by the commission addressed the overrepresentation of Indigenous women among the missing. At the conclusion of the inquiry, Justice Oppal made statements to the press asserting that Pickton got away with murder for years because of a systemic bias against poor Indigenous drug-addicted victims, who as a group were dismissed by police (Missing Women Commission of Inquiry, 2012).

Inequities in the justice system regarding the protection of vulnerable Indigenous women date back to the murders of Helen Betty Osborne in 1971 and Pamela George, a sex-trade worker, in 1995. In the George case, one of two young men convicted of her killing was reported to have said, "She deserved it. She was an Indian." The court's direction to the jury on the charge of first-degree murder, that they consider the issue of consent to sexual activity because of George's work in the sex trade, came under fire from both Indigenous and non-Indigenous rights organizations. Ultimately, George's killers—19 and 20 years of age—were convicted of only manslaughter and sentenced to 6.5 years' imprisonment for the murder (Commercial Sex Information Service, 2000).

Indigenous organizations, as well as Amnesty International, have called on the government of Canada to undertake a national inquiry into the missing and murdered Indigenous women. Following the 2015 federal election, the new government announced the first phase of a national inquiry, with the goal of beginning the inquiry itself in 2016.

The "Highway of Tears" awareness walk kicked off a 2005 symposium to address the issue of missing women who disappeared or were found murdered along the 724-kilometre stretch of British Columbia's Highway 16 between Prince Rupert and Prince George. The number of missing women combined with those confirmed murdered is believed to exceed 30; all but one of these victims were Indigenous (Highway of Tears Symposium, 2006). The communities in this area have struggled to bring the issue to the attention of law enforcement and government agencies since the pattern of disappearances began to emerge as far back as 1989. The long-term goals of the symposium echo many of the issues addressed throughout the chapters of this text:

1. Reduce Indigenous intergenerational poverty and post-secondary student temporary poverty, since poverty is the factor that makes both groups vulnerable to predators.
2. Increase outreach services to Indigenous communities along the highway specifically, and Indigenous communities in general, to reduce their need to hitchhike (due to poverty) to the nearest town or city.
3. Increase Indigenous youth recreation and social activities in the communities along the highway and generally, to prevent these youth from travelling (hitchhiking) to recreation and social activities in the nearest town or city.

Source: Highway of Tears Symposium (2006).

EXERCISE 2

Review the results of BC's Missing Women Commission of Inquiry and find three families' stories of their experience of a loved one going missing. Look for commonalities in the stories, then reflect on (1) how they could have been helped at the time of the disappearance, and (2) what measures could have prevented the disappearance.

Indigenous people are also twice as likely as non-Indigenous people to be the victims of spousal violence (Perreault, 2011, p. 10). Most of this violence is directed at women. For Indigenous victims of spousal assault, the frequency and severity of the assaults was found to be greater than for victims in the non-Indigenous population (Perreault, 2011, pp. 10–11). Twice as many Indigenous victims reported having been injured, and 48 percent (compared with 18 percent for non-Indigenous victims) reported that they feared for their lives (see Figure 5.2).

Causes of Overrepresentation

According to Aristotle, "poverty is the mother of crime." If he was correct, then the overrepresentation of Indigenous people in the criminal justice system is a natural consequence of the poverty and marginalization of Indigenous people in Canada today, as discussed in Chapter 4. The systemic failure to address this overrepresentation is also related to the vast difference between Indigenous and European concepts of justice, Canada's system being based on the latter.

There is good reason to associate Indigenous criminality with the effects of colonization, which has led to poverty and marginalization. Carole LaPrairie (2002) has sought to refine this general notion, asserting that if colonization and cultural conflict are the main source of Indigenous criminality, there should be no variation across the country in the levels of Indigenous overrepresentation, since all Indigenous people suffered colonization.

FIGURE 5.2   Self-Reported Spousal Victimizations, in the Preceding Five Years, Canada's Ten Provinces, 2009

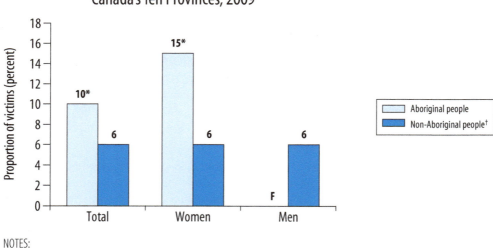

NOTES:

†   reference category

*   significantly different from reference category (p < 0.05)

F   too unreliable to be published

SOURCE: Perreault (2011, p. 10).

LaPrairie looked at provincial differences in Indigenous admissions to custody. The greatest overrepresentation, she noted, is in Saskatchewan, where Indigenous people are incarcerated at 10 times the rate of non-Indigenous people; in Alberta, at 9 times the rate; and in Manitoba, at 7 times the rate. According to McGillivray and Comaskey (1999), the highest enrollment rates at residential schools were also in these provinces. This suggests that assimilation and colonialism are primary factors in the overrepresentation of Indigenous criminality in Canada. Figure 5.3 demonstrates the overrepresentation of Indigenous people across Canada admitted to provincial or territorial custody in 2011 and 2012.

The crime statistics for urban Indigenous people, a fast-growing population, are higher than for Indigenous people living on-reserve. According to the 2011 census, 49 percent of Indigenous people live on reserves. A 1992 study revealed that only 19 percent of federally sentenced Indigenous offenders were from a reserve. In 1992, the Edmonton Inner-City Violent Crime Task Force found that 50 to 60 percent of incarcerated Indigenous offenders in Alberta came from urban areas (LaPrairie, 2002). LaPrairie conducted studies in 1992 and 2000 on urban Indigenous crime in Winnipeg; the results led her to argue that high Indigenous crime rates were related to disadvantaged living conditions. This hypothesis was tested again in 2008 by researchers Fitzgerald and Carrington (2008). Their results confirmed LaPrairie's earlier findings: the high level of police-reported Indigenous crime is related to the characteristics of the neighbourhoods in which Indigenous people tend to live—namely, neighbourhoods that experience low incomes, unemployment, low academic achievement, and a high incidence of family breakdown.

Enforcement directives differ greatly between on-reserve policing and urban policing. Urban police are more likely than on-reserve police to resolve criminal behaviour by laying charges; they are less likely to seek other means of resolving a situation. As a result, a relatively high number of charges are laid against urban Indigenous people. Many urban Indigenous people suffer from low socio-economic status and marginalization, and are isolated in high-crime

FIGURE 5.3   Admissions to Sentenced Custody by Aboriginal Identity and Proportion of Aboriginal People in Total Population, by Jurisdiction, 2011–12

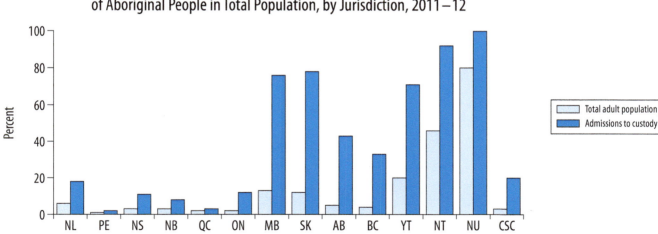

NOTE: The calculation of percentages excludes admissions for which Aboriginal identity was unknown. The term "Aboriginal identity" designates individuals who reported being an Aboriginal person, that is, First Nations (North American Indian), Métis, or Inuk (Inuit), and/or those who reported *Registered or Treaty Indian status*, that is, registered under the *Indian Act* of Canada, and/or those who reported membership in a First Nation or Indian band. The provincial/territorial figures represent admissions in provincial/territorial facilities. Correctional Services Canada (CSC) figures represent admissions to federal facilities.

SOURCE: Perreault (2014).

urban communities. This puts them doubly at risk—of being victimized and of engaging in criminal activity themselves.

Figure 5.4 shows the employment and education status of the prison population aged 20 to 34 in Alberta on census day, 2006. The figures suggest that lacking a high school diploma or a job contributes to the incarceration rate of Indigenous adults in this age bracket. But even when education and employment deficits for Aboriginal people are factored out, the risk of incarceration is still higher for Indigenous people than for non-Indigenous. This points to the likelihood that other factors are contributing to the high incarceration rate for Indigenous people, such as low income, inadequate housing, and the criminal justice process itself (Perreault, 2011).

Indigenous people see the family as central to the social health of their communities. Other marginalized groups view the family similarly. The assimilation process enforced by the federal government severely disrupted family relationships in First Nations communities. Residential schools caused the greatest damage; the abuse left the children with serious emotional scars. Those who escaped the worst abuse still suffered the loss of both language and family relationships. Some were unable to develop healthy relationships with their own children.

As the residential school system wound down in the 1960s, a new form of family dislocation occurred: the child welfare system. Cross-cultural adoptions and foster placements were so common that many communities lost almost an entire generation of children (see Chapter 3). Those adoptions rarely worked out; adoptive parents were often unprepared for the challenges of rearing an already troubled child whose problems were then compounded by discrimination (Wagamese, 1996). Communities reeling from the loss of their children continued to unravel (Fournier & Crey, 1997). In some penitentiaries, 95 percent of Indigenous prisoners are victims of the child welfare system, having been separated from family, culture, and community through adoption, foster care, and, eventually, custody (Royal Commission on Aboriginal Peoples [RCAP], 1996, p. 129). Figure 5.5 shows the statistics concerning involvement in the child welfare system for Indigenous and non-Indigenous inmates. In the Prairie provinces, an attempt was made to quantify the number of inmates who had been through the child welfare system

FIGURE 5.4   Incarceration Rate on Census Day, by Employment and Education Status, Population Aged 20 to 34, Alberta, May 16, 2006

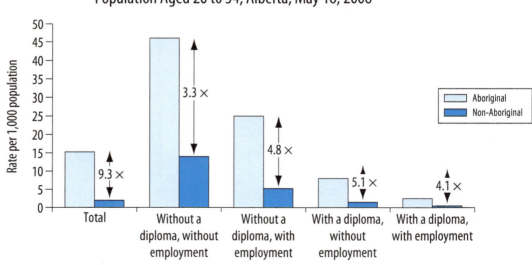

SOURCE: Perreault (2009).

FIGURE 5.5   Inmate Involvement in the Child Welfare System

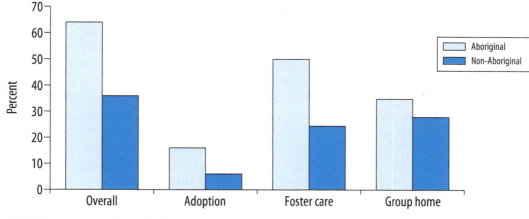

SOURCE: Trevethan, Auger, & Moore (2001).

compared with their non-Indigenous counterparts. It was found that 50 percent of Indigenous inmates had been through the system—twice the rate of non-Indigenous inmates (Trevethan, Auger, & Moore, 2001).

Loss of land through the colonization process and economic collapse in Indigenous communities led to extreme poverty and economic reliance on the Canadian government. At the conclusion of the era of colonization—an era that arguably continues to this day—Indigenous people endured "ill health, run-down and overcrowded housing, polluted water, inadequate schools, poverty and family breakdown/violence at rates found more often in developing countries than in Canada" (RCAP, 1996, p. 129). These problems reinforce one another, creating a circle of disadvantage for Indigenous people; swirling amid this circle is the prevalence of alcohol and substance abuse (discussed below).

Joan Sangster (1999) examined the historical overrepresentation of Indigenous women in custody at the Mercer Reformatory in Toronto between 1920 and 1960. Her study of admissions records at the Mercer Reformatory in the 1950s indicated that 70 percent of Indigenous women's admissions were for alcohol-related offences. Sangster (1999) writes, "When a middle aged woman, who lost all her eight siblings to disease and her father to alcoholism, told the Mercer doctor that her drinking is 'unfortunate but unchangeable' one can perhaps understand her tone of resignation." Sangster attributes the overrepresentation of Indigenous women in the criminal justice system to three factors. The first is material and social dislocation due to colonization. The second is gender and race **paternalism**, which translates into loss of autonomy and therefore agency over one's own actions. The third is the cultural gap between Indigenous ideas of justice rooted in healing and restoration and European ideas of justice rooted in crime and punishment. The three factors Sangster cites are rooted in the Indigenous experience of colonization.

paternalism
a system in which a dominant person or institution assumes authority for supplying the needs and regulating the conduct of those under its control

Alcohol, Substance Abuse, and Criminality in Indigenous Communities

In the past, alcohol problems in Indigenous communities were examined from a biological perspective; problem drinking was seen as a weakness of race, and Indigenous people were believed to have a genetic predisposition to alcoholism. Several studies in the 1970s disproved this theory, but it continues to surface today. The disease model of alcoholism gained popularity after the demise of genetic- or race-based theories. Indigenous addiction workers quickly embraced this model, since it not only offered a reprieve from the victim blaming and racial bias intrinsic in the genetic theory, but also held out hope for treatment and recovery. More recent examinations of the disease model question its validity; they indicate that many problem drinkers are not alcoholics but binge drinkers who engage in violent behaviour (Thatcher, 2004, p. 21).

This chapter addresses the issue of alcohol because its use has a strongly positive correlation with crime and violence, particularly family violence. As mentioned previously, alcohol is very often a factor in homicides in which Indigenous people are involved, whether as victims or as accused. There are two theories on the prevalence of alcoholism in Indigenous communities. The first is that alcohol and substance abuse is a symptom of social problems such as poverty, ill health, and family breakdown. The second theory inverts the first: alcoholism is the primary factor in the ill health, family breakdown, and violence in Indigenous communities (Whitehead & Hayes, 1998, pp. 6–7). All things considered, it seems most likely that alcoholism among Indigenous people stems from their experience of colonization and the consequent social upheaval they endured.

For some Indigenous communities, alcohol-related crime and family violence have been the norm and not deemed to be criminal. In 2009, Correctional Service Canada reported that substance abuse was a problem for 80 percent of all adult male inmates, but for 95 percent of Indigenous inmates. Domestic violence, similarly, was not seen as criminal or deviant; it was ordinary. It was a situation where denunciation and deterrence (section 718 of the *Criminal Code*) as one of the aims of criminal sentencing in criminal law had become irrelevant. With domestic violence, there is a strong intergenerational correlation; that is, children who witness or experience abuse are more likely to become abusers. The intergenerational correlation likewise exists with alcohol and substance abuse; its onset takes the form of gas sniffing, which is a particular problem in more isolated and economically desperate Indigenous communities. Gas sniffing has been reported in children as young as four years of age.

This cycle seems almost impossible to stop. Nonetheless, many Indigenous communities are currently making serious efforts to confront these issues. Inuit communities in Nunangat, for example, have attempted to regulate alcohol in their communities, and others have done the same (see Figure 5.6). Other communities have prohibited alcohol altogether. Statistics show that the prohibition of alcohol has significantly reduced the incidence of violent crime in these communities, including cutting the rates of serious assault and homicide by more than half (Wood, 2011).

FIGURE 5.6   Serious Assault Rates (Three-Year Running Average), Wet and Dry Communities, Nunavut, and Canada, 1987–2005

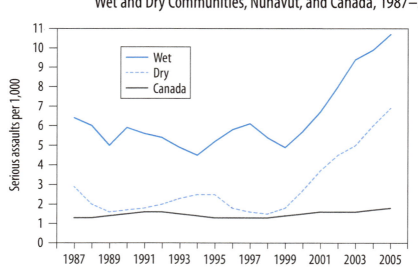

SOURCE: Wood (2011, p. 24).

Systemic Problems

Much attention has been paid in the last two decades to the overrepresentation of Indigenous people in the criminal justice system, including correctional facilities. Of grave concern are the matters of justice and economics. As we discussed in Chapter 4, the Indigenous population is increasing; according to the 2011 National Household Survey, between 2006 and 2011 the increase was 20.1 percent. The demographic statistics for Indigenous communities show an average age much younger than that of non-Indigenous Canadians. For example, in Maskwacis (Hobbema), more than half the population is 18 or younger (Offman, 2008). Since youth is recognized to be a contributing factor in criminal behaviour (most who engage in criminal activity are aged 18 to 35), there is cause for serious concern about the Indigenous population; the overrepresentation of Indigenous people in the criminal justice system will increase unless significant interventions occur. Inaction could have serious financial repercussions, too. The cost of incarceration in a federal penitentiary is approximately $111,000 per year for males and $214,000 per year for females (Office of the Correctional Investigator, 2013).

A number of studies have been undertaken with a view to establishing policy and action for intervention. One such study (Aboriginal Justice Implementation Commission [AJIC], 1991, p. 86) discovered the following:

- More than half of the inmates of Manitoba's jails are Indigenous.
- Indigenous people accused of a crime are more likely to be denied bail than are non-Indigenous people.
- Indigenous people spend more time in pre-trial detention than non-Indigenous people do.
- Indigenous people accused of crimes are more likely to be charged with multiple offences than are non-Indigenous people.
- Lawyers spend less time with their Indigenous clients than with their non-Indigenous clients.
- Indigenous offenders are more than twice as likely as non-Indigenous offenders to be incarcerated.

A report of the Office of the Correctional Investigator published in October 2012 repeated these same themes, indicating that little had changed since 1991. It showed that 21 percent of the federal inmate population was Indigenous and found the following facts:

- Indigenous offenders serve disproportionately more of their sentences behind bars before first release than non-Indigenous offenders do.
- Indigenous offenders are underrepresented in community supervision populations and overrepresented in maximum-security institutions.
- Indigenous offenders are more likely to return to prison on revocation of parole than non-Indigenous offenders are.
- Indigenous offenders are disproportionately involved in institutional security incidents, use-of-force interventions, segregation placements, and self-injurious behaviour. (Office of the Correctional Investigator, 2012)

CALL TO ACTION

31. We call upon the federal, provincial, and territorial governments to provide sufficient and stable funding to implement and evaluate community sanctions that will provide realistic alternatives to imprisonment for Aboriginal offenders and respond to the underlying causes of offending.

32. We call upon the federal government to amend the Criminal Code to allow trial judges, upon giving reasons, to depart from mandatory minimum sentences and restrictions on the use of conditional sentences.

33. We call upon the federal, provincial, and territorial governments to recognize as a high priority the need to address and prevent Fetal Alcohol Spectrum Disorder (FASD), and to develop, in
collaboration with Aboriginal people, FASD preventive programs that can be delivered in a culturally
appropriate manner.

**systemic
discrimination**
the enforcement
of laws and the
enforcement of
policies that are inher-
ently prejudicial to
a group or culture

These findings support the concept of systemic discrimination against Indigenous people.
Systemic discrimination is the enforcement of laws and the creation of policies that, while they
apply equally to all people, are inherently prejudicial to a group or culture. Sometimes treating
all people as equals does not amount to justice. The clearest example of this inequality is in the
sentencing process. Factors that judges must consider in providing custodial or non-custodial
sentences include socio-economic factors such as education level, family situation, having a
fixed address, and employment or prospects of employment. On the surface, these appear to be
neutral factors; however, as you will recall from Chapter 4, Indigenous people are most often
the unemployed, the transient, and the poorly educated, making them prime candidates for
custodial sentences. Manitoba's AJIC (1991, chap. 4) observed the following:

> Historically, the Justice system has discriminated against Aboriginal people by providing
> legal sanction for their oppression. This oppression of previous generations forced Ab-
> original people into their current state of social and economic distress. Now, a seemingly
> neutral justice system discriminates against current generations of Aboriginal people …
> of lower socio-economic status. This is no less racial discrimination; it is merely "laun-
> dered" racial discrimination. It is untenable to say that discrimination which builds upon
> the effects of racial discrimination is not racial discrimination itself. Past injustices cannot
> be ignored or built upon. … These statistics [of overincarceration] are dramatic. There is
> something inherently wrong with a system that takes such harsh measures against an
> identifiable minority. It is also improbable that systemic discrimination has not played a
> major role in bringing this state of affairs into being.

Racial profiling in policing is a problem faced by many minority groups in Canada, and
Indigenous people are no exception. This overpolicing of their populations generates more
charges against Indigenous people. Indigenous people are also overrepresented as victims of
crime; nevertheless, in the past, police have at times given less consideration to Indigenous
victims of crime than to non-Indigenous victims, such as in the cases of missing and murdered
Indigenous women.

Consider also the conclusions of the Royal Commission on the Donald Marshall, Jr., Prosecution (1989). Donald Marshall was falsely accused and convicted of murder and spent 11 years
in jail until witnesses heard the real murderer bragging about his deeds. The case was re-opened,
and Marshall was acquitted after witnesses in the original trial admitted to giving false evidence. The Royal Commission came to the following conclusion:

> Donald Marshall, Jr.'s status as a Native contributed to the miscarriage of justice that has
> plagued him since 1971. We believe that certain persons within the system would have
> been more rigorous in their duties, more careful, or more conscious of fairness if Marshall
> had been White.

Cultural Conflict and Alternative Justice

Besides systemic discrimination, the fact that Indigenous people's traditional notions of justice
differ from those of the dominant system is considered to be another cause of their overrepresentation in the criminal justice system. Recall that before European contact, Indigenous people
did not have jails, police officers, or courts. Each group had its own methods of social control
and its own manner of dealing with people who behaved outside what was accepted in the

community. Disputes were resolved through mediation, with elders playing a primary role. The focus was on restoring harmony within the community. Offenders were encouraged to accept responsibility for their offence and to make amends to the victim and the community. All community members played a role in restoring the offender to a harmonious relationship within the community.

Table 5.1 presents the broad principles of Indigenous justice, although each community had distinct ways of handling justice. Can and should pre-colonial systems be resurrected, and would they be successful in today's environment? Mary Ellen Turpel-Lafond addresses this question in the RCAP report on justice issues (RCAP, 1996, p. 65):

> Can the pre-colonial regime ever be reconstructed? In my own view no, not except as a relic of the past. It cannot be resurrected because we have all been touched by imperialism and colonialism, and there is no simplistic escape to some pre-colonial history except a rhetorical one. In my view, we [Aboriginal people] need to regain control over criminal justice, indeed all justice matter, but in a thoroughly post-colonial fashion. … One cannot erase the history of colonialism, but we must, as an imperative, undo it in a contemporary context. … We have to accept that there are profound social and economic problems in Aboriginal communities today that never existed pre-colonization and even in the first few hundred years of interaction. Problems of alcohol and solvent abuse, family violence and sexual abuse, and youth crime—these are indications of fundamental breakdown in the social order in Aboriginal communities of a magnitude never known before. A reform dialogue or proposals in the criminal justice field have to come to grips with this contemporary reality and not just retreat into a pre-colonial situation.

TABLE 5.1   Traditional Western Justice Versus Traditional Indigenous Justice

Traditional Western Justice	Traditional Indigenous Justice
Crimes as offences against the state	Crimes as offences against the family of the victim
Punishment for the protection of society	Restoration of peace and equilibrium within the community
Punishment as a means of making the deviant person conform	Reconciliation of the accused with his or her own conscience and with the person(s) who have been wronged
Laws enacted by elected or appointed members of government	Laws enacted by government, with governance structure differing between nations
Formal administration of justice, including policing	No specialized apparatus of law enforcement; justice informally administered by chiefs, appointed persons, or kin groups
Existence of "victimless crime," such as deviant sexual or religious conduct	Crimes defined by harm caused to the victim
Sanctions may include fines, imprisonment, or death	Sanctions may include compensation to the victim, corporal punishment, banishment, or death
Atonement or reparations made by the individual offender to the individual victim	Atonement or reparations made by the offender's family or clan to the victim's family or clan

SOURCE: Aboriginal Justice Implementation Commission (1999).

Indigenous people are infusing different approaches into criminal justice programs directed at their communities. In the traditional Indigenous justice system, authority is dispersed among many people, with consensus as a goal. This approach contrasts with the mainstream one, whereby sole authority for sentencing rests with one individual, such as a justice or a judge, and decision-making power is confined to the Crown, the defence attorney, and the justice. Another difference in the Indigenous justice system is that Indigenous women play a primary role in all stages of the process. Finally, when it comes to mediation or sentencing, the Indigenous process considers a large web of relationships, far beyond victims and offenders. This reflects the Indigenous world view that all things are connected and nothing can be addressed in isolation (RCAP, 1996).

The major changes we have seen in the last two decades within the court system in Canada have been largely borrowed from original themes in pre-contact Indigenous justice. We give them new names, such as "alternative justice" or "restorative justice," but they are ways of justice that have existed since time immemorial. Alternative justice and restorative justice programs include victim–offender mediation, sentencing circles, and traditional Indigenous justice.

Justice in Nunavut

Due to its majority Inuit population, Nunavut has had the unique opportunity to make major structural changes to its justice system. Upon the creation of the territory of Nunavut in 1999, the *Nunavut Judicial System Implementation Act* took effect. Whereas all other provinces and territories in Canada have a three-tier justice system composed of provincial, appeals, and superior or supreme courts, Nunavut has a one-tier court system. Due to the size of the territory and the sparseness of the population, through extensive community consultation and consultation with justice professionals, it was decided that Nunavut would have a one-tier system so that all judges would have the power to hear any case.

The per capita crime rate in Nunavut exceeds that of any other area in Canada. The police-reported crime rate is 9 times greater than in the rest of Canada, and the violent crime rate is 7.1 times higher. Between 1999 and 2004, while the rest of Canada saw a decrease in youth court cases due to the creation of the *Youth Criminal Justice Act*, Nunavut saw a 93 percent increase in youth court cases (Clark, 2011). This increased crime rate is influenced by social factors, including the age of the population, which is younger than the rest of Canada. Additionally, police service (the RCMP) has expanded in remote areas since 1999, which accounts for some of the increase in reported crime. Finally, the high crime rate is connected to colonization and the community relocations brought about in the last 50 years.

The Nunavut Court of Justice must cover the entire territory of Nunavut, which is 20 percent of Canada's landmass. There are 25 communities across the territory that must be served by the court. The court travels to communities based on need—it can hold court in each community anywhere from once every six weeks to once every two years, depending on the number of cases. The circuit court consists of a judge, clerk of the court, court reporter, Crown prosecutor, and defence attorney. Interpreters are often present, since for many Inuit, English is not their first language—in fact, they may not speak English at all. Court is held in schools, community centres, and other locations as they are available, and the circuit court almost always flies into each community.

In addition to this circuit court, there are justices of the peace (JPs) who reside in the communities. Ideally, these are Inuit from the communities they represent who also speak the language. The JPs can deal with summary conviction matters and show cause hearings, and issue search warrants when necessary.

CLOSE-UP   Community Justice in Iqaluit

The Government of Nunavut has breathed new life into restorative justice efforts in Iqaluit by resurrecting its community justice committee. "Crimes concern a whole community and that's why I'm part of the committee—because I feel that personal responsibility," said Romani Makkik, who will chair Iqaluit's committee.

"I grew up in Igloolik, where I'd like to think I'm a prime example of that saying, 'it takes a community to raise a child.' Everybody in town had a part in the person I've become," Makkik added during a July 14 interview.

"And that's grounded in Inuit societal values, which this committee is very much grounded in."

Iqaluit-Niaqunnguu MLA Pat Angnakak has been a vocal supporter of restorative justice measures to divert offenders from what she called Nunavut's "inadequate" corrections system June 1 in the territorial legislature.

The outspoken MLA said the revival of Iqaluit's justice committee is welcome news.

"I think it's very good news, and a long time coming. ... Justice committees provide a really important contribution to justice in Nunavut. If we can send some of those people who've broken the law to the justice committees instead of through court, all the better," Angnakak said July 14.

The Iqaluit Alluriarvik justice committee—which means in English "a place to step forward to"—will work alongside elders to incorporate three main Inuit social values, Makkik said: respect for others; serving family and community; and working together for a common cause.

Both the RCMP and Nunavut's Crown prosecution office can refer those accused of a summary crime to the committee, explained Lisa Tootoo, a community justice specialist with the GN.

Summary crimes are generally less serious crimes than indictable offences such as homicide, sexual assault and crimes against children.

If the accused admits to the crime, and is willing, his or her case will be dealt with by two facilitators and one or two elders on the local justice committee, Makkik said.

Unlike the court system, the community justice model is a collaborative process, Tootoo said, because it brings victims, if they so choose, and others impacted by a crime, together with community members to talk about how it affected their lives.

That collaborative process includes the offender, Tootoo added.

"Offenders have a direct say in what they can do to make things right, and are involved with coming up with an agreement. It's a safe place for them to discharge some of that shame that comes with offending and allows them to be a part of the solution."

The agreement will be unique to each case, Tootoo said, and could include things like community volunteer work, financial restitution or hunting on the land for those impacted by the offence.

In the court system, by contrast, lawyers speak on behalf of accused offenders and the judge hands out a sentence if the accused is found guilty, Tootoo said.

"In court, it's justice that's done to people, and here in community justice, it's justice that's done with people."

Source: Rohner (2015).

This system is far from perfect. Some of the inherent flaws are as follows:

- In isolated communities, the circuit court visits are infrequent, which places strain on victims, witnesses, and the accused while they await closure from the court. This strain is increased if the matter is a domestic abuse situation.
- Funding for legal aid and Inuit court workers comes from the Nunavut Legal Services Board. The salaries are significantly lower than those of professionals who work for other legal organizations, so retaining quality staff is difficult.
- The Nunavut court faces a higher cost of delivery per case due to isolation travel expenses and the volume of legal aid cases.
- Circuit courts may lack credibility in the community because members of the court are not from the communities that they serve and are thus viewed as having a limited stake in those communities. Therefore, the sanctions imposed by the court may also lack legitimacy in the community's view.

As previously mentioned, due to the majority Inuit population, there is an opportunity to infuse traditional justice into the system. In 2015 the four regions of Nunavut had 25 justice committees providing both adult and youth diversion and victim support services. In 2012–13,

137 cases were diverted using community justice committees. By the end of that year, 92 cases had been completed, 29 were pending completion, and only 12 were referred back to court (Nunavut Tunngavik, 2014).

Proposed Solutions

According to a 2009 report released by the Office of the Correctional Investigator (Mann, 2009), Correctional Service Canada has not done enough to ensure that Indigenous offenders have sufficient access to culturally sensitive programming and services—factors that may reduce incarceration and **recidivism**. Ongoing problems include delays in the implementation of Indigenous programming, a shortage of links to the Indigenous community at the time of release, a shortage of Indigenous elders within the prison system, and insufficient staff to deliver programming.

There are a number of proposed solutions to address the failure of Canada's mainstream criminal justice system. Patricia Monture-Angus (2000, p. 167) suggests creating one autonomous Indigenous system. This has been recommended in many comprehensive studies and inquiries. Another option involves creating autonomous but government-funded Indigenous agencies to work within the dominant system or, preferably, to integrate Indigenous ideas and people into the dominant system (Monture-Angus, 2000, p. 167).

Creating an autonomous Indigenous system has been recommended by academics, policy advisers, and both the Royal Commission on Aboriginal Peoples and the AJIC of Manitoba. Community justice initiatives, such as the one used in the Hollow Water community (see Close-Up: Hollow Water later in this chapter), hold great promise, but they must have points of contact with the mainstream criminal justice system. For this reason, a two-track approach is recommended: reform of the non-Indigenous system and creation of an Indigenous system. These two efforts must occur simultaneously, with close attention to how they will work in partnership.

CALL TO ACTION

42. We call upon the federal, provincial, and territorial governments to commit to the recognition and implementation of Aboriginal justice systems in a manner consistent with the Treaty and Aboriginal rights of Aboriginal peoples, the *Constitution Act, 1982*, and the *United Nations Declaration on the Rights of Indigenous Peoples*, endorsed by Canada in November 2012.

Autonomous government-funded agencies have been created to work within the dominant system. Examples of this include Indigenous court liaison officers and corrections inmate liaison officers. These agencies will be discussed in the following sections.

The integration of Indigenous ideas and people into the dominant system is happening currently as Indigenous people gain entry into all levels of the system, as police officers, justices, lawyers, and correctional officers. Currently, however, Indigenous people are underrepresented in all these areas.

The solutions generated in the past 15 years have been developed in consultation with Indigenous political organizations. Some suggested solutions are as follows:

- "Indigenizing" existing criminal justice structures by increasing Indigenous representation within the system. This includes creating a policing policy for Indigenous-run law enforcement agencies on reserves, and other initiatives.

- Implementing sentencing reforms, such as new sentencing directives, including section 718.2(e) of the *Criminal Code* and the subsequent creation of alternative measures, sentencing circles, and diversion programs.
- Amending the *Corrections and Conditional Release Act* (including ss. 79 to 84) to recognize the needs of Indigenous offenders.
- Implementing the Correctional Service Canada (CSC) Strategic Plan for Aboriginal Corrections, which provides for culturally appropriate rehabilitation programs in custody facilities (CSC, 2011).
- Developing programs through the Department of Justice Canada's Aboriginal Justice Strategy to build community capacity to prevent crime and provide community justice solutions to ongoing crime problems (see Department of Justice Canada, n.d.).

Indigenization

Indigenization—that is, the incorporation of Indigenous people as employees into the justice system—currently presents a number of challenges. First, as some academics have argued, the incorporation of a people does not guarantee the incorporation of their values and thought. The incorporation of Indigenous police officers, court workers, lawyers, and judges does not change the adversarial nature of the judicial system, which is intrinsically opposed to Indigenous values.

indigenization
the incorporation of Indigenous people into a social system, such as the justice system

Policing

The evolution of First Nations policing began in 1969 when the Department of Indian Affairs and Northern Development (DIAND) encouraged bands to hire "band constables" to enforce band bylaws. In 1971, DIAND extended this authority, encouraging bands to hire "special constables." The authority of these officers was limited; they did not carry firearms and received very low pay. In 1973, a study by DIAND led to the prospect of employing Indigenous people in a comprehensive policing role. One option was to establish autonomous police forces on reserves; another was to develop the role of special Indigenous constables attached to existing police forces. The latter was the most common choice, with larger forces including Indigenous contingents.

In 1991, the federal government announced a new on-reserve policing policy, making Indigenous policing increasingly autonomous. First Nations reserve policing would now come under the authority of the solicitor general. With the assistance of the solicitor general's office, provincial, federal, and First Nations governments now partner in agreements over police services that will meet the needs of each community. Agreements must be reached regarding cost-sharing for the creation and maintenance of police services.

Under the federal government's First Nations policing policy, created in 1991, a number of forms of policing can exist. One is the First Nations–administered police service—for example, the Nishnawbe Aski Police Service, which serves 35 Ojibwe and Cree communities in northern Ontario. A First Nations–administered police service is run by a board of directors consisting of representatives from First Nations communities, and its officers either are Indigenous or are trained in policing in an Indigenous context. It is modelled on the structure of an independent municipal police service: it has its own police services board, is accountable to the community it polices, and is not governed by a provincial or federal service. Another option is to have Indigenous officers employed within the RCMP, the provincial police, or the many municipal police services across Canada with dedicated responsibilities to Indigenous communities, including urban Indigenous communities—since, as we saw in Chapter 4, more than 50 percent of Indigenous people now live in urban centres. The governance of these specialized units or branches comes through the chain of command of the larger services to which they belong, with consultation for special community needs.

Today, 118 of the 134 Indigenous communities in Ontario have their own police services, with additional support units provided by the OPP. Of the 55 First Nations in Quebec, 51 are served by police services under community policing agreements with additional support units available through Quebec's provincial police (Sécurité publique Québec, 2013). In Alberta, the RCMP provides 36 members located in 12 Indigenous communities. However, three Indigenous communities have tripartite agreements with the province for the creation and maintenance of an on-reserve police service, with 52 percent of the cost coming from federal funds and 48 percent from provincial funds designated for policing services.

Currently, northern Manitoba is served by the RCMP, but communities are demanding expanded police services that could include fully trained Indigenous police services rather than the current band constable model. This is possible under contract provisions allowed under the provincial *Police Services Act*.

In British Columbia, there are 55 community tripartite agreements that provide policing services to 130 Indigenous communities and one Indigenous-administered policing service, the Stl'atl'imx Tribal Police.

Clearly, as Indigenous communities chart their path toward self-governance, self-administered police services will be a goal for many Indigenous communities. In March 2013, there were concerns that as part of budget cutbacks, the federal Ministry of Public Safety was intending to discontinue funding the First Nations Policing Program, which would force the disbanding of tripartite and First Nations–administered policing, but at the end of March, the ministry committed to funding the program for another five years.

EXERCISE 3

Choose a First Nations police service to research online. Consider the positive and negative consequences of its funding being discontinued and a non-Indigenous police service taking over its role in the community. Would it be more cost-effective? Would it be better or worse for the community? Would it be better or worse for the police officers themselves?

The Royal Commission on Aboriginal Peoples identified as a matter for concern the fact that Indigenous police agencies are often modelled on mainstream police agencies. Indigenous communities must have more input into the structure, the function, and the mission statements of their police services. This can be accomplished only when control over policing and justice is connected to self-government. As discussed in Chapter 4, self-government requires an economic base.

Aboriginal Court Workers and Gladue Courts

Recently there has been an emphasis on recruiting Indigenous people into all levels of the court system, including Indigenous justices of the peace, judges, and jury members, particularly in areas of the country where there is a large Indigenous population.

Most provinces also have an Aboriginal Courtworker Program funded jointly by the provincial and federal governments. The need for the program was identified in a number of studies of Indigenous people in the justice system. One such inquiry in Toronto, in 1989, quoted a judge as saying, "Unfortunately, Indians are the ideal accused in the courts. They are quick to accept blame for their offences and they accept their punishment very passively. In many ways they appear to be the victims of the system" (RCAP, 1996, p. 97). Whether Indigenous defendants' easy admissions of guilt are based on culture or an unfamiliarity with the criminal justice system is unclear; however, the Aboriginal Courtworker Program was initiated to address these specific issues. The program's purpose is to have the system feel less alienating for Indigenous accused and to ensure they have a clear understanding of their rights as well as a person to advocate on their behalf as they make their way through the system. Low socio-economic status among Indigenous people has, in the past, forced offenders to rely almost solely on the legal aid process, which may partly explain why Indigenous accused spend less time with a lawyer and more time in pre-trial detention than do non-Indigenous accused. Furthermore, if they spend less time with legal counsel, they are less likely to be informed of available alternative justice programs.

Aboriginal court workers are intimately familiar with the issues that are likely to bring Indigenous offenders into court; they have a unique perspective on both Indigenous and non-Indigenous culture and can advocate for their clients to try to make the justice system work to their benefit in terms of healing and recovery.

Another initiative is the use of *Gladue* reports and the subsequent creation of *Gladue* courts. The implementation of the requirements under the *Gladue* case law differs from province to province; only a limited examination can be provided in this section. The *Gladue* reports, named for the 1999 Supreme Court of Canada decision in *R v. Gladue*, were initiated in Ontario by Aboriginal Legal Services of Toronto. In *Gladue*, an Indigenous woman who was charged with manslaughter as a result of a domestic dispute was not given access to sentencing reforms under section 718.2(e) of the *Criminal Code* because she was urban-dwelling, and the offence happened in a large urban centre. The court found fault with this; the sentencing reforms had been aimed at all Indigenous people. The *Gladue* decision marked the first time the court interpreted the amended section 718.2(e), which reads:

> A court that imposes a sentence shall … take into consideration the following principles: …
>   (e) all available sanctions, other than imprisonment, that are reasonable in the circumstances and consistent with the harm done to victims or to the community should be considered for all offenders, with particular attention to the circumstances of Aboriginal offenders.

According to the court, these amendments required a change in the way that judges should approach the sentencing process.

A more recent Supreme Court decision, *R v. Ipeelee* (2012), dictates that *Gladue* principles must be included in all sentencing. Manasie Ipeelee was of Inuit descent and had an extensive criminal record as both a young offender and an adult. His alcoholism began when he was only 12 years old. Ipeelee had spent most of his life in a correctional facility and was out on a long-term supervision order when he breached the conditions to abstain from alcohol. He was sentenced to an additional three years in custody as a result of the breach; he appealed the sentence because *Gladue* principles had not been considered by the judge. The appeal court confirmed that *Gladue* principles must be considered in all sentences, even in relation to breach of long-term supervision orders.

The onus for obtaining sufficient information on the Indigenous offender to satisfy section 718.2(e) of the *Criminal Code* lies with counsel and the judge. Case law demands that if counsel does not supply sufficient information to meet the *Gladue* requirement, the onus is on the sentencing judge to obtain the information. If the information is not procured by the sentencing judge, it will be grounds for appeal according to case law (*R v. Kakekagamick*, 2006, paras. 44–45).

Furthermore, the *Gladue* principles are not limited to minor crimes but must be met in all cases. The principles must be considered in all aspects of the justice system that involve incarceration, including bail, release, and parole hearings.

Prior to *Gladue*, various studies had pointed out the ways in which the Canadian justice system had failed the Indigenous peoples of Canada, due primarily to "the fundamentally different world views of Aboriginal and non-Aboriginal people with respect to such elemental issues as the substantive content of justice and the process of achieving justice" (RCAP, 1996, p. 309).

Gladue Reports

A *Gladue* report exceeds the depth of a pre-sentence report since it considers the specific experiences of the Indigenous offender, detailing family history, historical family participation in residential schools, community dysfunction, intergenerational trauma, and community supports available to the offender. In Ontario, these labour-intensive reports are researched and written by Aboriginal Legal Services of Toronto (ALST) rather than by probation officers. *Gladue* report writers are available in a number of Ontario cities, including Toronto, Guelph, Sarnia, Manitoulin Island, Thunder Bay, and London. These reports are less widely used than might be expected, since Aboriginal Legal Services of Toronto reports the creation of only 169 *Gladue* reports in 2012 (Ibbotson, 2013).

In British Columbia, trained Aboriginal courtworkers create a detailed report, at the request of defence counsel or the court, to cover all "*Gladue* impact factors." These reports are funded by the Legal Services Society of BC. All provinces have processes in place to meet the criteria set out in legislation and the ability to produce reports that detail the *Gladue* factors. It is important to recognize that the purpose of the reports is not to reduce jail time but to look at the options available to provide the accused's best chance of rehabilitation in order to prevent recidivism.

Gladue Courts

The first *Gladue* court began functioning in October 2001, in Toronto. At the time of writing, for Ontario there are four *Gladue* courts operating in Toronto, Sarnia, Brantford, and London. A *Gladue* court is one in which all Crown attorneys, defence counsel, and judges have received supplemental training with respect to the decision in *R v. Gladue* and to the history, culture, and experiences of discrimination of the Indigenous peoples of Canada, as well as the alternative programs available to Indigenous offenders. The court is available to all Indigenous persons—status and non-status Indians, Métis, and Inuit—who wish to identify as such and have their matter heard in a *Gladue* court. The accused is assigned a *Gladue* caseworker, who does extensive background investigation to determine what strategy would best ensure rehabilitation. In some cities, such as Hamilton, Milton, and Kitchener-Waterloo, Indigenous offenders can apply for a *Gladue* caseworker and a *Gladue* report will be prepared, but their cases will not be heard in a dedicated *Gladue* court, since none is available there at the time of writing.

In British Columbia, dedicated First Nations courts (*Gladue* courts) are in Vancouver, Duncan, and New Westminster, and a part-time Indigenous court has opened in Kamloops. In Manitoba, where much sentencing of Indigenous offenders takes place but where there are neither *Gladue* reports nor *Gladue* courts, probation officers still try to cover the *Gladue* principles by adding Indigenous-specific considerations into their pre-sentence reports (University of Manitoba Faculty of Law, 2012).

Gladue courts accept guilty pleas, conduct remands and trials, sentence offenders, and carry out bail hearings. Judges consider the unique factors that may have contributed to the offender's being charged and the sentencing procedures that may be appropriate, given the offender's Indigenous heritage. This includes examining alternative justice processes such as restorative justice.

Jury Selection

An area of the justice system that is noticeably lacking Indigenous participation is the jury selection process. This concern was raised in relation to fielding a jury in Ontario for an inquest into the 2007 death of 15-year-old Reggie Bushie. Bushie, from the Nishnawbe Aski Nation, like other teens in his community had to live in Thunder Bay in order to get a high school education. Bushie was the seventh teen from Nishnawbe Aski to die while attending school in

Thunder Bay; six teens drowned and one was asphyxiated. Bushie's family asked that the inquest proceedings be stopped so that Indigenous people could be part of the jury pool.

This incident led to an independent review of the jury selection process in Ontario by former Supreme Court justice Frank Iacobucci, who completed his report in February 2013. Iacobucci identified five key reasons why Indigenous people are reluctant to become involved in the jury selection system:

1. the perception that the legal system is not consistent with Indigenous traditional values, laws, or ideas;
2. the perception that the justice system discriminates against Indigenous people;
3. a lack of knowledge among Indigenous people about the functioning of the criminal justice system in general and the jury system in particular;
4. Indigenous people's desire for more control over the justice system as it pertains to them in their communities and to not have a jury selection system imposed on them from outside; and
5. concern in many Indigenous communities over the underresourcing of their police services, which contributes to an overall negative view of the justice system. (Iacobucci, 2013)

Iacobucci made 17 recommendations as a result of his consultation with Indigenous service groups and his meetings with the leadership of 32 different First Nations communities in Ontario. Some of these include:

- recommendations for economic support to overcome hardship for time spent on juries, including transportation and accommodation;
- instituting a process for Indigenous people to volunteer as jurors for inquests;
- instituting a process whereby Indigenous people with minor criminal records could still serve as jurors;
- embarking on an educational initiative with Indigenous communities to provide information on the jury selection process and the requirements and benefits of sitting on a jury;
- the creation of an advisory committee to the attorney general on matters affecting Indigenous people in the criminal justice system; and
- the creation and implementation of cultural training for justice system workers on Indigenous culture. (Iacobucci, 2013)

Cultural Awareness Training

Within the last ten years, there has been a focus on Indigenous awareness training for non-Indigenous employees of the criminal justice system. Studies in Indigenous issues have been included in college courses for prospective police officers and correctional workers. Police services and correctional staff now in the field have received training in Indigenous issues and in the Indigenous world view, so as to promote understanding and collaboration. This training continues in most provinces and territories, although much work remains to be done.

Recommendations for this training were put forward in the 1996 RCAP report and endorsed by the First Nations Chiefs of Police Association's 2000 study. In 2007, as a result of Justice Linden's report on the Ipperwash crisis, all OPP officers receive education in Indigenous issues. OPP crisis negotiators and tactical response unit officers also receive additional training on Indigenous matters, including history and legal and socio-economic issues. This training includes a one-week "Native Awareness Training" program, which includes Indigenous elders and Indigenous community partners in setting curricula. *Spirit Matters* (Office of the Correctional Investigator, 2012) recommends ongoing training for corrections workers in applying legislation that affects Indigenous inmates as well as in cultural issues.

Outside Ontario, First Nations–administered police services are less common. The RCMP serves 634 Indigenous communities across Canada. The RCMP reports that currently 67 percent of its detachments serve Indigenous communities and more than 1,500 of its members are Indigenous (Royal Canadian Mounted Police, 2011). The RCMP also provides its staff with training in Indigenous perspectives to help them understand and serve Indigenous communities.

Sentencing Reforms

As mentioned above, section 718.2(e) of the *Criminal Code* states that "all available sanctions, other than imprisonment, that are reasonable in the circumstances and consistent with the harm done to victims or to the community should be considered for all offenders, with particular attention to the circumstances of Aboriginal offenders." This provision, added in 1996, was intended to address the excessively high incarceration rate for Indigenous people.

Section 718.2(e) states that sanctions other than incarceration must be available; these include sentencing circles, alternative measures, and diversion programs. Since many offenders are in large urban centres, programs are required both on- and off-reserve. This is supported by the Supreme Court's decision in *R v. Gladue* in 1999, which states that urban Indigenous people must be considered in accordance with section 718.2(e) even if they are not connected to a particular Indigenous community. The alternatives created for sentencing by section 718.2(e) have been used widely by both Indigenous and non-Indigenous offenders, allowing for a more individualized and restorative approach to justice. There is concern, however, that these sentencing options, particularly conditional sentences, are being used more often as an extension of punitive power than as an alternative to incarceration. In the two years following the addition of section 718.2(e), 28,000 conditional sentences were ordered, but prison populations were not proportionately reduced (Roach & Rudin, 2000).

Alternative Measures

The alternative sentencing options under section 718.2(e) include approaches other than conditional sentences. Diversion programs are common for both Indigenous and non-Indigenous offenders, either pre-charge or post-charge. Diversion programs are used for a variety of criminal offences, particularly minor thefts. In a non-Indigenous context, a diversion approach might involve the offender's being required, for example, to attend an education session or write letters of apology. In an Indigenous context, cases more serious than minor theft may be subject to diversion, at the discretion of the Crown. The Crown may suspend the disposition of the case until the Indigenous panel or deliberative body has settled on an appropriate resolution for the case. In the case of minor and non-violent offences, charges against the accused are then generally withdrawn, having been adequately dealt with by the community.

Sentencing circles and elders' panels are common alternative sentencing options. They are based on traditional Indigenous justice structures and allow communities to have control over rehabilitation efforts for offenders. (Sentencing circles have also become commonplace for non-Indigenous youth offenders under the *Youth Criminal Justice Act*, although they are known as "youth justice committees.") This initiative addresses the problem of having an outside person pass sentence over an Indigenous person in an Indigenous community; people who, as well as sharing their culture, know the accused and the victim and have relationships with their families have insight that an outsider may not possess and that may be difficult to translate into a pre-sentence report.

An elders' panel consists of elders or clan leaders who sit with the judge and provide advice regarding an appropriate sentence. In a sentencing circle, community members are invited to sit in a circle with the accused and a judge to decide the sentence. There are prerequisites for a

CLOSE-UP   Hollow Water

The area of Manitoba in which Hollow Water is located is one hundred fifty miles northeast of Winnipeg and has a combined population of approximately one thousand people. The people live in four neighbouring communities (Manigotogan, Aghaming, and Seymourville, which are Métis settlements, and Hollow Water, which is a status Indian Reserve).

In 1984, a Resource Team was formed to work on healing and development in these four communities. The first disclosure of sexual abuse came in 1986. Before that time, no one talked about it. When Hollow Water people looked at their community before 1986, alcohol and drug abuse loomed large as a problem, as did unemployment and a need to reroute the education of their children in the cultural ways of their people. It became very clear that there had been a great deal of sexual abuse going on for many years, but that talking about it was taboo. They gradually discovered that as the blanket of alcohol abuse was removed, many of the people were holding on to acute anger, hurt and dysfunctional behaviour patterns that were related to sexual abuse or to some other violation that had been done to them in their past.

What followed was a very active period of learning and healing. The Resource Team soon realized that there was a fundamental conflict between what the justice system does with offenders and what the community needed to do. What was actually needed, they realized, was a new negotiated relationship with all the agencies who have a stake in dealing with sexual abuse cases. The new negotiated relationship would have to spell out a strict set of procedures about what to do at the time of disclosure and how a disclosure would be dealt with by the courts to allow for the healing process to take place. This model was named Community Holistic Circle Healing (CHCH), and works basically as follows:

1. An intervention team consisting of representatives of CHCH, Child and Family Services, and Band Constable conducts an initial investigation to find out what really happened.

2. Once it has been determined (beyond reasonable doubt) that abuse has taken place, the abuser is confronted and charged. At this stage, the combined power of the law and the community are used to force the abuser to break through his or her own denial to admit to the abuse, and to agree to participate in a healing process.

3. If the abuser agrees to the healing road, he or she then begins a three to five year journey, which ends in restitution and reconciliation between the abuser and the victim, the victim's family and the whole community. Abusers are asked to undergo a process of looking deeply into themselves to admit to themselves and others what they have done and how their actions have hurt others.

In all, the CHCH process for dealing with abusers has thirteen steps as follows:

1. Disclosures
2. Establish safety for the victim
3. Confront the victimizer
4. Support the spouse or parent of the victimizer
5. Support the families that are affected
6. A meeting between the Assessment Team and the RCMP
7. Circles with victimizers
8. Circles with the victim and the victimizer
9. Prepare the victim's family for the Sentencing Circle
10. Prepare the victimizer's family for the Sentencing Circle
11. A special gathering for the Sentencing Circle
12. A sentencing review
13. A cleansing ceremony

Today Hollow Water enjoys a fairly high level of sobriety (around eighty percent) and they are actively dealing with the sexual abuse issue.

Source: Bushie (1999).

---

sentencing circle. First, the accused must recognize his guilt and have a clear intention to rehabilitate and become a good citizen of his community. Second, the community must have a desire to intercede on behalf of one of its members. Third, the victim must also support the initiative.

Youth

All of these options are also available for youth sentencing. Although the absolute numbers of Indigenous youth in custody decreased from 1,128 to 720 between 2000 and 2003, Indigenous youth are still overrepresented in the criminal justice system. Statistics Canada reported that in 2014, 3,468 Indigenous youth were in custody, compared with all youth at 8,945 (Statistics Canada, 2015a). In the nine jurisdictions covered by this report, 41 percent of youth admitted to custody were Indigenous, even though they make up only 7 percent of the total youth population in the jurisdictions under study. A greater number of Indigenous youth are incarcerated for serious offences than are their non-Indigenous counterparts. Indigenous youth are also more likely than their non-Indigenous counterparts to receive custodial sentences and to receive longer periods of probation. In a 2009 study, it was found that 22 percent of youth gang members in Canada are Indigenous (Totten, 2009). Figure 5.7 shows Aboriginal youth admissions to correctional services for eight jurisdictions in 2010–11.

Without intervention, these youth will make their way into the adult system. To combat this, family group conferencing is available to all youth, particularly Indigenous youth. It is a process by which the youth and members of his or her family, a youth advocate, a police officer, a social worker, and other community members meet to decide what types of intervention are available to the youth and what strategies can assist him or her to become a productive member of the community. Family group conferencing can take place pre-charge or post-charge. Unfortunately, family support is often unavailable for Indigenous youth due to estrangement or family dysfunction, and often there is no youth advocate, particularly for those who are homeless.

In the one-day snapshot of youth in custody in 2001 reported by the Department of Justice Canada, it was found that only 23 percent of youth in custody were living on a reserve directly prior to admission; however, 65 percent of youth in custody spent the majority of their time on the reserve in the two years prior to their incarceration (Bittle, Quann, Hattem, & Muise, 2002).

Corrections and Conditional Release Act

Amendments to the *Corrections and Conditional Release Act* (CCRA), including sections 81 and 84, which recognize the needs of Indigenous offenders, provide for early release considerations by parole boards. This would reduce the cost of incarceration, but the processes must be in place within the community to assist the offender in successful readjustment. Considering the high rate of recidivism for Indigenous offenders, this has not been an area of strength for our corrections system. Efforts to partner with Indigenous communities and to allow their input into the release process are currently under way.

FIGURE 5.7   Aboriginal Youth Admissions to Correctional Services, by Province/Territory, 2010–11

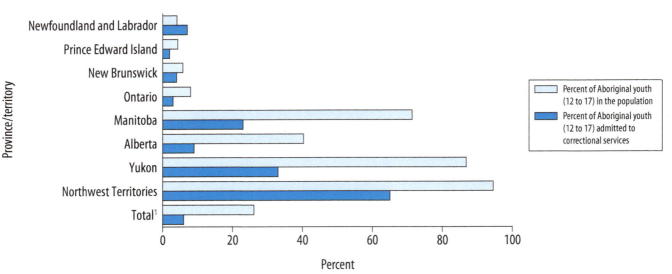

NOTE:
1. Excludes data from Nova Scotia, Quebec, Saskatchewan, British Columbia, and Nunavut.
SOURCE: Munch (2012).

Sections 81 and 84 were reviewed and evaluated by the Office of the Correctional Investigator in its 2012 report, *Spirit Matters*. These sections of the Act specifically deal with policy and structural adjustments that address the needs of Indigenous inmates. The report was critical of the action taken thus far to reduce the incarceration rate of Indigenous people in Canada. It asserted that the incarceration rate for Indigenous people had increased by 50 percent in the last decade, despite the *Gladue* reporting requirements and sections 81 and 84 of the CCRA. Although corrections is only one piece of the criminal justice system, it has serious influence over incarceration and recidivism rates for all clients, including Indigenous clients.

Section 81 Transfers

Section 81 of the CCRA provides for the transfer of an Indigenous offender from a correctional facility to an Indigenous community in a non-institutional setting where supervision, treatment, and programming are provided under the 24-hour supervision of community members for the term of sentence. Other types of arrangements can also be made under this section; an offender may be transferred to a spiritual or healing lodge, or a treatment facility in an urban centre or on reserve territory.

Section 81 reads as follows:

> 81(1) The Minister, or a person authorized by the Minister, may enter into an agreement with an aboriginal community for the provision of correctional services to aboriginal offenders and for payment by the Minister, or by a person authorized by the Minister, in respect to the provisions of those services. ...
>
> (3) In accordance to any agreement entered into under subsection (1), the Commissioner may transfer an offender to the care and custody of an aboriginal community, with the consent of the offender and of the aboriginal community.

To support these provisions included in the CCRA, eight healing lodges have been constructed. Four are run by Correctional Service Canada and funded under its model, and four are contracted and operated by the Indigenous communities themselves under section 81 of the Act. It is important to recognize the difference between the two types of lodges. For section 81 lodges, jurisdictional responsibility for corrections is not transferred to Indigenous communities; rather, the Act allows for certain services and programming funded by the Crown, including care and custody, to be delivered by Indigenous communities. Below are listed the four section 81 funding agreements between CSC and Indigenous communities. A total of 68 beds are available, and plans are under way to increase bed capacity (Office of the Correctional Investigator, 2012).

Facility	Opening date	Region	Bed capacity
Prince Albert Grand Council (PAGC)		Prairie—	
Spiritual Healing Lodge	1995	Saskatchewan	5
Stan Daniels Healing Centre	1999	Prairie—Alberta	30
O-Chi-Chak-Ko-Sipi Healing Lodge ...	1999	Prairie—Manitoba	18
Waseskun Healing Centre	2001	Quebec	15

The CSC has established four healing lodges that it operates as minimum-security institutions. They have significantly greater bed capacity: a total of 194 beds, with plans under way to soon increase spaces for both men and women. These are funded under a different model.

The plan for these lodges was not to compete with section 81 facilities but to ultimately transfer these facilities to community control under section 81 agreements. The negotiations for transfer were discontinued for three reasons according to the Office of the Correctional Investigator:

- The Indigenous communities enjoy the benefit of having the healing lodges without assuming full responsibility for them.
- The CSC healing lodges provide long-term stability rather than the five-year contracts negotiated under section 81.
- The funding for section 81 healing lodges is considerably lower than that for the CSC-run facilities.

Permanency and funding are two major factors affecting the operation of healing lodges. The discrepancy in funding between section 81 and CSC-operated lodges is significant despite the fact that CSC lodges provide more beds and also contribute to the operational funding of the department. In 2009–10, CSC's four facilities had a budget of $21.6 million, whereas the four section 81 lodges had a budget of $4.8 million. The cost per offender in CSC-run lodges is $113,450, compared with $70,845 in section 81 lodges. Since section 81 lodges pay lower wages, sometimes up to $30,000 less than in CSC lodges, their staff turnover rate is high. The five-year contracted budget means that staff are often laid off or transferred depending on budgetary needs and negotiations.

The CSC healing lodges are listed below.

Facility	Opening date	Region	Capacity
Okimaw Ohci Healing Lodge	1995	Prairie—Saskatchewan	30
Pê Sâkâstêw Centre	1997	Prairie—Alberta	60
Kwìkwèxwelhp Healing Village	2001	Pacific—British Columbia	50
Willow Cree Healing Lodge	2003	Prairie—Saskatchewan	80

According to the Office of the Correctional Investigator, Correctional Service Canada has received funding to enter into new section 81 agreements to increase the number of facilities and beds. The department changed direction in 2001–2 and decided to reallocate funds to create new Pathways healing units in medium-security penitentiaries. "In other words, the investigation found that Effective Corrections funding originally earmarked to enhance Aboriginal community reintegration was used largely to create new penitentiary-based interventions for Aboriginal inmates" (Office of the Correctional Investigator, 2012, p. 15).

CALL TO ACTION

35. We call upon the federal government to eliminate barriers to the creation of additional Aboriginal healing lodges within the federal correctional system.

This shift in direction may be occurring for two reasons. The existing healing lodge beds do not run at maximum capacity. CSC allows only minimum-security offenders to be transferred to a lodge. This restriction is not set out in the CCRA; however, it is meant to minimize risk. This poses some problems since in 2010–11, for example, only 22 percent of Indigenous offenders were classed as minimum risk under the custody rating scale. Furthermore, only 11 percent were housed in minimum-security institutions. The policy for transfer to healing lodges effectively excludes 90 percent of federal prisoners. The lodges could operate at maximum capacity based on the number of eligible inmates; it is unclear why this is not happening.

Facility	Capacity	2009–10		2010–11	
		Count	%	Count	%
PAGC Spiritual Healing Lodge	5	4	80%	4	80%
O-Chi-Chak-Ko-Sipi Healing Lodge	18	13	72%	13	72%
Stan Daniels Healing Centre.	30	13	43%	22	73%
Waseskun Healing Centre	15	13	86%	10	66%
Total/Average Percentage	68	43	63%	49	72%

(Office of the Correctional Investigator, 2012, p. 19.)

The second reason for the shift in direction is the recognition that there are too few successful culturally appropriate in-custody healing programs that would speed Indigenous inmates' progress toward minimum-security assessment and possible release. These in-custody initiatives will be discussed later in this section.

Section 84 Release Plans

Section 84 of the CCRA mandates that Indigenous communities be provided with the opportunity to participate in an offender's release plan once he or she is out of custody and on parole. The release plan balances the needs of the community with the needs of the offender. Successful reintegration is the primary goal for all parties: the victim, the offender, and the community.

Section 84 reads as follows:

> 84. If an inmate expresses an interest in being released into an aboriginal community, the Service shall, with the inmate's consent, give the aboriginal community
>
> (a) adequate notice of the inmate's parole review or their statutory release date, as the case may be; and
>
> (b) an opportunity to propose a plan for the inmate's release and integration into that community.
>
> 84.1 Where an offender who is required to be supervised by a long term supervision order has expressed an interest in being supervised in an aboriginal community, the Service shall, if the offender consents, give the aboriginal community
>
> (a) adequate notice of the order; and
>
> (b) an opportunity to propose a plan for the offender's release on supervision, and integration, into the aboriginal community.

To assist in the implementation of section 84, 12 Indigenous community development officers are responsible for bridging the best interest of the community and the offender prior to release. A section 84 release planning kit is available for those seeking this release option. The process is lengthy and time-consuming: there are 25 tasks to complete in a section 84 release application. A major obstacle in this process is that the community that receives the offender is not given resources to monitor the offender's compliance with release. Program and transportation costs must be listed in the release plan, but there is no guarantee that CSC will cover these costs, and the expense could fall to the community. As we know, over 50 percent of Indigenous people live in urban centres; this is true for Indigenous offenders as well. Many, other than Inuit who are mostly released into Inuit communities, would seek release to the urban centre they call home. There are organizations to help released offenders access services in urban centres, such as the Circle of Eagles Lodge in Vancouver and Friendship Centers in Saskatchewan, but many urban centres do not have the capacity to embark on a section 84 release with CSC. For these reasons, the number of section 84 release plans fluctuates. In 2010–11, for example, there were 593 offenders who expressed interest in section 84 release plans but only 99 were successful (Office of the Correctional Investigator, 2012, para. 67).

CALL TO ACTION

37. We call upon the federal government to provide more supports for Aboriginal programming in halfway houses and parole services.

Indigenous community involvement in justice issues marks the beginning of mainstream Canada's devolution of control over these matters where Indigenous people are concerned. However, it is only a beginning. The communities require funds to compensate members for the work of taking on these new responsibilities.

Culturally Appropriate Programs in Custody

CSC's *Strategic Plan for Aboriginal Corrections* (CSC, 2011) involves providing culturally appropriate rehabilitation programs to Indigenous people in custody. Under section 80 of the CCRA, CSC is required to provide programs designed to address the particular needs of Indigenous offenders. This section authorizes the solicitor general to enter into agreements with Indigenous communities to provide services to offenders, such as traditional healers and elders. Furthermore, it mandates the establishment of a national Indigenous advisory committee to advise CSC on how best to provide services to Indigenous inmates.

This is an important initiative for Indigenous inmates, since the chaplaincy program funded by CSC and other counselling programs are ill-equipped to deal with Indigenous experiences. Furthermore, some evidence supports the fact that exposure to Indigenous spirituality and connection to culture has been effective in the healing and rehabilitation of Indigenous offenders. In the Cawsey report, which was studied by RCAP, Justice Cawsey noted that "[e]verything that has worked for Aboriginal people has come from Aboriginal people" (RCAP, 1996).

CALL TO ACTION

36. We call upon the federal, provincial, and territorial governments to work with Aboriginal communities to provide culturally relevant services to inmates on issues such as substance abuse, family and domestic violence, and overcoming the experience of having been sexually abused.

In its quest for appropriate initiatives for Indigenous offenders, CSC (2011) has acknowledged the particularities of the Indigenous population in the criminal justice system and recognized that, compared with the average non-Indigenous offender, the Indigenous offender

- is younger;
- is more likely to have served a previous youth or adult sentence;
- is incarcerated more often for a violent offence;
- is at a higher risk of being placed in increased security institutions, which limits access to rehabilitative programs;
- is more likely to have gang affiliations;
- more often has increased health problems, including fetal alcohol disorders and mental health issues; and
- has a higher need rating when first admitted to custody.

With regard to needs, CSC assesses the needs of people who are admitted to custody in the following categories: employment, marital/family relationships, social interaction, substance abuse, community functioning, personal/emotional situation, and attitude. Because an assessment of these needs as medium or high is correlated with a greater risk of reoffending, these are areas in an offender's life that must be improved to increase the chances that the offender will be successfully reintegrated into his or her community. Currently, Saskatchewan and CSC collect data regarding offenders' needs (see Figure 5.8). In data collected for 2007–8, Indigenous adults admitted into custody had a higher number of needs on average than non-Indigenous people, in all areas of assessment (Perreault, 2009).

Table 5.2 compares the proportion of Indigenous and non-Indigenous offenders in Saskatchewan and federal institutions that demonstrate a particular need. The figures may go some way in explaining the overrepresentation of Indigenous offenders in custody; they suggest that the risk of recidivism—that is, the risk of returning to a correctional facility—may be higher for Indigenous offenders.

In addition to the fact that, compared with non-Indigenous offenders, a higher proportion of Indigenous offenders demonstrate needs, Indigenous offenders more often score as high risk (41 percent, compared with 22 percent among non-Indigenous inmates) on the Reintegration Potential Reassessment Scales (RPRS). According to measures of "low potential for integration," the non-Indigenous population has a 36 percent rating, whereas the Indigenous population has a 69 percent rating. It has been a priority of CSC to assess the risk-scoring process for bias against Indigenous people in custody. Because of the risk ratings, Indigenous inmates are paroled later than non-Indigenous inmates and less often complete sentences under community supervision. Indigenous inmates are more likely to be denied applications for full parole (24 percent, compared with 5 percent for their non-Indigenous counterparts). Finally, Indigenous inmates are more likely to waive parole application because of incomplete programs in custody (Mann, 2009).

Initiatives from CSC to address these matters include its Aboriginal Corrections Continuum of Care model, developed in consultation with Indigenous communities in 2003. The model was built around the traditional medicine wheel because research has indicated that connection to culture teachings and ceremonies is key in rehabilitation of Indigenous offenders. The model includes the following goals:

- Begin at intake to identify Indigenous offenders and encourage a reconnection with cultures and communities.
- Enable paths to healing in institutions to better prepare for transfer to lower security for eventual release.

FIGURE 5.8   Average Number of Needs by Aboriginal Identity, 2007–8

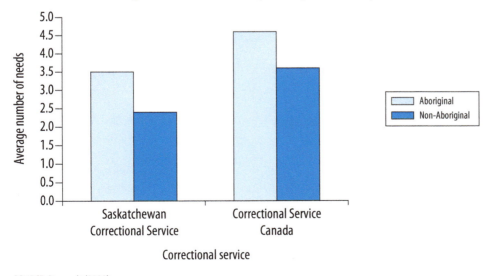

SOURCE: Perreault (2009).

TABLE 5.2   Proportion of Aboriginal and Non-Aboriginal Adults Admitted to Custody and Assessed as Having Needs, by the Type of Need, Saskatchewan and Correctional Service Canada, 2007–8

Type of need	Saskatchewan Correctional Service		Correctional Service Canada	
	Aboriginal	Non-Aboriginal	Aboriginal	Non-Aboriginal
	percent			
Employment	63	33	73	49
Marital/family relationships..............	48	33	51	32
Social interaction	76	51	72	61
Substance abuse	81	58	82	67
Community functioning	..	..	39	27
Personal or emotional...................	10	8	82	72
Attitude	71	52	58	55
Average number of needs................	3.5	2.4	4.6	3.6

NOTE: Represents individuals who were assessed as having either medium or high needs. For those who were admitted more than one time during the fiscal year 2007–8, information is based on the most recent admission.

SOURCE: Perreault (2009, July).

FIGURE 5.9   Corrections Continuum of Care

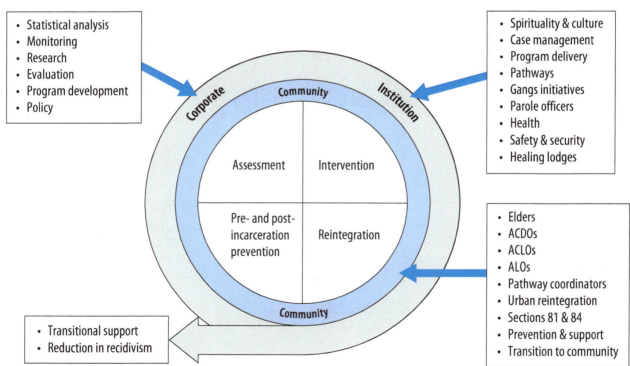

SOURCE: Correctional Service Canada (2012).

- Engage Indigenous communities to receive offenders back into the community and support integration.
- Create community supports for offenders to reduce risk of reoffending (Correctional Service Canada, 2012).

Under the institutional part of the model, during the initial intake the offender may indicate that he or she would like to work with an elder who would visit the inmate, review his or her circumstances, and submit a report based on these observations. The elder may continue to work with the offender and the case management team and incorporate into the offender's correctional plan any Indigenous-specific intervention programs that are available in the institution. If the offender demonstrates a commitment to traditional healing and ceremonies, he or she may request transfer to a Pathways unit in a medium-security institution.

The inmate must meet the criteria to gain access to a Pathways unit. These units provide a culturally appropriate environment for healing in intensive programs such as traditional talking circles, traditional parenting, and the "In Search of Your Warrior" program. Elders and spiritual advisers play key roles, and participants must verifiably abstain from substance abuse during their stay. Approximately 18 percent of the total Indigenous inmate population spent time in a Pathways unit with promising results. In a 2004 audit to justify the funding redirected from healing lodges to the Pathways units, it was found that Pathways participants' recidivism rate was 17 percent compared with 35 percent for non-participants one year after release from custody. The same audit revealed that Pathways participants were more likely to receive discretionary releases from custody: 37 percent of participants versus 22 percent of non-participants. In 2012, CSC reported that the service was planning for expansion to 17 Pathways units over the following five years (Office of the Correctional Investigator, 2012, paras. 75–78).

CLOSE-UP   Pathways

After two hours heading north on winding roads, the buildings of La Macaza Institution appear in the distance. The institution sprawls over a large area, which in the 1960s was the site of a U.S. army base, and later, an Aboriginal school. From there, you can see a longhouse and the tip of a great white tepee that pierces the blue sky. This medium-security institution houses about 257 offenders, of which nearly half are sex offenders undergoing intensive treatment.

According to the small team working on Pathways, the unit fosters a way of living that takes into account the actual experiences of Aboriginal, Métis and Inuit offenders—experiences marked by residential schools, life on reserves, forced assimilation, broken family ties and a pervading feeling of helplessness in the face of change.

Pierre Gervais explains: "Pathways is an initiative that tries to offer solutions to alleviate certain social problems by recreating a way of life that enables offenders to reconnect to Aboriginal culture and philosophy and take their needs—such as self-esteem—into account." Darryn Roy, Acting Manager, Aboriginal Initiatives Branch, National Headquarters, adds: "Pathways tries to create a special healing environment that encourages only positive behaviour. It is a considerable challenge, when considered in the context of a medium-security institution."

The Pathways team consists of three Elders, a liaison officer, two program officers and Coordinator Pierre Gervais. Together, they work with nearly 60 offenders, providing them with individual counselling, organizing sweat lodges and other ceremonies and crafts workshops, and preparing traditional meals. In addition, the team works with parole officers, building a relationship of increased trust that is essential to achieving positive outcomes.

"Pathways is a healing tool," says one offender, "a way to reconnect with my cultural heritage and with who I am. I used to be in a maximum-security institution in Kingston. I am here now, and I hope that the progress I've made will help me get into a minimum-security institution. I would rather talk to the Elders than to correctional officers. Their teachings are fantastic: respecting the land and the people. I prefer that to meetings with psychologists. Now, I make objects that are part of my culture and that I'm really proud of."

Gervais explains that offenders wishing to participate in Pathways must show genuine motivation and commit to making positive emotional, mental, physical and spiritual changes. They must also demonstrate responsibility and show respect for others and themselves. "An inmate interested in Pathways has to fill out the participation request form, explaining why he is interested in joining Pathways," he says. "After consultations with the Elders, the coordinator, the liaison officer, the correctional officer and the parole officer, the case is discussed by the Pavilion Board, and if the decision is favourable, we hold a welcome ceremony for the new member."

Elders Pierre Papatie, Colette Sabourin and Elizabeth Alikashuak work side by side with Pierre Gervais. When asked how they fit into Pathways, Elder Papatie says: "I think God chose me to play a role here. Pathways harmonizes body and soul through various activities. We must listen to them because their past is holding them back."

Métis Colette Sabourin, another Elder and former midwife, says that being there for offenders in their troubled times is crucial to the healing process. "I have been here with the team for two years. I was sent by the Creator. I have lived the cultural duality and today I'm proud of it, but it hasn't always been easy.

Self-acceptance is important. In Pathways, we focus on the offenders' best inner qualities rather than on their negative side."

Elizabeth Alikashuak has been in the institution for 13 years and works closely with Inuit offenders: "I try to work within a spiritual base. I talk to them about the old ways of life; I used to live in a tent in the middle of nowhere and I'm proud of who I am. I also encourage them to speak their mother tongue."

Offenders find that the arrival of Elders at the institution in 1997 changed their life for the better.

Source: Ammelal (2006).

EXERCISE 4

Read the box "A Community Fights Gangs and Guns," below, which discusses the Pê Sâkâstêw Healing Lodge, established by CSC in Maskwacis (Hobbema). How does the information further your understanding of the crisis in Maskwacis and some of the steps that can be taken to address it?

A Community Fights Gangs and Guns: The Pê Sâkâstêw Healing Lodge

In an effort to address the need for a more culturally specific approach to helping Aboriginal Canadians rehabilitate after becoming involved in criminal behaviour, the Correctional Service of Canada (www.csc-scc.gc.ca) constructed eight healing lodges across the country, including the Pê Sâkâstêw Healing Lodge in Hobbema, Alberta. All of the healing lodges strive to embrace Aboriginal traditions in an effort to allow the inmates to reconnect with their roots and find a way out of the criminal justice system and back into society. The Pê Sâkâstêw Healing Lodge is a 40-bed, minimum-security facility that has been serving Aboriginal inmates since 1997.

Counselors at the Pê Sâkâstêw Healing Lodge find they are teaching many Aboriginal inmates their traditions for the first time. Most inmates arrive without a real knowledge of their social, historical, and spiritual roots. The teaching of traditions takes the form of practical participation in Aboriginal rituals in what has been called the "In Search of Your Warrior" (ISYW) program. Pê Sâkâstêw Program Director Sharon Bell explains the rationale behind the program: "ISYW was created to treat traumatic experiences, to heal the scars of abuse, to get rid of the blinding rage and anger that inmates carry deep inside. Some of them, for example, are suffering from the effect that residential schools have had on their lives or on their parents'—residential schools established by the Canadian government that in the past aimed to assimilate Aboriginal people into white society. The scars from abuse and the loss of identity can have a terrible impact on a human being. That is why some of them strongly feel the need to refocus on themselves, to get back in touch with their real selves, to be able to face the future with hope."

So Bell and her staff help inmates to participate in Aboriginal rituals like the cleansing ceremonies known as smudging. In a smudging ceremony, those gathered form a circle. Sweetgrass is burned and carried around the circle. All participants wash themselves in the smoke of the burning grass, drawing the smoke toward them with their hands. After the smudging, inmates take turns holding an eagle's feather and giving voice to their thoughts and feelings while everyone gathered listens intently. This is just one of 75 healing activities that inmates can take part in at the healing lodge.

There are six units in the Pê Sâkâstêw Healing Lodge. The units are designed to capture some of the main teachings of Aboriginal spirituality. Circular patterns represent influence, unity, and social interaction. If you were to fly over the lodge, each unit is shaped like an eagle, which symbolizes the embracing of life and the effort to ward off evil. The colours used on the outside of each unit represent the all-pervasive presence of the Creator, with red representing the east, yellow representing the south, blue representing the west and white representing the north.

Overall, the Pê Sâkâstêw Healing Lodge provides a unique approach to rehabilitation. It strives to embrace the ideals of Aboriginal spirituality and give the inmates a sense of their own traditions. While people working at the lodge recognize that the program is not a cure for the Aboriginal community's ills, it does bring hope to a few of the community members who need help the most.

Source: CBC News (2008).

In regular institutions, there are a number of programs specifically intended for Indigenous inmates, including the "In Search of Your Warrior" program mention above, which is aimed at reducing serious violence. A review of this program (CSC, 2005) showed that offenders who completed the program were 19 percent less likely to be readmitted to custody. CSC seems to be making some progress in its rehabilitation focus for Indigenous offenders, but there is still much work to be done, and key resources are still lacking in many areas. For example, some institutions report that they do not have the services of an elder for extended periods of time, and the burnout of elders and spiritual advisers—due to lack of recruitment, retention, and operational requirements—means that the way in which services are delivered in practice is not in line with what was originally envisioned (Mann, 2009, p. 25). The incarceration rate of Indigenous people in Canada has increased in the past few years, and considering the social conditions and the demographics of the Indigenous population in Canada, the rate of incarceration can only increase if the criminal justice system and CSC do not make considerable efforts.

The Aboriginal Justice Strategy

Indigenous people are seeking to be responsible for their own populations and for addressing crime in their communities, and they should be empowered to find solutions in partnership with all levels of government. The Department of Justice Canada has developed the Aboriginal Justice Strategy to work in partnership with Indigenous communities. The goals are:

- To contribute to a decrease in the rate of victimization, crime and incarceration among Aboriginal people in communities operating AJS programs
- To assist Aboriginal people in assuming greater responsibility for the administration of justice in their communities
- To provide better and more timely information about community-based justice programs funded by the AJS
- To reflect and include Aboriginal values within the justice system. (Department of Justice Canada, n.d.)

The Aboriginal Justice Strategy has a very strict and onerous grant application system and does not cover any capital expenses for programs such as land, buildings, or vehicles. It limits administration costs to 20 percent of the funding grant. In 2014 its budget was $11 million for all of Canada to both support ongoing justice initiatives and create new ones.

The Department of Justice offers two funding streams for which Indigenous communities can apply. Both include only partial funding since the community must contribute either on its own or in partnership with provincial and territorial governments. One funding stream is the Capacity Building Fund for one-time funds to engage in studies, create capacity-building events, and provide training for existing programs. The other is the Community-Based Justice Fund, which supports Indigenous community-based programs including diversion programs, developing pre-sentencing and sentencing options, victim support programs, offender reintegration services, and Indigenous court worker programs. As of 2011–12 the Aboriginal Justice Strategy was funding 214 programs, up from 100 programs in 2006–7. One such program is the Community Council in Toronto operated through the Aboriginal Legal Services of Toronto. This is a criminal diversion program for youth and adult Indigenous offenders who live in Toronto. The project takes Indigenous offenders out of the criminal court system and brings them before members of the Toronto Indigenous community. The council develops a plan by consensus that will allow the offender to take responsibility for his or her actions and address the root of the problem, be it family dysfunction, drug or alcohol abuse, or any other personal matter that may have led to the offence. The concept of a community council reflects the way justice was delivered in Indigenous communities before the Canadian criminal justice system reached these communities.

This program reflects the truth of Justice Cawsey's statement, quoted earlier and repeated here: "Everything that has worked for Aboriginal people has come from Aboriginal people" (RCAP, 1996).

CHAPTER SUMMARY

The mainstream criminal justice system has been very slow to include traditional Indigenous forms of justice. In the last ten years it has begun to evolve much more quickly, to the benefit not only of Indigenous people but of all Canadians, as restorative justice processes become available to non-Indigenous as well as Indigenous people. Current measures for rehabilitation of Indigenous offenders appear to be lagging behind, though, as the number of Indigenous offenders incarcerated increases daily. Changes are not coming fast enough for those from Indigenous communities who are languishing in prison.

Indigenous efforts to create new programs for treatment of offenders and their communities are often hindered by lack of funding. Ultimately, if Indigenous communities were more affluent and economically independent they could finance those efforts themselves and have more autonomy and creative independence in community problem-solving.

Economic development and recovery are therefore vitally important in Indigenous communities. It is all interconnected: economic renewal and prosperity are tied to self-government and self-determination, which are tied to Indigenous control over justice service delivery. Economic renewal itself would address one of the root causes of crime, which is poverty.

The current legislative reforms in justice have shown some positive results but are not the only answer to the problem of Indigenous overrepresentation in the criminal justice system. First Nations territories and Indigenous communities Canada are diverse, complex, and various in their needs. Indigenous people need to lead the way in areas that are fundamental to their well-being. Indigenous people in Canada are working on all fronts to improve their situation; they need a strong partnership with the Canadian government, but one in which the government is willing to follow their lead.

REFERENCES

Aboriginal Justice Implementation Commission (AJIC). (1999). *Report of the Aboriginal Justice Inquiry of Manitoba* (Vol. 1). Winnipeg: Statutory Publications. http://www.ajic.mb.ca/volume1/toc.html.

Ammelal, D. (2006). The Pathways unit at La Macaza Institution: The path to personal growth and healing. *Let's Talk*, *31*(1), 8-9. http://www.csc-scc.gc.ca/publications/lt-en/2006/31-1/pdf/letstalk_31-1_e.pdf.

Bittle, S., Quann, N., Hattem, T., & Muise, D. (2002, March). *A one-day snapshot of Aboriginal youth in custody across Canada*. Ottawa: Department of Justice Canada, Youth Justice Research.

Bushie, B. (1999, August 7). *Community holistic circle healing*. International Institute for Restorative Practices. http://www.iirp.edu/article_detail.php?article_id=NDc0.

CBC News. (2008, November). A community fights gangs and guns. *CBC News in Review*. https://media.curio.ca/filer_public/33/f7/33f77dcb-80f2-41de-a095-8e60a7e01422/nov-08-gangs.pdf.

Clark, S. (2011). The Nunavut Court of Justice: An example of challenges and alternatives for communities and for the administration of justice. *Canadian Journal of Criminology and Criminal Justice*, *53*(3), 343–370.

Commercial Sex Information Service. (2000). Pamela George murder trial. http://www.walnet.org/csis/news/regina_96/pam_george.html.

Correctional Service Canada (CSC). (2005). The "In Search of Your Warrior" program for Aboriginal offenders: A preliminary evaluation. http://www.csc-scc.gc.ca/research/r172-eng.shtml.

Correctional Service Canada (CSC). (2011). *Strategic plan for Aboriginal corrections: Innovation, learning, and adjustment 2006–07 to 2010–11*. Ottawa: Correctional Service Canada. http://www.csc-scc.gc.ca/aboriginal/092/002003-1000-eng.pdf.

Correctional Service Canada. (CSC). (2012). Commissioner's directive 702—Aboriginal offenders. http://www.csc-scc.gc.ca/text/plcy/cdshtm/702-cde-eng.shtml#aB.

Corrections and Conditional Release Act. (1992). SC 1992, c. 20.

Criminal Code. (1985). RSC 1985, c. C-46.

Department of Justice Canada. (n.d.) Aboriginal Justice Strategy. http://justice.gc.ca/eng/fund-fina/acf-fca/ajs-sja/.

Fitzgerald, R., & Carrington, P.J. (2008). The neighbourhood context of urban Aboriginal crime. *Canadian Journal of Criminology and Criminal Justice*, *50*(5), 523–557.

Fournier, S., & Crey, E. (1997). *Stolen from our embrace: The abduction of First Nations children and the restoration of Aboriginal communities*. Vancouver: Douglas & McIntyre.

Gladue, R v. (1999). [1999] 1 SCR 688.

Highway of Tears Symposium. (2006). *Highway of Tears Symposium recommendations report*. Prince George, BC: Author. http://www.turtleisland.org/healing/highwayoftears.pdf.

Iacobucci, F. (2013, February). *First Nations representation on Ontario juries: Report of the independent review conducted by the Honourable Frank Iacobucci*. Toronto: Ministry of the Attorney General.

Ibbotson, H. (2013, April 8). Gladue reports: Boon or bane? *Brantford Expositor*. http://www.simcoereformer.ca/2013/04/08/gladue-reports-boon-or-bane.

Ipeelee, R v. (2012). 2012 SCC 13, [2012] 1 SCR 433.

Kakekagamick, R v. (2006). 81 OR (3d) 664 (CA).

LaPrairie, C. (2002). Aboriginal overrepresentation in the criminal justice system: A tale of nine cities. *Canadian Journal of Criminology*, *44*(2), 181–208.

Mann, M.M. (2009). *Good intentions, disappointing results: A progress report on federal Aboriginal corrections*. Ottawa: Office of the Correctional Investigator.

McGillivray, A., & Comaskey, B. (1999). *Black eyes all of the time: Intimate violence, Aboriginal women, and the justice system*. Toronto: University of Toronto Press.

Missing Women Commission of Inquiry. (2012, November 22). Media statement from Commissioner Wally Oppal, Q.C. http://www.missingwomeninquiry.ca/media-releases/.

Monture-Angus, P. (2000). Lessons in decolonization: Aboriginal overrepresentation in the Canadian criminal justice system. In D. Long & O.P. Dickason (Eds.), *Visions of the heart: Canadian Aboriginal issues*. Toronto: Harcourt Canada.

Munch, C. (2012). Youth correctional statistics in Canada, 2010/2011. *Juristat*. http://www.statcan.gc.ca/pub/85-002-x/2012001/article/11716-eng.htm#a4.

Native Women's Association of Canada (NWAC). (2010). *What their stories tell us: Research findings from the Sisters in Spirit Initiative*. Ohsweken, ON: Author.

Nunavut Tunngavik. (2014). *Annual report on the state of Inuit culture and society 13-14: Examining the justice system in Nunavut*. Iqaluit, NU: Author. https://www.tunngavik.com/files/2014/10/2013-14-SICS-Annual-Report-ENG.pdf.

Office of the Correctional Investigator. (2012, October). *Spirit matters: Aboriginal people and the Corrections and Conditional Release Act*. Ottawa: Author. http://www.oci-bec.gc.ca/cnt/rpt/oth-aut/oth-aut20121022-eng.aspx.

Office of the Correctional Investigator. (2013). *Segregation in Canadian federal corrections: A prison ombudsman's perspective*. Ottawa: Author. http://www.oci-bec.gc.ca/cnt/comm/presentations/presentations20130322-23-eng.aspx.

Offman, C. (2008, April 15). Hobbema, Alberta: A town in a "state of crisis." *The National Post*. http://www.nationalpost.com.

Perreault, S. (2009, July). The incarceration of Aboriginal people in adult correctional services. *Juristat*. http://www.statcan.gc.ca/pub/85-002-x/2009003/article/10903-eng.htm.

Perreault, S. (2011). Violent victimization of Aboriginal people in the Canadian provinces, 2009. *Juristat*. http://www.statcan.gc.ca/pub/85-002-x/2011001/article/11415-eng.pdf.

Perreault, S. (2014). Admissions to adult correctional services in Canada, 2011/2012. *Juristat*. http://www.statcan.gc.ca/pub/85-002-x/2014001/article/11918-eng.htm.

Roach, K., & Rudin, J. (2000). Gladue: The judicial and political reception of a promising decision. *Canadian Journal of Criminology*, *42*(3), 355–388.

Rohner, T. (2015). Nunavut's capital resurrects restorative justice committee. *Nunatsiaq Online*. http://www.nunatsiaqonline.ca.

Royal Canadian Mounted Police. (2011). Serving Canada's Aboriginal people. http://www.rcmp-grc.gc.ca/aboriginal-autochtone/index-eng.htm.

Royal Canadian Mounted Police (RCMP). (2014). *Missing and murdered Aboriginal women: A national operational overview*. Ottawa: Author. http://www.rcmp-grc.gc.ca/en/missing-and-murdered-aboriginal-women-national-operational-overview.

Royal Commission on Aboriginal Peoples (RCAP). (1996). *Bridging the cultural divide: A report on Aboriginal people and criminal justice in Canada*. Ottawa: Supply and Services Canada.

Royal Commission on the Donald Marshall, Jr., Prosecution. (1989). *Commissioners' report, findings and recommendations* (Vol. 1). Halifax: Province of Nova Scotia.

Sangster, J. (1999). Criminalizing the colonized: Ontario Native women confront the criminal justice system, 1920–1960. *Canadian Historical Review*, *80*(1), 32–60.

Sécurité publique Québec. (2013). Aboriginal nations police forces. http://www.securitepublique.gouv.qc.ca/en/police-prevention/aboriginal-police.html.

Statistics Canada. (2015a). Youth correctional statistics in Canada, 2013/2014, Table 5. *Juristat*. http://www.statcan.gc.ca/pub/85-002-x/2015001/article/14164/tbl/tbl05-eng.htm.

Statistics Canada. (2015b, November 23). Criminal victimization in Canada, 2014. http://www.statcan.gc.ca/pub/85-002-x/2015001/article/14241-eng.htm.

Statistics Canada. (2015c, November 25). Homicide in Canada, 2014. *The Daily*. http://www.statcan.gc.ca/daily-quotidien/151125/dq151125a-eng.htm.

Thatcher, R. (2004). *Fighting firewater fictions: Moving beyond the disease model of alcohol in First Nations*. Toronto: University of Toronto Press.

Totten, M. (2009, March). *Preventing Aboriginal youth gang involvement in Canada: A gendered approach*. Paper prepared for Aboriginal policy research conference, Ottawa.

Trevethan, S., Auger, S., & Moore, J.-P. (2001). *The effect of family disruption on Aboriginal and non-Aboriginal inmates*. Ottawa: Correctional Service Canada. http://www.csc-scc.gc.ca/research/r113-eng.shtml.

University of Manitoba Faculty of Law. (2012). *Gladue handbook: A resource for justice system participants in Manitoba*. Winnipeg: Author.

Wagamese, R. (1996). *The terrible summer: The national newspaper award-winning writing of Richard Wagamese*. Toronto: Warwick.

Whitehead, P.C., & Hayes, J.J. (1998). *The insanity of alcohol: Social problems in Canadian First Nations communities*. Toronto: Canadian Scholars' Press.

Wood, D.S. (2011). Alcohol and violence in Nunavut: A comparison of wet and dry communities. *International Journal of Circumpolar Health, 70*(1), 19–28. http://www.justice.gov.yk.ca/pdf/4_Alcohol_controls__violence_in_Nunavut_comparison_of_wet__dry_communities.pdf.

REVIEW QUESTIONS

True or False?

_____ 1. Statistics show that most incarcerated Indigenous offenders come from reserves.

_____ 2. The incarceration level of Indigenous people in relation to non-Indigenous people is declining.

_____ 3. Indigenous people are more frequently victims of crime than are other Canadians.

_____ 4. The report of the Royal Commission on Aboriginal Peoples stated that an exclusive pre-colonial Indigenous justice system can successfully be resurrected in today's society.

_____ 5. The Royal Commission on the Donald Marshall, Jr., Prosecution concluded that Donald Marshall Jr.'s status as an Indigenous person contributed to his false conviction for murder.

_____ 6. The Manitoba Aboriginal Justice Inquiry found that more than half the inmates of Manitoba's jails were Indigenous.

_____ 7. Alternative sentencing measures reflect Indigenous values and therefore are only available to Indigenous offenders.

_____ 8. Section 718.2(e) of the *Criminal Code* states that "all available sanctions other than imprisonment that are reasonable in the circumstances should be considered for only Aboriginal offenders."

_____ 9. To qualify for a sentencing circle, the accused must recognize his or her guilt and have a clear intention to rehabilitate.

_____10. The *Corrections and Conditional Release Act* has changed to allow Indigenous communities to participate in an offender's release plan.

Multiple Choice

1. Which of the following has not been a factor in Hobbema's descent into chaos?
   a. unemployment
   b. substance abuse
   c. the erosion of Indigenous traditions
   d. lack of access to natural resources

2. Joan Sangster attributed the overrepresentation of Indigenous women in the criminal justice system to three things. Which of the following is not one of those three?
   a. material and social dislocation due to colonization
   b. gender and race paternalism
   c. the isolation of Indigenous communities from the main cities
   d. the cultural gap between Indigenous ideas of justice and mainstream ideas of justice

3. The biological perspective of examining alcohol problems in Indigenous communities was popular prior to 1970. This perspective relies on the belief that
   a. problem drinking is a weakness of race and Indigenous people have a genetic predisposition to alcoholism
   b. all people have a predisposition to alcoholism; some people simply have more self-control
   c. problem drinking is not race-based but gender-based
   d. predispositions to alcoholism depend on the age of the drinker

4. The 1991 *Report of the Aboriginal Justice Inquiry of Manitoba* made several findings. Which of the following is not one of their conclusions?
   a. Indigenous offenders are more than twice as likely to be incarcerated as non-Indigenous offenders are.
   b. Lawyers spend less time with their Indigenous clients than with their non-Indigenous clients.
   c. Indigenous people spend more time in pre-trial detention than non-Indigenous people.
   d. Indigenous offenders are more likely to have their sentences reduced.

5. Which of the following is the definition of *systemic discrimination* as it pertains to the justice system?
   a. discrimination against a particular race in the delivery of any governmental service
   b. the enforcement of laws and policies that are inherently prejudicial to a group or culture
   c. lack of attention to the needs of a specific group in drafting legislation
   d. a purposeful exclusion of a group from certain sentencing options

6. Most comprehensive studies of the criminal justice system in relation to Indigenous people recommend
   a. an autonomous Indigenous system
   b. a dependent Indigenous system
   c. healing circles
   d. a system in which the Indigenous system and the dominant system are interrelated

7. Which of the following is not a feature of Indigenous traditional justice?
   a. Laws are formulated by the community through tradition and consensus.
   b. Traditional spirituality is the foundation of codes of behaviour.
   c. Personal offences are seen as transgressions against the state.
   d. Personal offences are seen as transgressions against the victim and the victim's family, and against the community when the peace is threatened.

8. Which of the following is the definition of *race paternalism*?
   a. a system under which the dominant group takes authority to supply the needs and regulate the conduct of a minority group
   b. an insistence that a group adopt the religion of the dominant culture
   c. an institutionally approved form of racism
   d. there is no such term

9. *Gladue* courts are
   a. mostly in Toronto
   b. courts where all Crown attorneys, defence counsel, and judges have received specialized training in Indigenous issues
   c. courts where only summary offences involving Indigenous accused can be heard
   d. courts where all Crown attorneys, defence counsel, and judges are Indigenous

10. One of the aims of Indigenous healing lodges is to
    a. increase the recidivism rate of Indigenous offenders
    b. help Indigenous offenders stay connected to their communities
    c. formally address the issue of substance abuse
    d. train Indigenous people to become elders

Glossary

assimilation: a process by which members of an ethnic minority group lose cultural characteristics that distinguish them from the dominant cultural group or take on the cultural characteristics of another group

British North America Act: a statute enacted on March 29, 1867, by the British Parliament providing for the Confederation of Canada

claims arising from Indigenous title: claims based on the allegation that lands traditionally used and occupied by Indigenous people were never surrendered to the Crown by Indigenous people

claims arising from the surrender for sale of reserve land: claims occurring when First Nations seek compensation for, or the return of, land that had been surrendered to the Crown for sale for the benefit of the band

claims relating to the fulfillment of terms of treaties: claims that are usually a result of disagreement between the Crown and First Nations about the size and location of reserves set aside by treaties

collateral victim: an unintentional but expected victim of an act

comprehensive land claims: claims to territory that are not covered by treaty or land -cession agreements

consensus government: a form of government that requires all parties to agree with a decision

covenant chain: first agreement entered into between the Five Nations of the Iroquois and the British; a clear recognition by both sides that their political systems would remain separate even as their systems of trade and alliance bound them

cultural genocide: the destruction of those structures and practices that allow a group to continue as a group, such as language, spiritual practices, and cultural values

direct victim: a targeted victim of an act

fee simple ownership: the right to exclusive use, possession, and disposal of a piece of land

fiduciary responsibility: the legal or ethical responsibility to manage something, usually money or property, in trust for another person (or people) and act in their best interests

Indian Act: a statute created in 1876 to consolidate all policies aimed at the administration of Indian populations in Canada and giving the federal government exclusive jurisdiction over Indians and reserves

Indian agent: a federal employee of Indian Affairs in charge of administration on reserves

Indian Residential Schools Settlement Agreement (IRSSA): an agreement by which Indigenous people who could prove their attendance in the residential schools became eligible to receive a "common experience payment" (CEP)

indigenization: the incorporation of Indigenous people into a social system, such as the justice system

Inuit Nunangat: the four regions in which Inuit live, including land, water, and ice: Inuvialuit, Nunatsiavut, Nunavik, and Nunavut

paternalism: a system in which a dominant person or institution assumes authority for supplying the needs and regulating the conduct of those under its control

patriation: the process by which Canada gained control over the Constitution; previously, amendments to the Canadian Constitution required an act of British Parliament

recidivism: the process of relapsing into crime

reconciliation: an ongoing process of establishing and maintaining respectful relations

residential schools: church-run, government-funded boarding schools for Indigenous children, designed to prepare them for life in white society

Royal Commission on Aboriginal Peoples (RCAP): a commission established by the federal government in 1991 to investigate the issues facing Indigenous people in Canada

Royal Proclamation of 1763: the cornerstone of Indigenous land claims today; has been called the "*Magna Carta* of Indian Rights" and has been deemed by the courts to have the "force of a statute which has never been repealed"

scrip: a one-time payment issued to Métis to discharge treaty rights

seigneurial farms: a system in which a man, usually a soldier, was granted land in the name of France

Sixties Scoop: the practice of removing Indigenous children from their communities and placing them in foster care or putting them up for adoption in non-Indigenous homes

specific land claims: claims that relate to specific misdealings of the Crown with relation to land or resources

subjugation: forcing obedience to authority

systemic discrimination: the enforcement of laws and the enforcement of policies that are inherently prejudicial to a group or culture

treaty: an agreement between two states that has been formally concluded and ratified

Index

Credits

CHAPTER 1

Chapter-opening photo: Library and Archives Canada c085137.

Wampum belt (photo): Courtesy of the Woodland Cultural Centre.

Figure 1.2: Indigenous and Northern Affairs Canada.

G'psgolox totem pole (photo): Bob Keefer.

Métis Provisional Government (photo): Library and Archives Canada PA-012854.

CHAPTER 2

Chapter-opening photo: Courtesy of Ossie Michelin and ATPN.

Torngat Mountains National Park (photo): © Parks Canada/ Heiko Wittenborn.

Figure 2.1: Implementation Monitoring Committee.

Figure 2.2: Indigenous and Northern Affairs Canada.

Figure 2.3: Indigenous and Northern Affairs Canada.

Indigenous Protestors (photo): JULIE OLIVER/Postmedia News.

The Nishiyuu Walkers (photo): Fred Chartrand/The Canadian Press.

CHAPTER 3

Chapter-opening photos: Provincial Archives of Saskatchewan R-A8223(1)-(2).

Inhumane Conditions at Residential Schools (box): Indigenous and Northern Affairs Canada.

George Cultesi (photo): University of Victoria, "George Clutesi presenting display of First Nations art," 1966, Item 038.0407.

I Lost My Talk (poem): Joe, R. (1998). I lost my talk. In D.D. Moses & T. Goldie (Eds.), *An anthology of Canadian Native literature in English*. Toronto: Oxford University Press.

Robert Houle (photo): TYLER BROWBRIDGE/Postmedia News.

Phil Fontaine (photo): Tom Hanson/The Canadian Press.

Appendix 3.1: Indigenous and Northern Affairs Canada.

CHAPTER 4

Chapter-opening photo: Mychaylo Prystupa.

Grassy Narrows (photo): Peter Power/The Canadian Press.

Figures 4.2–4.5: Indigenous and Northern Affairs Canada.

Figures 4.6–4.8: Employment and Social Development Canada.

Figure 4.11: Assembly of First Nations.

Figures 4.12–4.13: Public Health Agency of Canada © All rights reserved. *HIV and AIDS in Canada. Surveillance Report to December 31, 2014.* Public Health Agency of Canada, 2015. Adapted and reproduced with permission from the Minister of Health, 2016.

Dr. Stanley Volant (photo): Projet Innu Meshkenu. Reprinted with permission.

Table 4.4: Kirmayer, L.J., Fraser, S-L, Fauras, V., & Whitley, R. (2009). Current approaches to Aboriginal youth suicide prevention. Working Paper 14. Culture and Mental Health Research Unit, Institute of Community and Family Psychiatry, Jewish General Hospital, Montreal, Quebec.

Figure 4.15: © All rights reserved. *First Nations Mental Wellnessw Continuum Framework—Summary Report.* Health Canada and the Assembly of First Nations, 2015. Adapted and reproduced with permission from the Minister of Health, 2016.

Appendix 4.1: Blackstock, C. (2009). Jordan's story: How one boy inspired a world of change. *Canadian supplement to The State of the world's children 2009: Aboriginal children's health: Leaving no child behind*. Toronto: Unicef Canada. Reprinted with permission from Unicef Canada.

CHAPTER 5

Chapter-opening photo: Dave McCord/The Canadian Press.

A Community Fights Gangs and Guns (excerpt in case study): CBC News in Review November 2008. Reprinted with permission.

Figure 5.5: © Source: Correctional Service Canada, Inmate Involvement in the Child Welfare Systems. S. Trevethan, S. Auger & J-P Moore. http://www.csc-scc.gc.ca/research/r113 -eng.shtml. Reproduced with the permission of the Minister of Public Services and Procurement Canada, 2016.

Community Justice in Iqaluit (close-up box): Rohner, T. (2015). Nunavut's capital resurrects restorative justice committee. Nunatsiaq Online. http://www.nunatsiaqonline.ca.

Hollow Water (close-up box): Bushie, Berma. (1999, August 7). *Community holistic circle healing*. International Institute for Restorative Practices.

Figure 5.9: © Source: Correctional Service Canada, Strategic Plan for Aboriginal Corrections - Aboriginal Continuum of Care Model. http://www.csc-scc.gc.ca/text/pa/ev-ahl-394-2-49/healing-lodges-eng.shtml. Reproduced with the permission of the Minister of Public Services and Procurement Canada, 2016.

Pathways (close-up box): © Source: Correctional Service of Canada, 2006. Let's Talk: Vol. 31, No. 1. http://www.csc-scc.gc.ca/publications/lt-en/2006/31-1/6-eng.shtml. Reproduced with the permission of the Minister of Public Services and Procurement Canada, 2016.

A Community Fights Gangs and Guns (box): The Pê Sâkâstêw Healing Lodge: CBC News in Review November 2008. Reprinted with permission.

Royal Commission on Aboriginal Peoples (excerpt): RCAP. (1996). *Bridging the cultural divide: A report on Aboriginal people and criminal justice in Canada*. Ottawa: Supply and Services Canada. Permission granted by the Privy Council Office © Her Majesty the Queen in Right of Canada (2016).